PANDEMIC

'Catharine Arnold has done a remarkable job of relating
the tales of a diverse set of sufferers, crafting an arresting
and intimate narrative of the 1918 pandemic ... a gripping
tale that swoops down into the grisly detail, then soars up
to give a broad view over the landscape of this calamitous
moment in human history ... Arnold writes beautifully,
and starkly, of the tragedy that unfolded.'
New Statesman

'Arnold's pacy history focuses on the stories of
the individual, from scientists and politicians to
the ordinary men and women who suffered.'
History Revealed

'Meticulously researched ... vividly conveys
the terror of the disease.'
Professor Sheena Cruickshank, FRSA

NECROPOLIS

'Deeply pleasing ... Entertainment of the most garish and
exquisite kind ... A Baedeker of the dead.'
Peter Ackroyd, *The Times*

'Luminous and often touching ... Well-researched
and elegantly written.'
Sunday Telegraph

'Poignant or dramatic figures crowd these pages. Arnold's book
abounds in deliciously uncanny detail.'
Suzi Feay, *Independent on Sunday*

'Where Arnold's account really beguiles is in its eccentric social detail
... Enthusiastic, good-humoured and constantly engaging.'
Sinclair

BEDLAM

'Elegantly written and richly anecdotal.'
Daily Mail

'When you close this rewarding, informative and tastefully conceived book, you will be the richer for it.'
Sunday Express

'A finely written, thoroughly researched and humane book, packed with moving stories.'
Independent

CITY OF SIN

'Hugely entertaining ... Arnold is a delightful travelling companion through the centuries.'
Jeanette Winterson, *The Times*

'Often titillating, sometimes shocking, frequently entertaining ... The book is a lively affirmation of sexual desire in all its varieties.'
Observer

UNDERWORLD LONDON

'Catharine Arnold has assembled a history of British crimes to chill the blood but also titillate the reader.'
Mail on Sunday

'Arnold has a light touch when dealing with dark topics.'
Sunday Telegraph

About the Author

Catharine Arnold is the author of a number of much-acclaimed histories, including *Necropolis: London and its Dead*, *Bedlam: London and its Mad*, *City of Sin: London and its Vices* and *Globe: Life in Shakespeare's London*. Her first novel, *Lost Time*, won a Betty Trask Award. Catharine read English at the University of Cambridge and holds a further degree in psychology.

PANDEMIC
1918

THE STORY OF THE DEADLIEST
INFLUENZA IN HISTORY

CATHARINE ARNOLD

Michael O'Mara Books Limited

This paperback edition first published in 2020
First published in Great Britain in 2018 by
Michael O'Mara Books Limited
9 Lion Yard
Tremadoc Road
London SW4 7NQ

A CIP catalogue record for this book is
available from the British Library.

Papers used by Michael O'Mara Books Limited are natural,
recyclable products made from wood grown in sustainable
forests. The manufacturing processes conform to the
environmental regulations of the country of origin.

ISBN: 978-1-78243-808-3 in hardback print format
ISBN: 978-1-78929-293-0 in paperback print format
ISBN: 978-1-78243-810-6 in ebook format

1 2 3 4 5 6 7 8 9 10
www.mombooks.com

Cover illustration by Mick Wiggins
Cover design by Claire Cater
Typeset by Ed Pickford

Every reasonable effort has been made to acknowledge all
copyright holders. Any errors or omissions that may have
occurred are inadvertent, and anyone with any copyright queries
is invited to write to the publisher, so that full acknowledgement
may be included in subsequent editions of the work.

Printed and bound by CPI Group (UK) Ltd, Croydon, CR0 4YY

CONTENTS

'It was the beginning of the rout of civilisation, of the massacre of mankind.'

H. G. Wells, *War of the Worlds*

'The Captain looked suddenly tired. "Sometimes I think, Mr. Benson, that the very air is poisoned with the damned influenza. For four years now millions of rotting corpses have covered a good part of Europe from the Channel to Arabia. We can't escape it even when we're 2,000 miles out to sea. It seems to come as it did on our last trip, like a dark and invisible fog."'

Herbert Faulkner West, *HMS Cephalonia:*
A Story of the North Atlantic in 1918

Fly this plague-stricken spot! The hot, foul air
Is rank with pestilence – the crowded marts
And public ways, once populous with life,
Are still and noisome as a churchyard vault;
Aghast and shuddering, Nature holds her breath
In abject fear, and feels at her strong heart
The deadly fangs of death.

Susanna Moodie, 'Our Journey up the Country'

Dedicated to the memory of my grandparents Aubrey Gladwin and Lalage Bagley Gladwin, and the millions like them who perished in the Spanish flu pandemic of 1918–19.

An Ill Wind

<hr>

A S THE SUN sank over a windswept Yorkshire churchyard in September 2008, a battered lead-lined coffin was reburied hours after being opened for the first time in eighty-nine years. The familiar words of the burial service resounded through the twilight as samples of human remains were frozen in liquid nitrogen and transported to a laboratory with the aim of saving millions of lives.[1] Medical researchers had exhumed the body of Sir Mark Sykes (1879–1919) in order to identify the devastating 'Spanish flu' virus which killed 100 million people in the last year of the First World War. Sir Mark, a British diplomat, had succumbed to Spanish flu during the Paris Peace Conference of 1919, dying in his hotel near the Tuileries Gardens. Like many victims of Spanish flu, Sir Mark had been fit and healthy, a man in his prime at just thirty-nine years old.

Sir Mark's remains had been sealed in a lead-lined coffin, befitting his status as a member of the nobility, and transported to Sledmere House, the Sykes' family seat in east Yorkshire. Sir Mark was buried in the graveyard of St Mary's church, which adjoined the house. If his body had not been hermetically sealed by a thick layer of lead, his life might have passed quietly into history. But an accident of chemistry meant that the lead dramatically slowed the decay of Sir Mark's soft tissue, giving scientists investigating the H5N1 'bird flu' virus a unique opportunity to study the behaviour of its predecessor. One theory of the cause of the 1918–19 epidemic was that it originated with an avian virus, H1N1, which is similar to H5N1. Researchers believed Sir Mark's remains might hold valuable information about how the influenza virus leapt the species barrier from animals to humans.[2]

In 2011, there were only five useful samples of the H1N1 virus around the world and none from a well-preserved body in a lead-lined coffin. H1N1 had already been sequenced by scientists using frozen remains found in Alaska, but many questions remained about just how the virus killed its victims and the way it had mutated by 1919, when it killed Sir Mark Sykes.[3]

Professor John Oxford, the eminent virologist who led the team investigating Sir Mark's remains, told reporters that the baronet 'died very late in the epidemic, when the virus had almost burnt itself out. We want to get a grip on how the virus worked both when it was at its most virulent and when it was coming to the end of its life. The samples we have taken from Sir Mark have the potential to help us answer some very important questions'.[4]

After a two-year process of gaining permission from the Diocese of York to carry out the exhumation, involving a special hearing presided over by a High Court judge, Professor Oxford's team, wearing full bio-hazard kit and accompanied by medical experts, clergy, environmental health officers and Sir Mark Sykes' descendants, finally exhumed his grave. After a short prayer, the gravestone was removed and the coffin uncovered inside a sealed tent before researchers wearing protective suits and breathing apparatus opened the casket. After so many months of preparation, it was a tense and exciting moment. But the investigation seemed doomed to failure. A crack was discovered in the top of the lead lining, meaning that the chances of finding a pristine sample of the virus were remote. The coffin had split because of the weight of soil over it, and the cadaver was badly decomposed. Nonetheless, the team were able to extract samples of lung and brain tissue through the split, with the coffin remaining *in situ* in the grave during this process to avoid disturbing the body any further. Although the condition of the cadaver was disappointing, a study of the tissue samples taken from the remains eventually revealed valuable genetic imprints of H1N1 and its condition when Sir Mark died.[5]

The exhumation of Sir Mark Sykes' body represented just one attempt to find an explanation for the deadly disease that had devastated the globe during the last year of the Great War. In three successive waves, from spring 1918 to summer 1919, the phenomenon that became known as 'Spanish flu' killed an estimated 100 million people worldwide. The disease was not classified as 'Spanish flu', or the more fanciful soubriquet 'Spanish Lady', immediately. The shape-shifting creature that was Spanish flu was a slippery beast, difficult to define beyond the common characteristics of acute breathing difficulties, haemorrhaging and fever. As it progressed, many doctors and civilians would wonder whether this apocalyptic disease was actually influenza at all.

In terms of national identity, there was nothing inherently Spanish about Spanish flu. At first, in the early months of 1918, the majority of doctors believed they were dealing with nothing more serious than a particularly aggressive outbreak of common or garden influenza. But as the epidemic continued, and King Alfonso XIII of Spain fell victim along with many of his subjects, this virulent strain of influenza was discussed freely in the Spanish press. Debate of this nature was possible as Spain was a neutral country during the First World War. Elsewhere, in Britain and the United States, censorship made such speculation impossible beyond the pages of medical journals such as *The Lancet* and the *British Medical Journal*. Under 'DORA', or the Defence of the Realm Act, newspapers were not permitted to carry stories that might spread fear or dismay. As the term 'Spanish flu' entered the language in June 1918, *The Times* of London took the opportunity to ridicule the disease as little more than a passing fad. By the autumn of 1918, when the deadly second wave of Spanish flu was hitting populations worldwide, the implications of the disease proved impossible to ignore. The United States recorded 550,000 deaths, five times its total military fatalities in the war, while European deaths totalled over two million. In England and Wales an estimated 200,000, 4.9 per 1,000 of the total population, perished from influenza and its complications, particularly pneumonia.

Today, despite regular health scares about bird flu, SARS, HIV and Ebola, it is difficult to envisage a scenario in which something as common as influenza could cause widespread illness and death. Although most of us will contract influenza several times during our lifetimes, the influenza vaccination being only approximately 50 per cent effective, the majority will survive with a minimum amount of medical attention. What then was so different about Spanish flu and why did it have such a devastating impact?

To gain some understanding of these factors, we need to define the nature of influenza and consider a brief history of the disease. In general terms, influenza is a complex disease caused by an airborne virus which spreads between individuals in microscopic droplets, via coughing or sneezing. Bringing people together in close contact aids the spread of the infection, particularly in overcrowded communities such as schools, military camps and hospitals. In many cases, schoolchildren are the first to catch the virus and then transmit it to their families.[6]

Although Spanish flu constituted the most deadly mutation of the flu virus, flu itself is nothing new. References to influenza as an affliction date back to classical times, with Hippocrates witnessing an apparent epidemic of influenza in Greece in 412 BC and Livy recording a similar outbreak in his history of ancient Rome.

THE ACTUAL WORD 'influenza' dates from around 1500, when the Italians introduced the term for diseases that they attributed to the 'influence' of the stars. Another possible origin was the Italian phrase *influenza di freddo*, the influence of the cold.[7]

By the fifteenth century, the illness was referred to in England as a 'mure' or 'murre'; apparently it killed two monks at Canterbury Abbey, while an outbreak of the *sudor Anglicus* or 'English sweate' was recorded after the Battle of Bosworth in 1485.[8] By 1562, Lord Randolph was writing from Edinburgh to Lord Cecil describing the symptoms experienced by Mary, Queen of Scots. Lord Randolph's account will be familiar to anyone who has witnessed an outbreak of influenza:

> *Immediately upon the Quene's arrival here, she fell acquainted with a new disease that is common in this towne, called here the newe acquaintance, which passed also throughe her whole courte, neither sparinge lordes, ladies nor damoysells not so much as ether Frenche or English. It ys a plague in their heades that have yt, and a soreness in their stomackes, with a great*

*coughe, that remayneth with some longer, with others shorter
tyme, as yt findeth apte bodies for the nature of the disease. The
queen kept her bed six days. There was appearance of danger,
nor manie that die of the disease, excepte some old folkes.*[9]

By the eighteenth-century 'Age of Enlightenment', a spirit of
scientific enquiry enabled doctors and scientists to keep better
records of epidemics and speculate as to the nature of the
disease. As doctors came to realize that influenza was spread
via infection, rather than being caused by foul air and mists,
recording major epidemics became a matter of note. One
particularly virulent outbreak in 1743 originated in Italy, and as
it spread across Europe the term influenza became generally used
and was recorded in the *Gentleman's Magazine* in May 1743.[10] In
London the epidemic trebled the death rate in one week. Horace
Walpole, describing its effects in a letter dated 25 March 1743,
stated 'not a family in London has scaped under five or six ill;
many people have been forced to hire new labourers. Guernier,
the apothecary, took two new apprentices, and yet could not
drug all his patients.'[11] A generation later saw one of the worst
influenza outbreaks in history commemorated by Edward Gray
as 'An Account of the Epidemic Catarrh' in 1782 at the request
of the Society for Promoting Medical Knowledge.[12]

The first influenza epidemic of the nineteenth century appeared
in Paris, and then Britain and Ireland in 1803, by which time
some doctors were investigating the process of transmission by
social contact and the possible benefits of isolation or quarantine.
In 1831, a lethal strain of influenza swept across Europe, with
pneumonia a common complication. This epidemic occurred in
three waves, the second wave appearing in 1833 and the third in

1837. The final deadly wave claimed 3,000 lives in Dublin alone and was described by one London doctor as one of the 'more direfurl scourges'.[13]

In 1847–8, another influenza pandemic claimed an additional 5,000 lives in London over and above a normal influenza season and was compared to cholera. Over a period of six weeks it spread across Britain. Many died of pneumonia, bronchitis, asthma and similar ailments associated with influenza.[14]

Many of the doctors treating patients during the 1918 epidemic could recall the influenza pandemic of 1889–91, which probably came from southern China but was called Russian flu. Russian flu also hit the United States, with poor European immigrants being blamed for bringing it to the New World by steamship.[15] In America, a quarter of a million people died from Russian flu, and it subsequently spread to Japan, Latin America and Asia. Russian flu appeared in Britain four times between 1889 and 1894, killing approximately 100,000 Britons. After 1894, however, there were no further widespread epidemics until Spanish flu was unleashed upon an unsuspecting world in 1918.

Although influenza viruses as such were not isolated until the 1930s, medical scientists were already attempting to understand the nature of influenza. The eminent virologist Jeffery Taubenberger, a leading authority on influenza, has offered a lucid explanation of the stage researchers had reached by 1918:

Influenza was not known to be caused by a virus at that point – though the idea that viruses existed was beginning to be accepted by the scientific and medical literature. Virus, of course, just means 'poison' in Latin. A virus is nothing but a package of genes inside some proteins. So whether it's alive or not is kind of debatable. It's either a kind of a complex chemical or a very simple life form.[16]

Scientists did, however, understand the nature of bacteriology by 1918 through growing specimens of suspected bacterial material in laboratories and then attempting to strain out the infection matter through a filtration process. 'They were able to culture and identify and speciate a large number of bacteria,'[17] reports Taubenberger. 'They knew how big they were, and they developed filters that should block the passage of all the bacteria that they knew about.'[18]

However, the scientists discovered that bacteria was still coming through the filters, despite the filtration process designed to remove it, and the resulting liquid was still infectious. 'So they had the idea that what was infectious was a chemical, a poison, a "virus"; it wasn't actually an organism,'[19] Taubenberger explained. This was before the invention of electron microscopes, and it was impossible to see a virus through a light microscope, so scientists were unable to understand what a 'virus' actually was. It was merely an infectious 'thing' that slipped through the filters. 'Whatever these viruses were, infectious organisms, agents, teeny tiny bacteria or whatever, they were so small that they couldn't be seen, couldn't be cultured, couldn't be filtered. So they didn't know that influenza was a virus; they thought it was a bacterial disease.'[20]

Taubenberger has described viruses in anthropomorphic terms as 'very clever little beasts'.[21] 'Personally I think of viruses as living and sort of my adversaries!'[22] he commented in one interview. In the case of the virus that caused Spanish flu, medical scientists were up against a very clever 'little beast' indeed.

By January 1918, the world was still in the grip of the Great War, a global conflict on an unprecedented scale that had led to the death of 38 million people. While the war still raged, along came an outbreak of the H1N1 influenza virus that would inflict higher casualties than the war itself, from Europe to Africa, from the Pacific to the Arctic, from India to Norway. Ten to 20 per cent of those infected died, a third of the world's population. As many as 25 million are believed to have perished during the first twenty-five weeks of the epidemic, leading historians to refer to Spanish flu as the greatest medical holocaust in history, killing more than the Black Death. In India, 17 million are estimated to have died, 13.88 million of these in British India. In Africa, 2 per cent of the entire population was wiped out, 100,000 in Ghana alone. In Tanzania, an estimated 10 per cent of the population died, and the epidemic was followed by a famine which killed thousands more. In the United States, the figure was over half a million. Given censorship, lack of accurate records and inaccurate death certificates, the total global mortality may be even higher. According to Professor Oxford, the figures from China, which were low by comparison with data from other parts of the world, have yet to be confirmed, while the circumstances of many servicemen's deaths were concealed to safeguard morale. But whatever the final tally, there is no doubt that the 1918 influenza outbreak was one of the deadliest natural disasters in human history.

In 1918, mass troop movements spread Spanish flu among the military, while 'bond drives', aimed at persuading citizens to contribute to the war effort, and victory parades in the United States dispersed influenza among the civilian population. In Philadelphia, one such bond drive was to have devastating consequences and send the mortality rate soaring in the City of

Brotherly Love.[23] In Britain, Whitehall chiefs were reluctant to introduce quarantine restrictions on buses and trams for fear of damaging morale.[24]

The end of the war did not bring an end to Spanish flu. As the death rate soared, the joyful crowds gathered to welcome the Armistice in Albert Square, Manchester, unwittingly inviting the Spanish Lady to join them, and the killer virus remained active well into 1919.[25]

The most terrifying aspect of Spanish flu, in addition to its astonishingly transmissible nature, were its horrifying symptoms. By comparison, in a conventional case of influenza, the victim incubates the virus for at least twenty-four hours and up to four or five days before the disease becomes obvious. The first signs are headache, chills, dry cough, fever, weakness and loss of appetite. Generalized fatigue and, in some, bronchitis and pneumonia ensue. Recovery to full strength following influenza may take several weeks or longer. What can confuse the matter is that although influenza is a distinct and recognizable clinical entity, many patients and some physicians tend to group most respiratory ailments under a blanket term of 'flu'.[26] For most of us a case of flu means little more than a few days off work, paracetamol tablets and hot lemon drinks on the sofa.

But Spanish flu, by contrast, was far more aggressive and fast acting. During the devastating second wave of the epidemic, which began in the summer of 1918, victims collapsed in the streets, haemorrhaging from lungs and nose. Their skin turned dark blue with the characteristic 'heliotrope cyanosis' caused by oxygen failure as their lungs filled with pus, and they gasped for breath from 'air-hunger', like landed fish. Those who died quickly were the lucky ones. Others suffered projectile vomiting and explosive diarrhoea, and died raving as their brains were starved of oxygen. Those who recovered were often left with a lifetime's legacy of nervous conditions, heart problems, lethargy and depression. Doctors and nurses worked heroically to care for the sick, often falling ill themselves. Dr Basil Hood, medical superintendent of St Marylebone Infirmary, London, left a devastating account of conditions at his hospital, which he described as 'the most distressing occurrence of my professional life'.[27] On the Western Front, nursing staff had to cope with an endless stream of corpses, dark blue and putrescent within hours of death,[28] in addition to treating combat injuries.

On the battlefield, both Allies and Germans sustained massive losses. Out of the 100,000 casualties suffered by the US military, 40,000 troops died from Spanish flu. As troop movements dispersed influenza to every corner of the globe, the Spanish Lady travelled alongside innocent doughboys, from the United States to France. On one such journey, the doomed voyage of the USS *Leviathan* in September 1918, over ninety-six men succumbed to Spanish flu in hellish conditions while dozens more perished once they disembarked.[29]

Life on Civvy Street was no better, with entire families struck down in their homes. Children starved to death as their parents lay helpless in their beds; deranged men murdered their children, convinced that their offspring would starve without them. In South Africa, the bodies of dead and dying mine workers were thrown from trains and left along the trackside.[30] In New York, 600 children ended up in orphanages. Across the globe, entire cities became ghost towns as daily life ground to a halt. In Washington and Cape Town, undertakers ran out of coffins, while in Philadelphia a shortage of burial space meant the city council resorted to excavating mass graves with steam shovels.[31] As the spectre of the Spanish Lady conjured up visions of the Black Death of 1348, the great plague of 1665 and the terrible waves of cholera and typhus that devastated Europe in the 1840s, some speculated that this was not influenza at all, but plague itself, and feared that the human race would be wiped out. As the American epidemiologist Dr Victor C. Vaughan pointed out in 1918, the doctors of the day 'knew no more about the flu than fourteenth-century Florentines had known about the Black Death'.[32]

Combatants and civilians on both sides of the divide now discovered that Death was the new enemy. As isolated outbreaks formed into the terrible pattern of a pandemic, the world responded as if at the mercy of some alien invasion; Spanish flu became reminiscent of H. G. Wells's science fiction classic *War of the Worlds*.

Another disturbing feature of Spanish flu was the age of the casualties. Normally, it is the very young, the very old and patients with compromised immune systems who are most susceptible to dying of influenza. But the majority of victims in the Spanish flu epidemic were healthy young men and women, wiped out in their prime. Pregnant women were particularly vulnerable, Spanish flu killing both them and new mothers and their babies. In Massachusetts, one midwife helped a young woman deliver her premature baby, only to have both die within hours.[33]

Between spring 1918 and summer of 1919, the Spanish Lady continued her dance of death, attacking without warning, and seemingly at random. As if in a disaster movie, there was no telling which members of the worldwide cast would live or die. Those who survived included Franklin D. Roosevelt, who arrived in New York after a near fatal voyage on the unlucky

USS *Leviathan*;[34] British Prime Minister David Lloyd George also almost lost his life to influenza, a death which would have caused dreadful loss of morale to the Allies;[35] it was thought that Mahatma Ghandi wouldn't survive, and Kaiser Wilhelm suffered alongside his subjects. The great American novelist John Steinbeck recovered, as did the author Mary McCarthy, film star Lillian Gish, and Groucho Marx and Walt Disney. The experience of Spanish flu appears to have had a significant psychological impact; writers in particular noted the changes. It is said that Steinbeck's perspective was forever changed by the experience,[36] while Katherine Anne Porter, author of the Spanish flu memoir *Pale Horse, Pale Rider*, regarded the disease as an epiphany that altered the direction of her life.[37] Thomas Wolfe, one of the greatest American novelists, left a spellbinding and compelling account of his brother's death from Spanish flu in his most famous novel, *Look Homeward, Angel*.[38]

Spanish flu presented the wartime medical profession with its greatest challenge: how to tame the epidemic through cure, control and containment. Given the huge impact of the disease on both sides, much of the research was conducted by the military. While the civil authorities dismissed influenza as a distraction when all thought should be of the war, military doctors in Britain and the United States began to look for a solution based on their existing research into other epidemic diseases such as typhoid and cholera; but their hands were tied. They did not know exactly what they were dealing with. With the benefit of hindsight, we know that influenza is caused by a virus; but in 1918 scientists believed it was a bacterial disease, characterized by the presence of Pfeiffer's *bacillus*. Ultimately, the research conducted during these dark, terrifying times would lead to great scientific breakthroughs, such as the recognition that influenza can affect humans, birds and pigs, and the classification of the three subtypes of the influenza virus as type A (Smith, 1933), type B (Francis, 1936) and type C (Taylor, 1950).[39] But back in the autumn of 1918, as medical scientists struggled to develop a vaccine with their colleagues dropping dead around them, it must have seemed a desperate race against time.

Apart from the Spanish Lady herself, the most distinctive image of Spanish flu is the mask. While the mask itself provided little protection from the disease, it has become the icon of the epidemic. Generally white and fastened behind the head, the mask graduated from medical staff to the civilian population; in many towns and cities it became an offence to go outside without one. Policemen directed traffic in masks, entire family groups were photographed in their masks, including their cats and dogs; a honeymooning couple in San Francisco shyly confessed to their doctor that they wore their masks and nothing else when making love.[40] Surreal and haunting, the photographs of masked figures from this period resemble scenes from a science fiction film.

One of the most contested aspects of the Spanish flu epidemic remains its origins, as researchers and historians continue to debate the causes of the epidemic and indeed the very nature of Spanish flu. While some still argue that Spanish flu originated in the battlefields of France, as a mutation from animal flu,[41] others claimed that Spanish flu was not influenza at all but a strain of bubonic plague from China which travelled to the United States and Europe with the Chinese labourers supporting the Allied armies.[42] War is a great time of conspiracy theories so it comes as no surprise that many believed the flu to be man-made in origin, with claims being made that it had been distributed by

German U-boats on the Eastern seaboard or circulated in Bayer aspirin packs.[43] In highly religious communities, Spanish flu was even seen as divine punishment for humanity's sinful nature in general and in starting a war in particular.[44] Many survivors and eyewitnesses speculated that the original cause was the millions of corpses rotting in No Man's Land, combined with the lingering effects of mustard gas.[45] These explanations continue to be discussed to this day.

One aim of *Pandemic 1918* was to examine the impact of Spanish flu from the point of view of those who witnessed it, either famous or obscure. To this end, I present the memories of East End schoolgirls, Mayfair debutantes, Boston schoolboys and Italian immigrants. In this book you will find Lady Diana Manners, 'the most beautiful woman in England',[46] and her fiancé Duff Cooper, overwhelmed with despair on Armistice night;[47] the war poet Robert Graves losing his mother-in-law to Spanish flu after a night at the theatre; Vera Brittain of the Volunteer Aid Detachment, and author of *Testament of Youth*, surviving what seems to have been an early attack of Spanish flu,[48] and countless other nurses battling to cope with influenza cases at the Front. Here too are the forgotten heroes, Dr James Niven, Chief Medical Officer of Manchester, whose advice spared the lives of many, but not enough, in his own view; the medical researcher Walter Fletcher, who devoted his life to finding a solution to influenza; and Major Graeme Gibson, the doctor who became a martyr to his own research. But while Spanish flu killed many famous individuals, including the Austrian painter Egon Schiele, the majority of its victims remained unknown and unmourned outside of their immediate families, my own grandparents included. In numerous parts of China, Africa, India and Russia (in the maelstrom of revolution) the lack of accurate records meant that many millions of victims went unrecorded, their stories lost in the horror of the pandemic. For this reason, I have chosen to focus on the personal stories that have been preserved and handed down through family memories, documents, memoirs and the lives of more famous individuals. As the majority of these have been drawn from the British and American experience of Spanish flu, the emphasis of this book is unavoidably Western, although I have attempted to touch upon the impact of Spanish flu in British India, South Africa and New Zealand.

In the last chapters of the book, I explore research into the H1N1 virus carried out by Jeffery Taubenberger, the ill-fated excavation in Norway to extract samples from the bodies of Norwegian miners buried in the Arctic permafrost and the horrifying implications of the 1997 Hong Kong bird flu outbreak during which six people died including two children. I also attempt to take a glimpse into the future and consider the disturbing possibility that the Spanish Lady might stage a return visit, albeit in a different guise.

Finally, I would like to explain just why I have chosen to use the term 'Spanish Lady' as a description of the fatal virus that killed over 100 million people during the period 1918–19. As the first wave of Spanish flu broke across Europe in June 1918, cartoons and illustrations appeared depicting the disease as 'the Spanish Lady'. Spanish flu was personified as a death-headed, skeletal woman in a black flamenco dress, complete with mantilla and fan. The subtext of this gothic creation implied that the 'Spanish Lady' was a prostitute, free with her favours, and infecting everybody at the same time. Often parodied in political lampoons, the Spanish Lady became an iconic symbol of the influenza epidemic (the other being the face mask), featuring in countless publications across the globe throughout the epidemic. The Spanish Lady lost none of her power to fascinate decades later, when she lent her name to the title of Richard Collier's excellent history, *The Plague of the Spanish Lady*.

When I first came to write about the 1918 influenza pandemic, I rejected the description 'Spanish Lady' as an unhelpful concept, little more than a weary misogynistic cliché. But as the months went by, I began to appreciate the Lady for what she was; a fictional creation who enabled the world to make sense of its suffering at some subconscious level. The Lady has her origins in the world of Greek mythology, as an avenging goddess, a Eumenides; there is something of Kali, the Hindu goddess of destruction, about her, too. In Christian iconography, the Spanish Lady is the shadow side of the Madonna, a *mater dolorosa*, an exterminating angel punishing the world for its destructive acts of war. She is also a classic *femme fatale*, a woman in black. She is our lady of sorrows, the Spanish Lady, our torment. As a cultural phenomenon, she is impossible to resist. And this is her story.

CHAPTER ONE

A Victim and a Survivor

A S DAWN BROKE over a military hospital in northern France, another young soldier was pronounced dead. Sadly, this was a common occurrence at 24 General Hospital, Étaples, the biggest field hospital in France. Hundreds of men had already died here, from disease or wounds. When Private Harry Underdown, a farmer's son from Kent, died on 21 February 1917, he appeared to be just one more statistic. Even the words on Harry's death certificate seemed commonplace. At twenty years old, Harry was the latest victim of 'widespread broncho-pneumonia', a complication following an attack of influenza,[1] but he may also have been one of the first victims of the disease that would morph into the terrifying entity that was Spanish flu.

Harry's short life was tragic but unremarkable; yet another young man among the millions killed during the First World War. Born near Ashford, Kent, in 1897, Harry grew up on the family farm, named 'Hodge End'.[2] When war was declared, Harry initially chose to stay on at Hodge End, later describing his occupation as that of a 'hay trusser'.[3] But then, at the end of 1915, Harry changed his mind and decided to enlist. At just 5 feet 1½ inches tall, and 132 pounds in weight, Harry was passed fit for military service and joined the Army Reserve, under a scheme whereby he was 'required to serve one day with the Colours and

18

the remainder of the period in the Army Reserve . . . until such time as you may be called up by order of the Army Council'. [4] So, although he now formed a part of the Army Reserve, Harry returned to his farm. In April 1916, Harry was called back to the army, and, as a private in the 12th Battalion, Queen's (Royal West Surrey) Regiment, he was sent for training at an army depot. But within four months he had fallen ill, and was hospitalized with tonsillitis. Harry appeared to recover, then came a relapse, and he was not finally 'discharged cured' until 5 August 1916.[5]

Almost immediately, Harry was sent over to France. Within a few weeks, he became a casualty, after being buried in debris when a shell exploded nearby. Although not physically harmed, Harry was invalided home, suffering from shell shock, the Great War's euphemism for combat stress. At Bagthorpe Military Hospital in Nottingham, Harry was found to be 'very shaken', with 'loss of speech and memory'.[6] 'Rest & bromides' formed the course of treatment prescribed.[7]

Despite these misfortunes, Harry was determined to stay in the army. In November 1916, he left hospital and returned to his regiment. After being detained in England for a few weeks, Harry crossed back to France in February 1917. Within a fortnight he had been struck down by 'widespread broncho-pneumonia', as it was named by Lieutenant J. A. B. Hammond of the Royal Army Medical Corps.[8] Lieutenant Hammond observed Harry's condition with sympathy and intense professional interest; he had witnessed similar symptoms in previous patients at Étaples, none of whom had recovered.[9]

At first, Hammond noted that Harry's symptoms seemed consistent with ordinary lobar pneumonia, 'with the sounds of crackling *rales* [popping sounds] clearly audible at the root of the patients' lungs'.[10] What was different, however, was the amount of purulent pus Harry produced, together with a terrible breathlessness that made him visibly distressed, panicking and attempting to leap out of bed. There was worse to come; as Harry's condition deteriorated, his skin began to acquire a 'dusky heliotrope type of cyanosis of the face' due to lack of oxygen.[11] Harry Underdown died soon afterwards.

Noting that this was the twentieth fatal case of 'widespread bronchial pneumonia' since the year began, Lieutenant Hammond and his colleagues became intrigued and concerned by this development, speculating that it was an unusual condition and might perhaps be war related. Lieutenant Hammond conducted a study of the condition with army pathologist Captain William Rolland and Dr T. H. G. Shore, the officer in charge of the Étaples mortuary and laboratory. Hammond's findings were eventually published in *The Lancet* in July 1917.[12] The article came to the attention of Sir John Rose Bradford RAMC, consultant physician at Étaples. Bradford, a future president of the Royal College of Physicians, was 'an enthusiastic advocate of laboratory based research'[13] and had been sent out to Étaples to do his part for the war effort. At first, Bradford had found himself frustrated by the lack of professionally interesting medical cases, freely admitting the fact in letters home to his wife. But the emergence of 'widespread bronchio-pneumonia' piqued his curiosity; the disease that killed Harry Underdown had eventually caused the death of 156 soldiers at Étaples during February and March 1917.[14] Bradford recruited Hammond to conduct further research into the condition.

One aspect of the disease only became evident after death. During autopsy, in a case of lobar pneumonia, pathologists would expect to find damage to one of the lobes of a patient's lungs. However, in the case of these patients, there was widespread bronchitis. On being sliced open, the smaller bronchi oozed thick yellow pus and in some cases contained *H. influenzae* and other bacteria.[15] Of the 156 soldiers who had been diagnosed with and died of purulent bronchitis in the winter of 1917, 45 per cent had purulent excretions blocking the smaller bronchi. As 'the disease assumed such proportions as to constitute almost a small epidemic' at Étaples, Hammond decided that these features constituted a 'distinctive clinical entity' and named the disease purulent bronchitis in a paper for the *British Medical Journal* published the following year.[16]

The most disturbing aspect of the 'purulent bronchitis' outbreak of winter 1917 was its resistance to treatment. Doctors resorted to every conceivable type of approach, including oxygen therapy, steam inhalation, even blood-letting, but without effect.

While Hammond and his team were investigating the phenomenon of purulent bronchitis in Étaples, a similar outbreak occurred at an army barracks in Aldershot, England. RAMC Major Adolphe Abrahams, older brother of the Olympian champion Harold Abrahams, was in charge of the Connaught Hospital at Aldershot during 1916 and 1917, where a series of patients had presented with purulent bronchitis in the winter months. The symptoms which these patients presented were disturbingly similar to the ones witnessed at Étaples, including coughing up yellow pus and cyanosis, and the disease was resistant to every form of treatment and had a high fatality rate.

Abrahams and his colleagues conducted their research at Aldershot entirely independently from Bradford and Hammond, with the researchers only realizing that they were dealing with the same disease when both published papers in *The Lancet* in summer and autumn 1917. Abrahams came to the conclusion that the disease was more widespread than he had envisaged, and, more disturbingly, that it would continue to flourish during the winter months, increasing the need to develop a form of prophylaxis.[17]

If, as Abrahams suggested, purulent bronchitis was more widespread than had been realized, the question arises as to how it was transmitted. Had Harry Underdown contracted purulent bronchitis earlier in his military career, becoming infected at Aldershot, or Bagthorpe? In his bid to stay in the army, and keep fighting despite his own poor health, had Harry inadvertently transmitted the prototype of the deadly disease across the Western Front? It is tempting to conclude that Harry Underwood, who lies buried at the military cemetery in Étaples, might have been the original 'Patient Zero', but in fact Harry's fate represented that of many like him who joined up and died, not in battle, but from the deadly disease that would become known as 'Spanish flu'. The origins of the disease itself and the virus that caused it proved to be far more complex.

Perhaps the answer lies in Étaples itself, a massive military base which is a strong contender for the birthplace of Spanish flu. A small town in the Pas-de-Calais, some fifteen miles south of Boulogne, Étaples Base embraced port facilities, railway yards, stores, hospitals, prisons, training areas and all the encumbrances of an army at war. In addition, there were infantry depots, training grounds, a firing range, cemetery, laundry and two post offices.[18] As horses still played a significant role in combat, there were stables for the thousands of horses that needed veterinary attention during the conflict.[19] For food, there were piggeries, ducks, geese and chickens. The coexistence of animals alongside humans had been a familiar feature of warfare for hundreds of years. Little did doctors suspect, during the First World War, that ducks operated as a 'reservoir' for bird flu viruses, littering the soil with faeces that were then snorted in by pigs grubbing for food, and that the pigs would subsequently incubate avian viruses and combine them with the human flu viruses acquired through contact with people.[20] It would not be until the last decades of the twentieth century that virologists such as Professor John Oxford and Jeffery Taubenberger discovered that avian flu could leap the species barrier and mutate into an influenza virus capable of infecting and killing humans.[21]

ANOTHER ELEMENT ADDED to this deadly petri dish was the presence of Chinese labourers, who were brought over to support the war effort. Recruited by the British in Northern China, their task was to ensure the smooth running of the Allied forces by ferrying munitions and food from the Channel ports to the camps. The presence of the animals, and the Chinese labourers, at Étaples was simply a familiar aspect of army life. At the time, the presence of the labourers was not regarded as a health issue, despite the Manchurian pneumonic 'plague' of 1910–11 which had killed between 43,000 and 60,000 people, the equivalent of the death toll during London's great plague of 1665. In hindsight, virologists such as Dr Kennedy Shortridge of Hong Kong University have identified China as 'the epicentre for influenza epidemics',[22] due to the ingrained Chinese habit of living at close quarters with their animals, keeping vulnerable piglets in their homes, for instance. 'The ingredients are here – ducks, pigs, people, in close contact,' he said.[23]

Conditions – ducks, pigs, people – were similar at Étaples, and were combined with the infectious diseases that beleaguer all military camps. Étaples consisted principally of a series of Infantry Base Depots (IBDs), gathered on the rising ground to the east of the railway that runs north–south beside the town. Drafts from England for numerous infantry divisions passed through the IBDs where, according to unit, they were regrouped, put through a period of training, and sent forward to the Front.[24] Also in the depots were to be found men transferring to other theatres of the war or consigned to the category of 'Temporary Base' after hospital and convalescence.[25] These included the interminable convoy of sick and injured Tommies and German prisoners of war from the Front nursed by a young Englishwoman, Vera Brittain, and her comrades in the Volunteer Aid Detachment or VAD at No. 24 General Hospital.

Étaples was a bleak spot at the best of times. Lady Olave Baden-Powell, wife of the founder of the Scouting movement and Chief Guide in 1918, volunteered in the YMCA huts at the base and dismissed Étaples as 'a dirty, loathsome, smelly little town'.[26] While officers managed to escape from the base camp to the smart beach resort of Le Touquet, the troops encountered oppressive conditions, with no rest for the weary. At the 'Bull Ring', as the training grounds were called, soldiers barely discharged from hospital and men who had seen much service in the trenches were put through the same training as the latest drafts from England.[27] A course in gas warfare and two weeks at the Bull Ring was the usual programme; two weeks of marching across the dunes, supervised by officers and NCOs (non-commissioned officers) of the 'blood on the bayonet' school.[28] The NCOs in charge of the training, known as the 'canaries' on account of their yellow armbands, also had a reputation of not having served at the Front, which inevitably created a certain amount of tension and contempt.[29] While conditions were poor, marching to and from the Bull Ring, and the training itself, took up the entire day. Although Étaples was a permanent base, the men were confined to tents and the main meal of the day consisted of two slices of bully beef, two biscuits and an onion. One officer remembered the training as 'demoralising beyond measure'[30] while another man recalled that the Bull Ring was like 'passing through hell for two weeks'.[31] One corporal encountered several men returning to the Front with wounds that were far from healed. 'When I asked why they had returned in that condition they invariably replied: "To get away from the Bull Ring."'[32]

Conditions and morale deteriorated to such an extent that there was a mutiny at Étaples on Sunday, 9 September 1917. Vera Brittain recalled an atmosphere of rumour and secrecy, with female personnel locked up in their hospitals for their own safety, and concluded that the mutiny had been the result of harsh conditions.[33]

The war poet Wilfred Owen, based at Étaples at the end of 1917, held an equally jaundiced view of the base, describing it in a letter home to his mother on New Year's Eve:

Last year, at this time, (it is just midnight, and now is the intolerable instant of the Change) last year I lay awake in a windy tent in the middle of a vast, dreadful encampment. It seemed neither France nor England, but a kind of paddock where the beasts are kept a few days before the shambles. I heard the revelling of the Scotch troops, who are now dead, and who knew they would be dead. I thought of this present night, and

*whether I should indeed – whether we should indeed – whether
you would indeed – but I thought neither long nor deeply, for I
am a master of elision. But chiefly I thought of the very strange
look on all faces in that camp; an incomprehensible look, which
a man will never see in England, though wars should be in
England; nor can it be seen in any battle. But only in Étaples.
It was not despair, or terror, it was more terrible than terror,
for it was a blindfold look, and without expression, like a dead
rabbit's.*[34]

For all its disadvantages, Étaples was the perfect spot for a
military hospital. The base was close to the railway lines running
south to Abbeville and the Somme, making it easy to bring the
wounded in from the battlefield and send them back to the Front
as soon as they were ready to fight again. Étaples was also close
to Boulogne, offering a short hop across the Channel to England,
an important consideration with German submarines patrolling
the Channel.

Vera Brittain, who had abandoned her studies at Oxford
University to volunteer as a nurse, first arrived at No. 24 General
Hospital on 3 August 1916. Vera described Étaples poetically
as lying 'between the sand hills and the sea',[35] with 'vivid light'
hanging over the marshes.[36] The officers and men, with a blunter
turn of phrase, referred to Étaples as 'the sandheap'.[37]

The camp seemed more like a small town than a military
base, extending as far as the eye could see, with row after row of
tents for the doctors and huts for the nurses stretching across the
fields on either side of the railway line. No. 24 General Hospital
itself, which had enough beds for 22,000 patients, consisted of
twelve long wooden huts covered with nasturtium plants and

chintz curtains at the windows. But with the distant sound of gunfire, there was no escaping the purpose of the hospital and the constant atmosphere of tension. 'Everyone and everything' at Étaples was 'always on the move; friendships were temporary, appointments were temporary, life itself was the most temporary of all'.[38]

No. 24 General Hospital at Étaples had been built to cope with the huge number of casualties from the Western Front, and the diseases that accompany war. Initially, these were the traditional wounds of warfare, although these grew increasingly worse as the war progressed due to innovations in weaponry, including high-explosive shells and machine guns. Vera's duties, when she first arrived, consisted of nursing prisoners of war housed in damp, overcrowded marquees, changing dressings and draining wounds in temperatures of 90° F. By September, as the weather remained unseasonably warm, the nursing staff developed a gastric bug, which they named 'Etaplitis'.[39] With men packed so closely together, there was a real danger of dysentery and typhoid. The next problem was sepsis, and the danger that wounds sustained in the trenches would fester. The men also suffered from trench foot, a hitherto unknown condition in which the men's toes developed gangrene and dropped off, and trench fever, later discovered to have been transmitted by a louse, *Pediculus humanus*.[40] There was also another new condition known as 'war nephritis', which presented with headache, fever and kidney damage, and the consequences of mustard gas, which led to chest infections, pneumonia and the dreaded 'pulmonary bronchitis' that had killed Harry Underdown and his comrades. Demoralized by war, their immune systems weakened, the convalescent troops were weak and vulnerable.

These conditions, new and old, were sufficient to keep the medical teams working flat out for the duration of the war. On any given day, there were 10,000 medical personnel at Étaples, male and female, while a hundred trains a day pulled into the camp's railway sidings, bearing casualties from the Front. Stretched to capacity, the medical staff could scarcely cope, and many of them fell victim to illness and disease themselves, Vera among them. When Vera received a letter from her brother Edward on 12 January 1918, asking her to accompany him on leave in England, she understandably seized the opportunity.

But two days later, having arrived in Boulogne too late for the boat across the Channel, Vera found herself spending a feverish night at the port, aching all over and with a splitting headache. Next morning, a rough crossing and a freezing train journey from Folkestone did nothing to improve her condition and she reached the family home in Kensington 'in a state of collapse'.[41]

The following morning, Vera woke with a temperature of 103 degrees, and was advised to prolong her leave until she had recovered. Vera appeared to be suffering from 'PUO' (Pyrexia [fever] of Unknown Origin) also known as 'trench fever',[42] a catch-all for many wartime afflictions. Vera's symptoms are also consistent with the early onset of Spanish flu, although she mercifully escaped the latter symptoms of purulent bronchitis, cyanosis and air-hunger. Had Vera already been exposed to an early form of the virus while nursing, and acquired immunity?

Whether Vera had been infected at Étaples, or been exposed to the virus during her voyage back to England, we shall never know. Unlike Private Harry Underdown, she survived and went on to record her experiences in *Testament of Youth*, one of the most compelling memoirs of the Great War. The destinies of Private Underdown and Vera Brittain were, like their lives, very different, but both their stories serve to illustrate the medical mysteries surrounding the origins of Spanish flu.

CHAPTER TWO

'KNOCK ME DOWN' FEVER

———◆·◆———

O NE FREEZING NIGHT in February 1918, Dr Loring Miner was called out to a patient in Haskell County, Kansas. Dr Miner had been informed that the old lady was suffering from 'knock me down' fever, the traditional name for fever, coughing and chills. For most patients, influenza was a fitful fever that passed within days. Only the very young and the very old had reason to fear it, since complications were lethal for the vulnerable. Seizing his leather bag, Dr Miner climbed into his horse-drawn buggy and headed for the remote farmstead. A craggy figure with a distinctive handlebar moustache, Dr Miner was much loved in this harsh rural outpost. It was said that Dr Miner's patients would rather have Dr Miner drunk than any other doctor sober.[1]

Dr Miner was shocked by what he found when he reached the farmstead. The patient, an elderly woman, had developed 'heliotrope cyanosis', and was turning blue from lack of oxygen. Fighting for her life, she was racked with coughing fits and struggling to breathe; her family crowded round with bowls and towels as she suffered one catastrophic haemorrhage after another, blood frothing up from her lungs. Dr Miner immediately diagnosed pneumonia, following the initial onset of influenza, but never before had he witnessed such virulent symptoms.

The patient died in agony soon afterwards. Over the following days, Dr Miner scarcely had time to record his patient's unusual symptoms, for he was rushed off his feet by a flurry of similar cases. Night and day, local families knocked at the door of Dr Miner's house or appeared in his drugstore begging for help. Many of the victims were previously fit and healthy, farm boys and young women struck down without warning. Influenza, potentially fatal for infants and the elderly, seemed to be targeting the healthiest folk in the community. Fascinated and appalled, Dr Miner threw himself into solving the riddle of this mystery affliction. He even administered diphtheria and tetanus injections to stimulate his patients' immune systems. But there was little time for research, as Dr Miner chased the influenza the length and breadth of Haskell County. Although he had an automobile, one of the first in the county, he relied on his old horse-drawn buggy. He was frequently so exhausted that he fell asleep in the buggy, leaving his horse to find the way home.[2] On rare breaks between house calls, the doctor consulted medical textbooks, wrote to other physicians and analysed blood and urine samples from his patients in a search for a cure. He suspected, but could not prove, that the outbreak had something to do with animal husbandry, due to the frequency of outbreaks in remote farmsteads, but he was battling in the dark. In 1918, our modern concept of a virus was unknown to medical science. It was understood that particles existed that were smaller than bacteria, but it would not be until 1938, with the invention of the electron microscope, that scientists would begin identifying viruses.[3]

While scientists were already researching bacterial vaccines for many diseases including smallpox, anthrax, rabies, diphtheria and meningitis, bacterial vaccines for influenza were of limited availability. Doctors could only rely on the classic treatments for influenza: bedrest, opium to suppress coughing and relieve pain, and quinine, an extract of tree bark. Traditionally used to treat malaria, although no longer recommended for this purpose, quinine was thought to aid recovery by enabling the patient to sweat out infection. Many patients turned to folk remedies, some more palatable than others. While lemon, whiskey and garlic were traditional 'cure alls', along with herbal remedies, more bizarre suggestions included castor oil and kerosene on a sugar cube.

As Haskell County held its breath and feared for its loved ones, the local newspaper, the *Santa Fe Monitor*, performed its traditional task of informing readers about the day-to-day activities of its readers: 'Mrs. Eva Van Alstine is sick with pneumonia', the paper announced, and as if by way of consolation: 'Her little son Roy is now able to get up.'[4] A day or two later came the announcement that 'Ralph Lindeman is still quite sick. Goldie Wolgehagen is working at the Beeman store during her sister Eva's sickness.'[5] Readers were also informed that while 'Homer Moody has been reported quite sick, Mrs J S Cox is some better but is very weak yet', and 'Ralph McConnell has been quite sick this week.'[6] The *Monitor* concluded that 'most everybody over the county is having lagrippe or pneumonia'.[7]

These blunt descriptions downplayed the impact of the influenza outbreak in Haskell County. Descriptions such as 'sick' or 'weak' did not do justice to the sheer terror experienced by patients and their families, the speed with which the influenza outbreak took hold, and the appalling symptoms of cyanosis, haemorrhages and the sinister 'air-hunger' that left patients clawing at the air and gasping for breath.

Within weeks, the influenza outbreak in Haskell County subsided as quickly as it had begun, but Dr Miner refused to forget the experience, which had begun with the death of the elderly lady on the farmstead. The doctor had lost three patients to secondary pneumonia, a common complication of influenza, and was deeply concerned about the prospect of another outbreak. He wrote to the government in Washington, warning them about the outbreak in Haskell County and recommending precautions against an epidemic, but he was largely ignored. Influenza was not a 'notifiable disease', meaning that it had to be reported to the public health authorities, and the government was preoccupied with the war effort. This would be the first occasion when the government suppressed warnings of a lethal influenza virus for the sake of national morale. Dr Miner's reports were eventually published, tucked away from prying eyes within the unsensational pages of a professional journal, the *Public Health Reports* for 5 April 1918: 'INFLUENZA Kansas Haskell On March 30, 1918, the occurrence of 18 cases of influenza of severe type, from which 3 deaths resulted, was reported at Haskell, Kans.'[8]

Meanwhile, back in Haskell County, the *Santa Fe Monitor* continued to report the minutiae of small-town life. Young Dean Nilson returned home on leave from the army and the paper concluded that 'Dean looks like soldier life agrees with him.'[9] At the same time as Dean arrived home, Ernest Elliott embarked on his journey to Camp Funston, Fort Riley, to visit his brother. This military reservation, 300 miles from Haskell County, was the same place that Dean Nilson had just left. When Ernest Elliott set off, his young son Mertin was unwell. While Ernest was away, the little boy's condition deteriorated.

The ever informative *Sante Fe Monitor* noted that 'Mertin [*sic*], the young son of Ernest Elliot, is sick with pneumonia.'[10] Mertin had contracted the potentially lethal strain of influenza, and his father, although not a victim, was clearly a carrier, bringing the contagion with him to Fort Riley. A few days later, Dean Nilson arrived back at the same camp. Both men unwittingly spread the virus; an unforeseen consequence of America's entry into the war.

America in 1918 had become a nation at war. Led by President Woodrow Wilson, the United States had declared war on Germany the previous year, galvanizing the country with draft call-ups, troop shipments and bond drives. By spring 1918, the nation was poised to play a decisive role in the conflict. Over 4 million men from all backgrounds volunteered or were conscripted to serve their country in a climate of patriotic fervour. Recruited from rural backwaters and sprawling cities, from Midwest prairies and the depths of the South, these men found themselves quartered in army camps, undergoing the basic training that would enable them to fight on all fronts against a common enemy. Tragically, these were also the ideal conditions for an outbreak of disease, according to epidemiologist Dr Victor C. Vaughan, writing with hindsight in his 1936 memoirs:

The procedures followed in the mobilization of our soldiers in the World War brought into every cantonment every infection then existent in the areas from which the men came. Drafted men were assembled at some point in each state. They came from every community; they came in their ordinary clothing; some clean, some filthy. Each one brought many samples of the bacteria then abounding in his own neighborhood. They brought

*these organisms on and in their bodies and on and in their
clothing. They were crowded together at the state rendezvous
and held here for varying periods of time, long enough to pass
through the stages of enlistment. Then they filled troop trains
and were transferred to their respective cantonments.*[11]

While Vaughan was referring to measles in this broadside, the
same rules applied to the epidemics of influenza that broke out
in army camps in 1918. But at the time, his words and those of
fellow medics fell on deaf ears: 'The dangers in the mobilization
procedures followed by us in the World War were pointed out
to the proper authorities before there was any assembly, but the
answer was: "The purpose of mobilization is to convert civilians
into trained soldiers as quickly as possible and not to make a
demonstration in preventive medicine."'[12]

But, of course, Vaughan stated, the worst place for an infection
was an army camp: 'The more densely people are packed together
the more difficult it is to control the spread of infection. There
are no other conditions under which men are so closely and so
continuously in contact as in an army camp.'[13]

Camp Funston, Fort Riley, Texas, was just such a camp, a
typical example of the camps that were rising up across the
United States. Located on the Fort Riley military reservation near
Junction City, Kansas, Camp Funston, named after Brigadier
General Frederick Funston, was the largest of sixteen divisional
cantonment training camps built during the First World War
to house and train soldiers for military duty. Construction had
begun in July 1917 and buildings were laid out uniformly in city
block squares with main streets and side streets on either side.
An estimated 2,800 to 4,000 buildings were constructed at the

camp to accommodate more than 40,000 soldiers from the US Army's 89th Division, who were stationed at the facility. The camp cost roughly $10 million to build.[14]

More like a city than an army camp, Camp Funston contained housing and training centres, general stores, theatres, social centres, infirmaries, libraries, schools, workshops and even a coffee roasting house. The sleeping barracks were 43 feet by 140 feet and two storeys high. In them was a kitchen, mess hall, company commander's office, supply rooms and squad rooms or dormitories. There were 150 beds in each sleeping room, as that was the size of an infantry company in 1917.[15]

Camp Funston's main purpose was to train soldiers drafted in Midwestern states to fight overseas. Men would spend their hours drilling and learning new military techniques, and many officers were brought in from other countries such as France and Britain to train the Midwest soldiers. In their free time soldiers could see a show at the theatres or visit one of the social centres, although many pined for life back home. James H. Dickson, who served in the 356th Infantry Regiment of the 89th Division, wrote to his friend: 'Eunice don't be to [sic] long about writing for news is scarce out in Kansas the wind blows it all away.'[16] The reference to the wind is significant. Soldiers often complained about the inhospitable weather conditions at Camp Funston, the bone-chilling winters and sweltering summers. First Lt Elizabeth Harding, army nurse corps and the first chief nurse at Fort Riley, recalled that 'I arrived at Fort Riley about the middle of October, 1917, in a snow storm! I spent the coldest winter of my life and the hottest summer that I can remember.'[17] As if the climate were not enough to contend with, conditions were made worse by the blinding dust storms, which in turn were intensified by manure fires. Fort Riley was the centre of the US Cavalry and thousands of horses and mules were stationed there; soldiers learned the skills of horsemanship, from veterinary science to farriery to harness-making and saddlery. The future General George Patton was to be seen there, playing polo and show jumping at weekends.[18] The horses produced around nine tons of manure a month, and burning was the accepted method of disposal. As a result, the dust, combined with the ash of burning manure, created a stinging, stinking yellow haze. The grains of fine grit aggravated lungs and bronchi, leaving men miserable and prone to asthma, bronchitis and pneumonia, while thick black smoke hugged the ground for hours and further irritated respiratory tracts.[19]

One of the biggest problems at any military camp was the spread of communicable disease. All soldiers were inoculated against 'battlefield' diseases such as cholera and dysentery upon entering the camp, and any men thought to have any communicable disease were immediately quarantined until they either recovered or were no longer considered contagious. In 1918, the commandant of the base hospital at Fort Riley was Colonel Edward Schreiner, a surgeon who had entered federal service as a contract surgeon, joined the regular medical corps and commanded the cantonment hospital on the Mexican border in 1916.[20] Army nurses had arrived to bleak conditions just a year earlier. First Lieutenant Elizabeth Harding recalled that 'barracks were being converted into hospitals. At first it was very primitive with no toilet or bath facilities except in the basement of the buildings. Hot water and heat were scarce.'[21]

On Saturday, 9 March 1918, Fort Riley endured a significant dust storm, one of the worst that the men could remember. It was said that the sun went black in Kansas that day. Trains had to halt on the tracks and Fort Riley was covered in soot and ash. Men were assigned to clean up the mess, but it did not occur to their commanding officers to issue them with masks. The following Monday, 11 March, company cook Private Albert Gitchell reported sick, suffering from a sore throat and a headache. The duty medical officer suspected Private Gitchell's symptoms were caused by the dust storms and the after-effects of manure bonfires, but, since Private Gitchell was running a temperature of 40° C, he was confined to an isolation bed.[22] Soon afterwards, Corporal Lee W. Drake and Sergeant Adolph Hurby presented themselves. At 41° C, Private Hurby's temperature was even higher than Gitchell's, and he suffered from an inflamed throat, nasal and bronchial passages. As a steady stream of sick men formed an orderly queue, the duty medical officer called in Colonel Schreiner for back-up. By noon, Colonel Schreiner and his assistants had seen over 107 sick men; by the end of the week there were 522 cases at Camp Funston, and by the end of March, 1,100 men were sick, so many that a hangar had to be requisitioned as a ward.[23] In paying attention to this outbreak of influenza, and fulfilling the duty of care to the men, Colonel Schreiner was being ultra-cautious following events of the previous year. In 1917, an army officer, John Dwyer, had been court martialled following the death of recruits from influenza. Dwyer was found guilty of neglect, having ordered one flu victim to take on additional duties despite the fact that he was severely ill. Dwyer was dismissed from the army.[24]

This outbreak was severe, but not unexpected. Outbreaks of contagious disease were common in barracks, where so many men were crushed in together, in cramped conditions. First

Lieutenant Harding noted that 'As usual in large groups as were housed together at Camp Funston, there were many epidemics. Many of the troops came from the farms where they had never come in contact with contagious diseases.'[25] But this outbreak was different.

Colonel Schreiner's initial diagnosis suggested that his patients had succumbed to influenza. Their symptoms resembled a classic case of influenza, with a chill followed by a high fever, headache and back pain. But some patients were too weak to stand, and their symptoms included violent coughing, projectile nosebleeds, and air-hunger, some choking to death. The death toll was unusually high: while most patients recovered within five days, forty-eight died of complications such as pneumonia and haemorrhages. As the virulent strain of influenza cut a swathe through Camp Funston, Colonel Schreiner telegraphed the US Army's GHQ in Washington on 30 March: 'Many deaths influenza following immediately two extremely severe dust storms.'[26] The authorities treated Colonel Schreiner the same way they had treated Dr Loring Miner: they did not take his warnings seriously.

Dust storms were nothing new in Kansas; neither were outbreaks of contagious diseases in army camps. But put together, the two seemed to suggest some new and hitherto unknown menace. Dr Miner and Colonel Schreiner were both aware that plague, in the form of pneumonic plague, represented a real threat. Pneumonic plague, the 'Black Death' of medieval history, was transmitted by breath, just like influenza, and as noted in the previous chapter, there had been an outbreak of pneumonic plague in Manchuria. Some 200,000 labourers from North China had passed through North America, to work with the Allies in France. Had they brought pneumonic plague with them, which now, after modification by the new environment, was appearing as the new and deadly strain of influenza? This theory, of course, does not explain the outbreaks in the remote farmsteads witnessed by Dr Miner.

Colonel Schreiner seemed to believe that the dust storm itself had triggered the epidemic, but in hindsight there were other possibilities: had swine flu mutated from animals kept on the base, or had horse flu, known as 'the Strangles', mutated from the camp's a thousand cavalry horses?[27] It is entirely possible that some of those horses were suffering from a strain of flu, which was then spread across the camp by the burning of manure. In practical terms, while the dust cloud may not have caused the influenza, it certainly helped it on its way, leaving the soldiers breathless and wheezing for days, ideal conditions in which a flu virus might flourish.

And then, just as before in Haskell County, the influenza vanished as swiftly as it had begun, and was forgotten in the ferment of preparation for the war in Europe.

CHAPTER THREE

THE KILLER WITHOUT A NAME

$\longrightarrow$

A S THE AMERICAN war effort intensified in the spring of 1918, outbreaks of a particularly severe strain of influenza flared up across the military camps apparently simultaneously, from New York to Florida, California and Alabama. Although influenza was a regular hazard of army life, the consequence of overcrowding and insanitary quarters, a number of officers became alarmed about the rapidity and severity of the outbreaks. The new strain of deadly influenza also began to make inroads among the civilian population, targeting those places where people were gathered together at close quarters, such as schools and prisons. The following series of events indicates the arbitrary manner in which the 'First Wave' of Spanish flu, as it would become known, occurred across the United States.

In the US army, Colonel Edward Schreiner had already expressed unease about the outbreak of influenza at Camp Funston. Major General Hugh Scott, commander of the 78th Division at Camp Dix in New Jersey, soon became similarly concerned. In April 1918, Major General Hugh Scott wrote to US Surgeon General William Crawford Gorgas about the spread of disease at Camp Dix, in particular influenza, which was responsible for an increasing number of pneumonia cases.

Major General Scott was at a loss to explain the cause for such an epidemic, as 'the camp is as clean as a hound's tooth'.[1]

In his letter to General Gorgas, Major General Scott described the sanitation measures he had ordered at Camp Dix and asked Gorgas to come and visit the camp and 'give us the once over'.[2] Major General Scott could not rest easy until he could be certain that he had done everything he could to prevent his men from becoming infected.

For his part, General Gorgas took Major General Scott's plea very seriously, having conquered yellow fever in the American army. Yellow fever, so called because in its second, toxic, stage it causes jaundice, is a viral disease spread by infected female mosquitos. Gorgas had famously tackled the virus with a programme of sanitary precautions, and was eager to tackle an outbreak of pneumonia in the same ruthlessly energetic fashion. General Gorgas was convinced that one reason for this particularly virulent outbreak was overcrowding.

'I haven't the least doubt that if you, tomorrow, could give every man in Camp Dix his own individual hut, that pneumonia would ease at once,'[3] he declared, explaining that this was his chosen method for fighting pneumonia among construction workers on the Panama Canal, adding that 'we have a number of the best scientists in the United States studying this question of transmission of pneumonia and may be [sic] we will be as successful with pneumonia in this as we were with yellow fever and malaria in the Spanish-American War'.[4]

One victim of the outbreak at Camp Dix was Private Harry T. Pressley of the 15th US Cavalry. Pressley caught influenza during the spring epidemic at Camp Dix, but was not considered sick enough to be taken off duty. Fortunately for Private Pressley, he had an office job which limited his physical activity. Pressley's buddy, Cid Allen, had also fallen sick, but he was 'ordered to keep on drilling' and was still sick when they shipped out to France in April 1918.[5]

It was only when further outbreaks of this particularly severe strain of influenza struck simultaneously that the US military conceded that there might be a problem. Outbreaks of influenza occurred at army camps in California, Florida, Virginia, Alabama, South Carolina and Georgia.[6] General Gorgas reported epidemic influenza at Camps Oglethorpe, Gordon, Grant, Lewis, Doniphan, Fremont, Sherman, Logan, Hancock, Kearney, McClellan and others.[7]

Outbreaks were not restricted to the military. Back in Haskell County, source of the disturbing outbreak witnessed by Dr Miner, influenza hit Haskell County Indian School, where young Native Americans were trained for the workforce. Out of a population of 400 children, three died. Fatal cases of influenza also appeared in Chicago and Detroit, where a thousand workers at the Ford Motor Company came down with influenza in March 1918.[8] The mystery disease was on the move, and it was travelling fast. While it was clear to doctors such as Colonel Schreiner that this lethal strain of influenza took a different form, they didn't even have a new name for this old enemy. One army doctor did attempt to find a label, however. In *H. Camp Kearney Division Surgeon's Reports*, the local term 'Japanese influenza' was erroneously given to the disease, believed to have been started by the arrival of a squadron of Japanese warships at San Diego during the first week of April with a number of cases of influenza.[9]

Lack of documentation made the outbreak difficult to track. While the military authorities were compelled to keep medical records of troops, their fitness to serve being critical to their role in the army, no such records were available for the civilian population, as influenza was not a notifiable disease. The only acknowledgement of the lethal outbreak in this period is the brief mention of the outbreak at Haskell County in *Public Health Reports*, 5 April 1918.[10]

Influenza flourished inevitably in schools. One victim was sixteen-year-old John Steinbeck. The future author of *The Grapes of Wrath* returned home from his Californian school one day looking 'pale and dizzy'[11] and collapsed into bed, much to the horror of his mother, Olive. John's temperature shot up and he became delirious. 'I went down and down,' he remembered, 'until the wingtips of angels brushed my eyes.'[12] A local surgeon, Dr Merganser, was called in, and promptly turned the master bedroom into an operating theatre.

> He opened the teenager's chest under ether, removing a rib to gain access to the infected lung, which was then drained of pleural pus. 'We thought surely he would die on us,' his sister says. 'John looked horrible, horrible. We did everything we could for him. And then he had a relapse. It took a long time, but he was all right in the end. I must say, we were scared to death.'[13]

This drastic treatment worked, and John recovered sufficiently to attend the last three weeks of school before the summer recess, but he was left with lung problems for the rest of his life. The experience bestowed a strange psychological legacy, leaving Steinbeck with a profound sense of vulnerability which shaped him as a writer. 'It seems to have given him a sense of himself as someone on the edge of life,'[14] wrote his biographer, Jay Parini. Like so many other

Spanish flu survivors who we will meet in the course of this book, Steinbeck was marked for life by the experience.

America's prisons were prime targets for influenza, which spread rapidly between overcrowded prison populations. The 1918 outbreak at San Quentin, California, where 500 of the 1,900 prisoners were affected, was a notable example, the prisoners appearing to have been victims of a notorious medical experiment.

The influenza epidemic at San Quentin was unremarkable given conditions at the prison. Resident physician Dr Leo Stanley had been appalled at the lack of hygiene when he arrived in 1913. 'The ventilation was abominable, the beds were crowded together, air space was extremely limited,'[15] he wrote, in his account of the outbreak. Stanley was particularly concerned about the spread of tuberculosis, a major killer at the time, and also reflected the prejudices of his age by expressing disgust at the lack of racial segregation. 'Whites, Negroes and Indians commingled here indiscriminately,'[16] he wrote, and the 'surroundings were extremely sordid'.[17] Despite his evident shortcomings, Stanley became an apparently model prison doctor, devoting himself to his work. With a team of four paid assistants, and inmate clerks and nurses, Stanley developed an efficient treatment system, with prisoners lined up in 'pill lines' morning and afternoon.[18] It was Stanley who, in his efficient way, chronicled the onset of influenza at San Quentin when it first arrived in April 1918.

The first outbreak at San Quentin began on 13 April when a prisoner, henceforth referred to as Prisoner A, arrived from Los Angeles county jail, where a number of other inmates had been ill. Prisoner A had been sick before he arrived at San Quentin, suffering from 'pains over his body accompanied by fever'.[19] When he entered San Quentin, Prisoner A 'mingled with the

1,900 men who were congregated in the yard on Sunday, April 14, ate in the general mess with them, and at night was locked in the receiving room with about 20 other newcomers'.[20] Prisoner A's condition deteriorated the following day and he was admitted to the prison hospital with 'a temperature of 101, chills, and an aching sensation in the back and bones'.[21] From this time on until 26 May, San Quentin underwent an epidemic of unusual severity, with 101 patients admitted to the hospital, of whom seven developed broncho-pneumonia, and three died.

The epidemic was at its height on Tuesday 23 April, when eight new cases were hospitalized; a further sixteen were admitted the following day, 24 April. On these two days, about half of the prison population was ill. According to Stanley,

> the records show that whereas ordinarily only 150 to 200 men call each day at the hospital for treatment, consultation, and advice, on these days 700 and 750 appeared.[22]
>
> Instead of the usual number of from 3 to 7 being excused from work on account of sickness, at this time there were from 25 to 62. All of these men excused from their ordinary tasks were quite ill, having temperatures ranging from 100 to 101, with pains in the back and severe prostration. They should have been placed in the hospital, but it was impossible to put them there on account of lack of facilities. They were allowed to stay in the open air and were not permitted to go to their cells until evening, because, it was believed that this unusual disease might be increased by confinement in stuffy rooms during the day.[23]

This move reveals one of the early treatment methods for influenza victims. Although doctors had no real understanding of influenza, there remained the prevailing Victorian conviction that fresh air was beneficial to patients, hence the countless entreaties encouraging families of flu victims to open a window.

Stanley was genuinely astonished by the number of flu victims at San Quentin, particularly as he maintained a profound belief that many prisoners faked their symptoms in order to avoid work details. In his memoirs, Stanley reflected on his capacity to 'distinguish the malingerer, the malcontent, and the hypochondriac'[24] although the 'talent I developed for recognizing faked illnesses has won me a fair share of hatred . . . I have been pictured as a medical sadist, gloating over tortured victims.'[25] As far as Stanley was concerned, this was the price he paid for being a stern, but fair, prison physician.[26]

But on this occasion, the men at San Quentin were genuinely sick. Although many prisoners who were obviously unwell carried on with their work, so many were ill that in 'the jute mill, tailor shop, furniture factory, and foundry it was almost impossible to keep up operations, and the governor considered a complete shutdown'.[27]

Stanley's article indicates how rapid the onset of influenza was. 'The weather at this time was warm and balmy, with much sunshine, and the men who felt ill were allowed to leave the mills for periods to go outside. Many felt too ill to return to work and lay down on the ground in the sunshine.'[28]

The epidemic at San Quentin gradually subsided, but in retrospect Stanley believed that over 500 of the prisoners were ill. Noting that 'the disease reached its height on Tuesdays and Wednesdays of the second and third weeks',[29] Stanley put forward an explanation. Every Sunday morning, the prisoners were permitted to watch a 'moving-picture show', with two screenings, one at eight o'clock and the other at ten. The room in which screenings were shown were partly underground, poorly ventilated, artificially lit and always 'tremendously crowded'.[30] Almost all of San Quentin's 1,900 prison population attended, and before the morning was over the room was 'moist, warm, and foul with smoke and human odours'.[31] Fans had been installed, but they were not efficient, and there was no time to air the room between shows. One body of prisoners entered the room as soon as the other left. Some prisoners remained for both shows.

Were these movie shows the ground zero of the San Quentin epidemic? Stanley seemed to think so.

> Assuming that this respiratory infection attacked its victims at the Shows on Sunday, it would seem that there was an incubation period of from 36 to 60 hours, which produced the sudden illness on the following Tuesday or Wednesday. A typical history of many of the cases is that on Sunday they visited the show, and that on Tuesday or early Wednesday they were seized with headache, fever, chills, bone ache, severe prostration, and sometimes nausea. It seems probable that the epidemic was started and introduced in this prison by the new arrival from Los Angeles, for he was the first one ill, and others became sick shortly after he arrived.[32]

Stanley admitted that Prisoner A associated closely with the other men, and could probably have passed on the disease by droplet infection. Stanley was also one of the first doctors to notice the peculiar trademarks of this specific strain of flu, including 'becoming dyspnoeic [distressed breathing], cyanotic [blue due to low oxygen in the blood], and often expelling a thin, sanguineous fluid from the lungs'.[33] Stanley also noted another aspect of the disease which had hitherto gone unrecorded: the repeat effect, during which patients would appear to recover, before relapsing and being readmitted. 'In this epidemic 9 per cent of the cases, after two or three days, had a subsidence of all symptoms and were discharged from the hospital, but in about 10 days returned with a recrudescence.'[34]

As it would later demonstrate to vicious effect, this new strain of influenza was colour blind and attacked all, regardless of race and creed. At San Quentin, victims were 73 per cent white, 18 per cent Mexican, 6 per cent African American and 3 per cent Chinese. A number of patients attacked by the influenza were so weakened that, according to Stanley, they developed tuberculosis, of which one died.

Stanley's hypothesis that Prisoner A spread the flu among his fellow prisoners appears to be convincing. But this hypothesis also raises issues about the treatment of Prisoner A from the time of his arrival. If, as Stanley stated, Prisoner A was already suffering from conventional flu, he should have been quarantined to stop the flu spreading. Instead, he was allowed to mix freely with his fellow prisoners and even attend a full house movie screening in a badly ventilated room. Was this carelessness, or was there another factor at play?

In his study of Dr Leo Stanley, the historian Ethan Blue makes it clear that Stanley was no ordinary prison doctor. Dr Leo Stanley was a eugenicist who later became famous for a bizarre series of medical experiments conducted upon the prison population of San Quentin. These included medical experiments of dubious ethical value, including attempting to treat older, 'devitalized men' by replacing their testicles with transplants from livestock and recently executed convicts. 'The practice was known as rejuvenation, the idea being that an aging man could have his testosterone levels renewed by having the testicles of a younger man implanted into him.'[35] Stanley had already begun the rejuvenation experiments in 1918, five years after taking the post at San Quentin. But Dr Stanley was concerned with more than restoring the virility of flagging older men. Motivated by his eugenicist beliefs, Dr Stanley wanted to remedy what he considered to be 'the plight of white masculinity in a country increasingly inhabited by a melting pot of races and ethnicities'[36] by encouraging white men to reproduce and so-called 'undesirables' to undergo sterilization.

Given Stanley's propensity for experimentation, it does not seem beyond the bounds of possibility that he allowed Prisoner A from Los Angeles County Jail to mix with the prisoners of San Quentin. The prison offered the perfect opportunity for a smart physician to watch the progress of the disease in laboratory conditions. Dr Stanley's observations about the spread of influenza throughout San Quentin remains an important source. Whether he deliberately tampered with the conditions in order to conduct an early medical experiment is a matter for conjecture, but it remains a convincing theory. Stanley certainly got more than he bargained for with this virulent strain of influenza.

Meanwhile, in the world outside San Quentin, the deadly new strain of influenza began to take its toll, silently, invisibly. The disease remained under the radar in the United States, breaking out here and there with sudden, dramatic impact and then vanishing again. Beyond the careful, record-keeping military and the diaries of strange Dr Stanley, its impact was hard to judge. By the early summer of 1918, the 'first wave' of influenza appeared to have receded.

In Europe it was a different story. Influenza was having a catastrophic effect on the war effort, impacting on both sides. One young American's story gives us some idea of the conditions and shows us what it was like for a man from the comparatively safe haven of mainland US confronted with the suffering in the Old Country.

In Cittadella, Italy, Second Lieutenant Giuseppe Agostoni was tending a 25-year-old soldier in an army hospital. A second-generation Italian-American, Agostoni had watched powerlessly as influenza had devastated his regiment. He and his comrades had never witnessed anything like it. Men were coughing up blood and choking to death on their pus-filled lungs; their faces turned blue and their laboured breathing produced a duck-like quack. In an effort to do something, anything, Agostoni drew out a syringe and attempted to draw blood from the soldier's arm, rationalizing that draining some of his blood might relieve the congestion. But instead, the blood clotted after 10cc; it had become black and gummy, viscous as tar.[37] He did not know it, but as Agostoni gazed hopelessly at his dying patient, similar scenes were being enacted across the entire continent of Europe. He was not alone, but he was just one man in a massive struggle against an invisible enemy: Death, and its sinister agent, the deadly disease with no name.

CHAPTER FOUR

THE INVISIBLE ENEMY

———

A S THE GERMAN army was launching its massive attack on France in spring 1918, both sides were being attacked by the lethal new strain of influenza. The Allies and the Germans did not realize it at the time, but they were dealing with an enemy mightier than any man-made army.

The German army had launched its attack on France with the conviction that it would win the Great War. With Russia having withdrawn from the war, the Germans were able to deploy over one million experienced men and 3,000 guns to the Western front, where Germany had numerical superiority. Thirty-seven infantry divisions were placed at the Western Front, with another thirty in reserve. In several sectors, the British and French were outnumbered by the German forces by a ratio of four to one.[1]

While the French position was desperate, the British army had sustained serious losses at the battle of Passchendaele. The Germans, knowing that the Allies were depleted, knew that their main hope of success depended on attacking early before the arrival of the American forces.[2]

Initially, it seemed as if the Germans were winning, gaining over 1,250 square miles of French soil within four months. By May 1918, the German army had reached the Marne River, and its heavy artillery was within range of Paris. As a result, more than one million people had already fled the French capital.[3]

But, as the Germans attacked, an invisible enemy was creeping through the Allied Expeditionary Force in France, with doctors and pathologists reporting a widespread fever in Rouen and Wimereux in the 'ill-famed Ypres salient, where disease of all sorts seemed to flourish'.[4] This development obviously raised concerns as the British and the newly arrived American forces on the Western front braced themselves for a major assault from the Germans.

Although other military diseases such as typhoid had been contained, and the British army was in relatively good physical shape despite four years of war, outbreaks of influenza were a regular occurrence. But there was something different about this one.

A rash of articles in medical journals attests to the sudden onset of this epidemic and how it differed from normal influenza. Doctors were intrigued and dismayed by this development, which resisted the traditional classification of 'la grippe' or 'trench fever'. There was clearly something different about this new condition. While Hammond and Rolland had proposed their theory of 'purulent bronchitis' for the disease they had witnessed at Étaples, there was considerable disagreement as to the aetiology of this new disease.

While the British Expeditionary Force was succumbing to the mystery illness, reports emerged in March 1918 that influenza had struck the American Allied Expeditionary Force (AEF) crossing the Atlantic to serve in France. In March, 84,000 American 'doughboys' had set out for Europe, unaware that influenza had travelled with them on their troopships. The 15th US Cavalry was hit by a pneumonia epidemic on the voyage to

Europe, suffering thirty-six cases and six deaths. Private Harry Pressley, who had survived the influenza epidemic at Camp Dix, was among those on board. Private Pressley's buddy, Cid Allen, who had been forced to carry on drilling at Camp Dix despite his obvious illness, died two days out. Private Pressley never found out whether his friend was buried at sea, or in France.[5]

By the end of March, as the killer flu continued its remorseless progress through the ranks, one of its most distressing features, acute cyanosis, had become a regular occurrence. On 1 April 1918, American nurse Shirley Millard wrote in her diary: 'We are swamped with influenza cases. I thought influenza was a bad cold, something like the *grippe*, but this is much worse than that. These men run a high temperature, so high that we can't believe it's true, and often take it again to be sure ... When they die, as about half of them do, they turn a ghastly dark grey and are taken out at once and cremated.'[6]

Despite this disturbing development, the Allies rejoiced at the arrival of their American reinforcements. On 13 April 1918, VAD Vera Brittain looked on as a large contingent of troops arrived at Étaples and a cry went up from the nurses: 'Look! Look! Here are the Americans!'[7]

I pressed forward with the [other nurses] *to watch the United States physically entering the War, so god-like, so magnificent, so splendidly unimpaired in comparison with the tired, nerve-racked men of the British army. So these were our deliverers at last, marching up the road to Camiers in the spring sunshine. There seemed to be hundreds of them, and in the fearless swagger of their proud strength they looked a formidable bulwark against the peril looming from Amiens.*[8]

The tragic truth was that, although there were already outbreaks of influenza in France, the magnificent doughboys had unwittingly brought another, more virulent strain of the disease with them from the home. On 15 April, the first cases of epidemic influenza in the AEF appeared at a camp near Bordeaux, one of the chief disembarkation ports for American troops.[9] Those handsome, healthy farm boys were to pay the price for America's entry into the war. In the words of epidemiologist Dr Vaughan: 'City dwellers acquire some degree of immunity to respiratory diseases because they live in an atmosphere frequently or constantly bearing these infections. Country boys are more highly susceptible to the respiratory disease.'[10]

Influenza killed these young men in their thousands. Indeed, by the end of the war, more Americans would have died from Spanish flu than perished in the war. When Vera Brittain and her comrades greeted the doughboys with such enthusiasm, little did they know that many of these youths were doomed.

Colonel Alfred Soltau of the British Army Medical Service noted that the first outbreaks 'occurred in the ill-famed Ypres salient, an area where disease of all sorts seemed to flourish'.[11] Initially, Colonel Soltau regarded this development impassively; influenza had always been a constant feature of army sick lists.[12] As the epidemic spread, the colonel still saw no cause for alarm, but instead found a name for this malaise, christening it 'three day fever – three days' incubation, three days' fever, and three days' convalescence'.[13] Apart from the high rate of patients, he concluded that this illness gave 'very little cause for anxiety'.[14]

By the end of May, the first wave of infection had died down, but it recurred dramatically in early June, in rapidly mounting numbers, reaching its height in the third week.

As far as Colonel Soltau was concerned, the most disturbing aspect of the epidemic was that as the epidemic increased in numbers, it became more virulent. While the earlier patients had recovered swiftly and seldom experienced complications, the second onset brought an increasing number of respiratory complications. In June it was estimated that of the cases admitted to the special influenzal centres, some 2 per cent developed serious pulmonary lesions, of whom a very considerable proportion died. This was particularly the case in patients suffering from 'any old-standing renal lesion. In such cases a rapid increase in the renal inadequacy and a profound toxaemia led almost invariably to a fatal termination.'[15]

As a soldier, Colonel Soltau was well aware that the epidemic of spring 1918 had significant military implications. Entire units were put out of action; one army brigade of artillery had at one time two-thirds of its strength laid up, and was unable to go into action, though badly needed, for three weeks. In military terms, the killer flu proved to be a blessing in disguise for the Allies. As the German army suffered heavily, Allied Intelligence learned that, according to the colonel, 'this was one of the factors which caused the postponement of a certain contemplated attack of very critical importance'.[16]

Colonel Soltau was one of the first to suggest that troop movements and drafting were responsible for spreading the epidemic. The colonel cited Major Zinsser, of the American Medical Corps, who had argued that 'a formation of troops may develop a certain immunity to its own organisms, but breaking up and re-distribution of such a formation may lead to epidemics, as such immunized men are brought into contact with other strains of organisms, or take to other formations strains which are new to the latter and therefore not guarded against'.[17]

By May, influenza was widespread among French troops, and the military authorities were calling for all outbreaks of *la grippe* to be reported via telegraph. As the first wave of influenza seemed to be receding in the United States, it was making a spectacular entrance in Europe.

On 9 May, the 26th Division of the American army suffered a heavy gas shell attack in the midst of an epidemic of 'Three Day Fever'.[18] In the middle of the month, the fever hit the 42nd Division, filling hospitals to the brim. While the majority of soldiers shrugged off the disease, some developed a secondary pneumonia of 'a most virulent and deadly type'.[19] The new influenza proved astonishingly contagious, with 90 per cent of the 168th Infantry Regiment and the sailors of the US Navy Seaplane Station at Dunkirk affected to a greater or lesser degree.[20]

By May, influenza had crossed effortlessly over 'No Man's Land' to hit the German army. Known to Germans as *Blitzkatarrh*, the disease affected 139,000 men during June and peaked in early July. Lasting for four to six days on average, it left troops debilitated and brought the German army to a state of near exhaustion.[21] In late June, German commander Eric von Ludendorff noted that over 2,000 men in each division were suffering from influenza, that the supply system was breaking down, and that the troops were starving. As the German high command struggled to replace more than 900,000 casualties, influenza put ever-increasing numbers of German soldiers out of commission. By late July, Ludendorff was blaming influenza for halting the German attack.

'Our army suffered. Influenza was rampant,' von Ludendorff wrote in his memoirs. 'It was a grievous business having to listen every morning to the chief of staff's recital of the number of influenza cases, and their complaints about the weakness of their troops if the English attacked again.'[22] Influenza had brought the all-conquering German army to its knees, while the Allies, stricken too, took advantage of their enemy's weakness to regroup.

By the end of June 1918, *The Times* of London reported a successful advance by British troops in the Forest of Nieppe, during which more than 300 prisoners were taken, providing

> confirmation of the tales which we have heard of the prevalence of influenza in the German Army. Reports have been current for some time past that the malady was sufficiently serious to have constituted one reason why the Germans have been so slow in pushing the offensive, divisions intended for the attack being so prostrated as to be unable to fight . . . They say that the disease is widespread in all departments of the Army.[23]

The first wave of influenza also made a significant impact on the Royal Navy, with outbreaks in Scotland at the Navy's Grand Fleet at Scapa Flow, in the Orkney Islands and at Rosyth in the Firth of Forth, in April.[24] According to Surgeon Lieutenant Commander Dudley, influenza had first appeared at Scapa Flow, headquarters of the British fleet, during May to June 1918. The hospital ship Agadir recorded only a few mild cases at this stage among her own ship's company, with the Grand Fleet reporting that an estimated 10 per cent of men had been struck. According to Surgeon Commander Raymond, the source of infection in May had been traced to the return to the ship of stokers who had been engaged on a light cruiser attending to an oil fuel course where cases of influenza had developed.[25] As a result, by 1 July 1918,

First Sea Lord Admiral Sir Rosslyn Wemyss was telling Cabinet Secretary Sir Maurice Hankey that 'the influenza is rife in the Navy [with the result that] many destroyers have been unable to go to sea, so that the loss of several merchant ships is directly attributed to this issue'.[26]

In late May, reports had begun to arrive from Valencia, Spain, regarding 'a disease of undetermined nature . . . characterised by high fever, to be of short duration, and to resemble *grippe*'.[27] The spring epidemic of influenza had crossed the Alps into Italy and demonstrated its impartiality by appearing in neutral Spain. When 'a strange form of disease of epidemic character'[28] was reported in Madrid, the city responded by closing theatres and stopping trams. The price of lemons, a traditional remedy, spiralled, but the outbreak was not considered serious, with the Madrid daily *El Liberal* informing its readers on 30 May 1918 that there was no reason for alarm.[29]

Even when King Alfonso XIII fell ill after attending Mass in the Palace chapel, and government ministers Miguel Villanueva, Santiago Alba and Eduardo Dato became sick, there was no immediate panic. Poet Juan Pérez Zúñiga scoffed at the outbreak, dismissing it as 'the fashionable illness':

> *There is no more remedy, sirs*
> *Than to speak a little*
> *Of this illness, whose rigours*
> *Has all of Madrid crazy.*[30]

Journalist Mariano de Cavia was equally dismissive: 'What's the big deal with this silly *trancazo* that is content with three days' bed rest and a medicine cabinet?'[31]

King Alfonso recovered, and the mysterious new disease was immortalized as 'Spanish flu', depicted by cartoonists worldwide as the ghoulish 'Spanish Lady', a nightmare lady grinning skull dancing across headlines in a black flamenco dress.

Thanks to the neutrality of Spain, the progress of the so-called 'Spanish flu' was freely reported by the warring nations and could be read about and discussed by doctors in medical journals. This excerpt from the *British Medical Journal* provides an insight into the questions doctors were asking themselves about the epidemic in Spain.

The widespread epidemic of an acute catarrhal affection in Spain, which was stated in our last issue to be most probably influenza and attended by little or no mortality, is now reported to have caused 700 deaths in ten days, but if the number of cases has been as large as reported the case mortality must have been very low. The Times of 3rd June quoted Dr Pittaluga to the effect that the disease attacks the respiratory rather than the abdominal organs; that relapses frequently occur within a few days; and that, although the disease is clearly of the character of influenza, bacteriological examination has not resulted in the discovery of the influenza bacillus, but has revealed an organism described as the parameningococcus. It is well known that the Bacillus influenzae is quite commonly absent in cases clinically characteristic of influenza, and that Micrococcus catarrhalis, which has some superficial resemblance to the parameningococcus, is very commonly found. Although, as recent reports of the Medical Research Committee have shown, an epidemic of meningococcus carriers may reach a very high percentage amongst contacts, we are not cognizant of any previous outbreak of cerebro-spinal fever in any degree comparable in extent to the epidemic in Spain. Before coming to any conclusion it is obvious that further bacteriological information must be awaited.[32]

Dr Gustavo Pittaluga, Chair of Parasitology and Tropical Pathology at the University of Madrid, was one of the first doctors to argue that the new disease was not influenza at all. 'The epidemic we're suffering from differs from *grippe* for the following fundamental reasons: (a) because the set of symptoms is much more uniform ... (b) because of the near constant absence of bacterial forms identifiable with Pfeiffer's *bacillus*, the pathogen that causes influenza.'[33] Pittaluga's comments, and the responses of his 'most vocal antagonist', Gregorio Marañón, who was convinced that what they were dealing with *was* influenza, constituted the early salvos in a medical controversy which raged for longer than the epidemic itself.

Initially, many Spanish journalists dismissed the impact of the influenza epidemic as negligible, while others were more guarded. The commentator Antonio Zozaya, writing in the same newspaper two days later, reminded his readers that life possessed greater threats than the influenza outbreak, on a daily basis. Citing the dangers of public highways, railways and even suicide, he nevertheless conceded that the epidemic was serious and urged his readers to take a stoic approach: 'The epidemic has arrived. It's an unpleasant contingency. We do not find ourselves more oppressed or helpless in this merciless valley because of it. Let us try to live prudently, to proceed as good people do and suffer with dignity.'[34]

Meanwhile, grim scenes were being enacted in Spain that would become familiar across the world in the months to come:

A funeral that was making its way along a central street saw, to the amazement of those who witnessed it, the coach driver fall from his seat to the ground dead, as if struck by lightning, and one of the mourners keeled over on the ground, having also died suddenly; panic gripped the others who were part of the procession and they scattered, leaving the coach abandoned. An ambulance had to come collect the dead and a municipal guard tied a cord to the horse's bridle and walking ahead some twelve meters pulled the coach to the cemetery.[35]

CHAPTER FIVE

ONE DEADLY SUMMER

———◆———

T HE 'SPANISH LADY' had already set foot at Scapa Flow in May 1918. Later that same month, she arrived in the Scottish dockyards, causing three deaths on ships moored in Glasgow harbour. The slums of Govan and the Gorbals in Glasgow swiftly succumbed to an eight-week influenza epidemic, with the *Glasgow Herald* reporting thirteen deaths from influenza and twenty-six from pneumonia on 17 July. A week later the toll was even higher: fourteen deaths from influenza and forty-nine from pneumonia.[1]

As Spanish flu travelled south from Scotland, homecoming military personnel also brought the disease home with them. Influenza arrived in Portsmouth and other Channel ports, and was carried on to London, Birmingham and the northern cities of Leeds, Manchester and Liverpool, and west towards Bristol and Cardiff. In July 1918, nearly 1,000 of 3,000 German prisoners of war interned at Bramley Camp, Hampshire, were reported to be ill,[2] and had to be taken to nearby civilian hospitals.

One famous victim of the Spanish Lady's arrival in Britain was Mrs Rose Selfridge (1860–1918), Chicago-born wife of Harry Gordon Selfridge, founder of the eponymous department store in London's Oxford Street. When the family moved to Highcliffe Castle, Dorset, in 1916, this energetic, active woman joined the Red Cross along with her two oldest daughters. Following a stint nursing at nearby Christchurch Hospital, Rose had opened a convalescent hospital for American soldiers at Highcliffe Castle after the United States joined the war. According to Hayden Church, an American reporter who visited Rose at Highcliffe, she was very enthusiastic about her hospital. 'The Christmas gift of this American business man to his wife was a perfectly equipped convalescent camp,'[3] wrote Church.

The former cricket pavilion with thatched roof that must be over a century in age has been transformed into an office for the commandant and into a kitchen and cheerful dining room, in which the convalescent 'Sammies' take their meals. The huts in which they live number 12, with quarters for two men in each, and each of these huts whose open side is protected against the elements by a thick rubber curtain, which is mounted on an axis in such a way so that it may always face the sun. Then there is a recreation hut provided with a gramophone, games, books, maps, writing material and other things to make the men who use it comfortable. Lastly, there is another building known as the 'Medical Ward,' which provides quarters for the permanent American non-commissioned officer who is responsible for the discipline of the camp and which also houses the linen room and the men's bathroom.[4]

Tragically, Rose developed influenza herself, as a result of her nursing duties, and contracted pneumonia. Rose Selfridge died on 12 May 1918 and was buried in the churchyard of St Mark's church at Highcliffe, near the castle.[5] Rose's widower, Harry Selfridge, continued the work at the convalescent camp, in her honour.

*

WHILE SPANISH FLU had insinuated itself into Britain by a number of points of entry, the North was initially hit hardest, particularly the northern industrial cities.[6] The silent menace travelled undetected through shops, businesses, public transport and person to person, before gradually spreading out into rural communities. In Newcastle, labour was becoming scarcer by the hour as up to 70 per cent of employed men fell sick, while Durham also suffered an outbreak. At a time of coal shortages, when Britons were being exhorted to burn as little fuel as possible to conserve stocks for the war effort, mineworkers appeared susceptible to developing secondary respiratory infections. According to *The Times*, coalminers were particularly prone to attack by influenza, while the Nottinghamshire press reported that 'in Northumberland and Durham the rapid spread of the disease is seriously affecting the collieries, in some cases 70 per cent of employees being off work'.[7] In Nottinghamshire itself, 'a number of employees from the Digby Collieries . . . had to be taken to their homes suffering from the malady'.[8] Nottinghamshire collieries were struggling, 250 men succumbing to the infection at the Mansfield pit in one day.

On 22 June 1918, *The Times* reported that influenza similar to that being experienced in Spain had appeared in Birmingham, resulting in critical labour shortages in the munitions factories and ironworks. 'Birmingham was the first provincial city to experience a sudden and sustained rise in influenza mortality with deaths also occurring in neighbouring Wolverhampton and Coventry at about the same time.'[9] Two weeks later, influenza appeared in South Wales: *The Times* reported that there were hundreds of influenza cases in the Monmouthshire collieries.[10]

In Lancashire, one textile house employing 400 workers was reduced to making do with just 100, as three-quarters of the workforce was laid up.[11] In Sheffield, the *Yorkshire Telegraph* reported that 15 per cent of employees were off at one factory, and there was a run on quinine. As the body count rose, Sheffield's deputy town clerk appealed for gravediggers. 'People are lying dead in their houses seven days, and sometimes nine. The position is very serious indeed.'[12] Fearing that the disease was caused by soldiers home on leave, Sheffield's council banned military personnel from cinemas and other places of entertainment.

Influenza hit the East Midlands at the end of June, wreaking havoc on factories and coal mines. The local press reported that the infection was prevalent in Derby and affecting work and education, although it was thought to be only a mild form of the disease. At the beginning of July, the *Leicester Mercury* stated that there were already 'a considerable number of cases of the new influenza' in the town and even one fatality, a nineteen-year-old woman.[13] The following day the same newspaper announced that 'The influenza epidemic has reached North Nottinghamshire where there are many hundreds of cases.'[14] The *Loughborough Herald* carried a similar story but also indicated that there did not seem to be cause for great anxiety: 'There are further reports of the spread of influenza in many parts of the Kingdom, and in the large towns especially . . . Some fatal cases have occurred, but it is the opinion of the medical Officers of Health . . . that the epidemic, though so widely prevalent, is for the most part of mild type.'[15]

But by 11 July the *Herald*'s mood had darkened, with reports of several deaths from influenza in the village of Barrow upon Soar, three deaths occurring in one family.[16] Thirty miles north, in Nottingham, the *Nottingham Journal* stated: 'As far as this country is concerned the epidemic continues to be more severe in the Midlands and the North than elsewhere ... Although it cannot be said that the malady is present in Nottingham in grave epidemic form, there are nevertheless quite a number of cases.'[17]

As reporting continued on the progress of the influenza pandemic across the county throughout July, it was clear that the situation was much worse than had originally been thought; reports of deaths and disruption began to fill the newspapers. Under the front page headline 'The "Flu" Scourge: Extension of its Ravages Locally', the *Nottingham Journal and Express* declared it to be spreading across Nottinghamshire and Derbyshire and spoke of deaths in Derby and Lincoln, the closure of schools, delays in carrying out important work and victims collapsing in the street.[18] In the Leicester press, the report of the death of a woman showed how quickly the disease could overtake a victim: 'A doctor was stopped in the street by a woman who said she was suffering from influenza and while he was talking with her she collapsed and died almost immediately.'[19]

The Spanish Lady arrived in Salford, Greater Manchester, in late June. The *Salford Reporter*, 25 June 1918, announced that 'the epidemic of influenza has reached Salford and if it is not of the old "sneezing variety", it is very prostrating. Hundreds of cases have occurred in the borough during the week, and doctors are extraordinarily busy.'[20] The paper instructed its readers to go to bed as soon as they started to experience the symptoms and included an interview with a doctor who commented: 'If you get about and try to shake it off it becomes much worse.'[21]

Over in Manchester, resourceful Chief Medical Officer of Health Dr James Niven tackled the influenza epidemic with a formidable mixture of clinical experience and public information. Niven had experienced epidemic influenza before. In 1890, Niven had been working in Oldham when the city was hit by an outbreak of 'Russian flu'. Niven's prompt response, ordering isolation for the sick and cleansing of infected premises, undoubtedly saved lives, and when 'Russian flu' returned to Oldham in 1891 and 1892 the city fared better than its neighbours. In June 1918, Niven responded with the same tactics, having 35,000 handbills printed and distributed to local factories and businesses, with information and instructions in clear plain English. Niven also recommended that any infected individuals should quarantine themselves for three weeks before returning to work, to prevent the further spread of influenza. On 18 July 1918, Manchester's education committee agreed to close all the schools on Niven's recommendation after the shocking news that children had died at their desks, 'like a plant whose roots have poisoned, the attack being quite sudden, and drowsiness a prominent symptom'.[22]

There is no doubt that Niven's approach saved many lives: 100,000 Mancunians contracted influenza during the spring and early summer, but only 322 died, 'a relatively low mortality rate',[23] which may be taken as a testimony to Niven's organizational skills. While Niven had responded admirably to this challenge, he realized that he was dealing with something different; there were two anomalies in this new outbreak. This form of influenza targeted the fittest and healthiest members of a workforce or community, instead of the very old, the very young and the vulnerable, as was traditional. The other anomaly was that the outbreak had arrived in the summer, and not in the traditional winter flu season.[24] Niven could only hope that those people who had been infected and survived had developed immunity if the influenza was to return.

Down in London, morale was high. The public mood had been boosted by the latest developments in the war, with reports coming from the Western Front that the Allies had the upper hand. After four long years of food shortages, food rationing, Zeppelin raids and bereavement, the end was in sight. The *Manchester Guardian* reported that 'The whole temperature of London has gone up in these two days of good news. Although there will be no flags or bells for some time yet the look on the faces of the people is like flags and bells.'[25]

At this exciting time, an unseasonal outbreak of influenza seemed unusual but of no great significance. *The Illustrated London News* observed in its science column that 'luckily the complaint – which, as a matter of fact, now recurs annually, is this year of a type so mild as to show that the original virus is becoming attenuated by frequent transmission'.[26] Meanwhile, *The Times* had adopted the new name for this curious manifestation. Under the headline 'The Spanish Flu – a Sufferer's Symptoms' the paper declared that the cause of the disease was 'the dry, windy Spanish spring . . . an unpleasant and unhealthy season at all times. A spell of wet weather or of moist winds would probably check the progress of the epidemic.'[27] In the same article, the newspaper claimed, with a leaden attempt at humour, that 'The man in the street, having been taught by that *plagosus orbilius* war to take a keener interest in foreign affairs, discussed the news of the epidemic which spread with such surprising rapidity through Spain a few weeks ago, and cheerfully anticipated its arrival here.'[28]

While Spanish flu rampaged across the rest of the country, Londoners basked in 'the almost tropical heat',[29] and life was positively idyllic for some. Under the sub-heading 'That Active Microbe' the women's editor of the *Evening Standard* commented light-heartedly that 'A glance at the calendar shows that the hot weather we've been having, so far from killing the charity and matinee microbe, has stimulated it to a pitch of feverish activity, with the result that the philanthropic have a busy time ahead of them for the next few weeks.'[30]

In the same article, readers were presented with breathless accounts of what the most glamorous chorus girls were wearing in their West End shows. Gaiety Girl Ruby Miller dazzled in *Going Up* in 'an aluminium grey frock of satin beaute with pannier draperies at the sides and slit up in front to show a ribbon-trimmed petticoat'[31] and 'an evening gown of cyclamen mauve georgette with . . . harem hem and cummerbund of silver tissue'.[32] Marie Lohr, meanwhile, appeared at the Globe in 'her white cloth frock with its slender lines of jade green embroidery and wide folded belt, caught at one side with three large green and white buttons, and the long straight, green-lined rap of white cloth, with its black velvet collar and array of pearl buttons worn over it'.[33]

Despite the war, the *Manchester Guardian* newspaper detected 'the ghost' of a London social Season in the West End, alongside the 'extraordinary greenness of the grass and leafiness of the trees'.[34] West End shopkeepers were carrying on as normal: 'Painting and pointing' had been carried out in Grosvenor Street and other areas of Mayfair, and 'Regent Street, despite its lack of paint, looks gay with its summer fashions'.[35]

While weekending in country houses had declined, with so many men away fighting, and at a time when 'hardly anyone is entertaining except in small restaurant parties',[36] St James's

Park had returned to its origins as a stylish pleasure garden, in 'a sort of revival of the eighteenth century ways'.[37] The big art shows were continuing as usual, while the Summer Exhibition at the Royal Academy attracted a 'large attendance, especially from convalescent soldiers'.[38] Even the summer dances, those traditional fixtures of the Season, had seen a small revival, as high society mothers did their best to marry off their daughters to the rapidly diminishing pool of eligible men.

Fashionable London had changed dramatically in one respect, and that was the presence of the Americans. The entry of the United States into the war had caused this major transformation. While wartime arrivals in London were nothing new, the city having already witnessed 'friendly invasions'[39] of Belgian nuns, Brussels dandies and the Anzacs (Australian and New Zealand Army Corps) with their tall, lounging, sinewy figures and grim faces, the fourth year of the war was the year of the American, according to the *Manchester Guardian*.

'The war year closes with the American in khaki and in blue almost in possession of London . . . In the last year many hundred thousands [*sic*] of Americans are actually passing through England to fight in France.'[40] American servicemen swelled the audiences of London's theatre district, where the seats were already dominated by young men in khaki and navy blue. Despite the war, London's West End was still going strong in 1918, with 'opera at Drury Lane and at the Shaftsbury, and a very good Gilbert and Sullivan production at the King's Theatre, Hammersmith'.[41]

Pacifist Caroline Playne recalled that 'during the summer of 1918 there was a great run on the theatres'.[42] Desperate to distract themselves from the horrors of war, soldiers, sailors and civilians alike crowded into the theatres and music halls. Tragically, live entertainment proved to be the perfect breeding ground for Spanish flu.

'In 1916 it seemed that there was no prospect of success in producing plays. In 1918 it was difficult to get seats at all even for the worst plays. Almost any production was a huge success. People were said to be fighting to fling their money into the box-office.'[43] Leasing theatres involved the payment of a high premium, with high prices for seats and talk of raising them further.[44] This came as no surprise given the shortage of other forms of entertainment.

'It was the vast prosperity of almost every class and the closing of other opportunities for pleasure that caused the theatres to be thronged. The use of motor cars was restricted to trade and professional necessities. Skating rinks and beanfeasts were no more.'[45]

Drury Lane still presented a brilliant spectacle on some nights, with 'jewels in the balcony and long strings of carriages waiting and even a footman or two'.[46] Among the soldiers and sailors, a few stalwarts of the *ancien régime* were still in evidence, with 'M. Nabokoff [*sic*] [father of the novelist Vladimir Nabokov] and a Russian diplomatic party'[47] in one box watching *Boris Godounov* with its scenes of Russian revolution – an incident more dramatic than anything on the stage itself.[48]

It was against this backdrop that Mrs Mabel Pride, the mother-in-law of poet Robert Graves, decided to fight off her influenza symptoms and go to the theatre with her son Tony while he was home on leave. We do not know which show they attended, but there was plenty of entertainment on offer. The attractions of summer 1918, when Mabel accompanied her son to the theatre, included Charles Hawtrey and Gladys Cooper in *The Naughty Wife* at the Playhouse; George du Maurier, father of Daphne du Maurier, in *Dear Brutus* at Wyndham's; while the notorious Canadian dancer Maud Allen starred at the London Pavilion. Maud had become the subject of wild allegations from a Tory MP, who had accused her of being the lesbian lover of Margo Asquith, wife of former Prime Minister Herbert Asquith, and a German spy. (It was debatable as to which of these allegations was regarded as the most shocking.) Those of a more serious disposition could go to see Ibsen's *The Master Builder* at The Court, while anyone desperate for a little light relief could do worse than head for *Chu Chin Chow* at His Majesty's or *Peg O' My Heart* at St James's.[49]

Desperate to go out on the town with her son, Mabel visited her doctor, took quantities of aspirin to reduce her temperature, and went off to the theatre with Tony. It was to be Mabel's last outing; her case of Spanish flu proved fatal, and she died two days later. Robert Graves later noted that 'Her chief solace, as she lay dying, was that Tony had got his leave prolonged on her account.'[50] Graves subsequently learned that Tony was killed in September.[51]

Mabel's death was but one among many. Despite the confident mood, Spanish flu had spread across London and was making deadly inroads into the population. Many of the victims were young, affluent and healthy, with Chelsea and Westminster struck down as well as impoverished Bethnal Green.[52] The writer Virginia Woolf noted on 2 July 1918 that 'influenza, which rages all over the place, has come next door'[53] the door in question being at Paradise Road, Richmond upon Thames. While Woolf's neighbour died, Woolf, despite being a lifelong invalid, survived.

Another writer, Lady Cynthia Asquith, recounted a dreadful encounter with the Spanish Lady.

Best remembered for her horror stories, Lady Cynthia at the age of thirty-one had already developed a literary career working alongside *Peter Pan* creator J. M. Barry and D. H. Lawrence, and her diaries contain entertaining and breathless accounts of life in wartime London. On this occasion, however, Lady Cynthia wondered if she was actually going to survive: 'Just before luncheon precisely the same symptoms as yesterday came on, only much worse. My temperature went up to 102°, and all the afternoon and evening I felt as wretchedly, humiliatingly ill as I ever have in my life – bursting head, painful pulses, aching legs, sick, burning with cold shivers. I tossed and groaned.'[54]

While Lady Cynthia Asquith's experience indicated the tendency of Spanish flu to attack the healthy and wealthy, the disease was also on the increase in other parts of London. American soldier Private Pressley, having survived the influenza outbreak at Camp Dix and lost his friend Cid on the voyage to France, was now in London. On 10 July, Pressley wrote to his girlfriend that 'London, in common with the rest of the Eastern World, has had an epidemic of Spanish flu. It seems to cause a heavy fever, with a complete feeling of weariness, and usually only confines the patient to bed for a few days.'[55]

On the same day, over in Walthamstow, East London, Elsie Barnett wrote to her husband in Mesopotamia: 'We have had a terrible doing from the Spanish Flu as they call it, but doctors are inclined to think it's malaria brought about by soldiers. Am thankful to say I've kept clear so far and we are warned to wear camphor about us as people are dying with it in a few hours if they don't lay up at once.'[56]

Young Margery Porter, from South London, also contracted Spanish flu that summer. She remembered:

I was an only child and I lived with my mother and father. When we all got the flu we couldn't do anything else but go to bed, because we just couldn't stand up. Your legs actually gave way, I can't exaggerate that too much. Everybody at our end of the street had it. Next door but one lived my grandparents and my three aunts. They all had it, but my grandfather was the only one who died in our family. The rest of us recovered but it took a long time, because the flu took charge of your whole body. I don't remember having a cold or sneezing. I just remember terrible pains in all my limbs, and I just didn't want to eat anything. I think my bout of flu lasted about two weeks until I started going back to school again. I was so lucky. That was the worst illness I've ever had.[57]

By August 1918, the Spanish Lady had departed Britain as swiftly and mysteriously as she had appeared four months earlier. An American doctor, writing home from London on 20 August, noted that 'the influenza epidemic described in recent letters has completely disappeared'.[58] But the outbreak had left a dreadful legacy. Over three weeks during July 1918, 700 civilian Londoners had died of influenza and a further 475 from pneumonia,[59] while a total of 10,000 influenza deaths had been recorded in Great Britain between June and July. By November 1918, this figure would exceed 70,000.[60]

CHAPTER SIX

KNOW THY ENEMY

H OWEVER PRESSING THE demands of the summer outbreak on the Home Front in Great Britain, Spanish flu was outranked by the war effort. The war dominated civilian life, half the country's medical professionals were away on military service and hospitals were dedicated to military requirements.[1] Medical science had little to offer in the way of prevention or cure, apart from the process of disinfection, notification and isolation as recommended by Dr Niven. There was little consensus on treatment apart from the traditional recourse to bed rest, opiates and folk remedies, while to make matters worse, significant individuals refused to take the threat of Spanish flu seriously.[2]

Sir Arthur Newsholme, Chief Medical Officer of the Local Government Board (LGB), pointed out that influenza travelled too rapidly to be stopped and could not be controlled: 'I know of no public health measure which can resist the progress of pandemic influenza.'[3] For this reason, Newsholme declined to issue an official LGB memorandum to civil authorities in the summer of 1918. Matters were not improved by the fact that, at this time, there was no actual Ministry of Health, which could have overseen a national prevention strategy or issued directives to prevent the spread of influenza. In 1918, public health was the responsibility of local 'sanitary authorities' and the local Medical Officers of Health who were appointed by city councils. Because influenza was not a notifiable disease, there was no legal requirement to put quarantine measures in place in the event of an epidemic. The LGB also maintained that nothing could be done to prevent outbreaks of influenza. Reflecting the government's all-consuming preoccupation with the war, Newsholme claimed that the nation's duty was to 'carry on' working, even suggesting that it was unpatriotic to worry about influenza when dealing with the threat to Britain's survival. Another factor that explains why the authorities seemed to do nothing in the face of a deadly epidemic was that there was no general consensus as to the cause.

The British army, however, took a very different approach. After the influenza epidemics struck France in spring 1918, the Army Medical Service had gone into overdrive, determined to combat the disease with typical military logic and energy. Research was conducted by the Medical Research Committee in London (which would later become the Medical Research Council) and in the army pathology laboratories, which had already been set up in hospitals on the Western Front. The army committed time and manpower to investigating the causes of the influenza epidemic in an effort to create a vaccine, a form of inoculation that had become increasingly common following the pioneering work of Louis Pasteur in 1881. The scientific community maintained that something constructive could be done to halt the inexorable progress of the killer disease, despite the fact that its origins remained mysterious. Army medical teams had successfully combated other diseases such as cholera and dysentery in the past, and so this new strain of influenza should not present a lasting problem. Resources were deployed to combat the mystery illness, with overall control coming from the Medical Research Committee.

The MRC had been founded in 1913 as part of the provisions of the National Insurance Act of 1911. In July 1914, Sir Robert Morant, the senior civil servant tasked with setting up the committee, recruited Walter Morley Fletcher (1873–1933), a brilliant Cambridge physiologist, to act as Secretary to the Committee. Fletcher had graduated from Trinity College Cambridge with first-class honours in Natural Science in 1891, before undergoing clinical training at St Bartholomew's Hospital and returning to Cambridge as a Senior Demonstrator at the Cambridge School of Physiology.[4] Elected to a fellowship at Trinity College, Fletcher was an outstanding character even by Cambridge standards, possessing a vivid personality, spectacular physique, striking features, dynamic energy, quickness of thought, and an elegance in the spoken and written word, set off by an endearing stutter when he became excited.[5] Warm and humane, Fletcher could also be masterful, principled and held an intense belief in the value of science in the service of humanity.[6]

But Fletcher also wanted more than the familiar routine of academic life, requiring a bigger arena for his intellectual versatility and flair for management.[7] This made Fletcher the perfect individual to steer the MRC through its first big challenge, the battle against influenza. When war broke out in August 1914, Fletcher had been appointed to the Army Pathological Committee working to combat sepsis, gas-gangrene and other 'diseases of war'.

Fletcher's ferocious work ethic proved injurious to his own health. In order to spend as little time away from his desk as possible, he lunched on a cup of coffee and a Welsh rarebit at the local ABC.[8] (The ABC tearooms, run by 'the Aerated Bread Company', were a familiar feature of London life.) According to his wife, Maisie, when Fletcher eventually reached home in the evening, after a day of innumerable meetings at the War Office, RAMC (Royal Army Medical Corps), Home Office, Air Force and Royal Society, dealing with the problems presented to medicine by the war, he would immediately settle down to a mountain of paperwork.[9]

This punishing schedule had led to Fletcher's own brush with death in February 1916, when he contracted double pneumonia, which was next door to a death sentence, according to Maisie.[10] Fletcher endured 'agonising pleurisy' (inflammation of the layer covering the lungs), with the ancient remedy of leeches being applied to add to the torment, and later a major operation for empyema (lungs filled with pus), which he barely survived.[11] Even then, Fletcher's ready wit did not desert him. 'He spoke his mind to his devoted, tireless doctors, when he saw the list of remedies and the medicine bottles that had been amassed in the weeks when he had been unaware of their doings. "That collection of stuff," said this pioneer of the New Age of medicine, "is worthy of the physicians of Charles II."'[12]

Returning to work at the MRC just as the first wave of influenza hit northern France, Fletcher's subsequent role consisted of overseeing the research being carried out in France at the hospital pathology labs. The research laboratories in France demonstrated 'the decisive role of British military medicine in shaping official strategies against the pandemic'.[13] Through the spring and autumn of 1918, the War Office, the Army Medical Services (AMS) and the Medical Research Committee (MRC), which had coordinated mobilization of

British medical science, jointly produced official knowledge and epidemic strategies. Prior to the epidemic, these authorities had worked together to create a system of military pathology, which linked pathological laboratories to base and field hospitals in France and Flanders. This system was organized to collect, isolate and identify pathogens from the battlefield, and to facilitate production of vaccines and antisera, a blood serum containing antibodies against specific antigens, injected to treat or protect against specific diseases. Military pathology delivered therapeutic and preventive measures against a range of battlefield diseases, and its planners trusted that it could do the same with influenza.

Combined efforts between the army and the medical researchers were aided by the fact that both organizations had many points of similarity. Medicine was traditionally organized along military lines in terms of discipline, organization, rank and uniform, relying on teamwork and specialization.[14] For this reason, medical research fitted comfortably into the war machine. Large-scale communication linked Casualty Clearing Stations (CCS) at the Front to field and base hospitals attached to each army division. Field hospitals were supported by 'territorial' hospitals in mainland England, which were connected to major London and provincial teaching hospitals and run by consultants who were given temporary ranks in the RAMC and paid part-time salaries.[15]

At the heart of this were the pathology laboratories, inspired by the success of bacteriology in civilian medicine and the development of public health.[16] The forward-looking RAMC had been training its doctors in pathology and bacteriology since 1903, while the pathology labs which developed during the war were justified by Fletcher as vital for the 'efficiency of the fighting forces'.[17]

For this reason, as soon as an influenza epidemic broke out in the army in spring 1918, the War Office, the Army Medical Service and the Medical Research Committee took the view that if the influenza germ could be identified, a preventive vaccine could be developed to protect soldiers and military interests.[18]

The military pathology laboratories had been established by Sir William Boog Leishman (1865–1926), a career military pathologist, specialist in tropical medicine and founding member of the MRC. Leishman was instrumental in spearheading the integration of pathology into military medicine.[19] In October 1914, Leishman had been appointed Advisor in Pathology to the Director-General of the AMS and detailed to establish pathological laboratories in France and Flanders. Leishman oversaw the deployment of almost one hundred pathologists at eighty-five hospital labs in France and Flanders, the development of a fleet of twenty-five mobile labs and provision of pathological services at the Front, and the creation of a central research lab in Boulogne.

The pathology department at the Royal Army Medical College in Millbank, London, was the hub of the operation, training pathologists, and developing preventive and therapeutic techniques and vaccines for cholera, plague and dysentery. These vaccines, developed in peacetime, had even greater significance during the war. As a result of developments in vaccination, fewer soldiers died of infections than in any previous war.

The AMS's central pathology laboratory at Boulogne was headed up by Sir Almroth Wright (1861–1947), the MRC's leading pathologist. Wright's two young assistants, Alexander

Fleming and Leonard Colebrook, worked alongside him on wound infections and antiseptics, and the Boulogne laboratory had links with Wright's Inoculation Department at St Mary's Hospital, Paddington.

Many historians have claimed that the British Military had attempted to conceal the epidemic of killer flu, by delaying reports of the outbreak and claiming that it was of Spanish origin. Historian Michael Bresalier, however, takes the view that this was less a matter of censorship, and more a consequence of the fact that military doctors were genuinely confused about the identity of this new strain of influenza.

Up until 1918, influenza had been assumed to be a bacterial disease caused by Pfeiffer's *bacillus*. Richard Pfeiffer (1858–1945), a leading German bacteriologist, had isolated what he believed to be the causative agent of influenza in 1892. According to Pfeiffer, the disease was caused by 'a small rod-shaped bacterium' that he isolated from the noses of flu-infected patients. He dubbed it *Bacillus influenzae* (or Pfeiffer's *bacillus*), which was later called *Haemophilus influenzae*. Pfeiffer's discovery was not questioned, chiefly because other human diseases, such as cholera and plague, had been shown to be caused by bacteria.[20]

This theory dominated the official strategy when the influenza epidemic hit the British Expeditionary Force in France and Flanders in March 1918. Working on the assumption that the epidemic of spring and summer 1918 was influenza, the AMS pathologists tried to isolate *B. influenza* from sick soldiers' sputum, nasal passages and blood, and from the lesions of the few cases that ended up on the autopsy table.[21] The doctors believed that if they could develop a vaccine based on Pfeiffer's *bacillus*, they could inoculate against flu, in the same way that inoculation had been developed against other diseases.

But, in the absence of Pfeiffer's *bacillus*, many doctors questioned whether they were dealing with influenza at all. Lacking a satisfactory definition of the disease, pathologists, as noted earlier, had classified it as 'Pyrexia [fever] of Unknown Origin' or 'PUO', also referred to as 'Three Day Fever', because, as Colonel Soltau of the Army Medical Service had observed, the disease consisted of 'three days' incubation, three days' fever, and three days' convalescence'.[22] Both these definitions were, like 'trench fever', 'clumsy catch-alls, for which neither specific causal agents nor pathognomonic signs could be determined'.[23] All through the summer of 1918, arguments raged across the pages of the learned journals as to the nature of the disease and the validity of a vaccine.

While the *British Medical Journal* claimed that 'the general consensus of opinion seems to indicate Pfeiffer's *Bacillus Influenzae* as the infecting agent despite the reports in the same journal',[24] *The Lancet* 'doubted whether the epidemic was influenza'.[25]

During the course of summer 1918, two loosely defined camps of pathologists clashed over the causal agent and identity of the epidemic. While the 'Pfeiffer School' argued that the epidemic was influenza, and said the failure to find the *bacillus* was due to technical problems, the 'anti-Pfeiffer' brigade suggested that either the disease was not influenza or the disease was caused by another organism.

The majority of military pathologists were familiar with Pfeiffer's *bacillus*. From as early as 1915, its isolation was used to distinguish the various atypical respiratory conditions encountered on the battlefield and local outbreaks of influenza in France. The *bacillus* had come to general military attention in late December 1916, when it was isolated from an epidemic of 'purulent bronchitis' at Étaples by Hammond and Rolland.[26] Purulent bronchitis was said to be the 'primary condition' in 45 per cent of all pulmonary autopsies performed in the hospital during February and March 1917,[27] with the majority having died of 'lung block' resulting from the accumulation of fluid and pus in the lungs, causing emphysema and cyanosis in an estimated 50 per cent of deaths.

What struck investigators was that in smears and cultures of sputa and lung samples from twenty cases they tested, *Bacillus influenzae* appeared to be the primary agent, even though the symptoms were different. Reports by a team of medical experts at Connaught Hospital at Aldershot Command in September 1917 supported this observation. The Aldershot team identified *B. influenzae* as the primary agent in the eight cases they tested and other well-known respiratory germs – particularly pneumococci, *Micrococcus catarrhalis*, and streptococci – as secondary infections. Like their counterparts at Étaples, the Aldershot group concluded that the isolation of *B. influenzae* from the majority of cases of purulent bronchitis indicated a 'serious form of influenzal infection'.[28] Pathologists and physicians working at the No. 3 Canadian General Hospital at Boulogne, who carried out a full clinical, pathological and bacteriological study of purulent bronchitis, supported this conclusion. From all but one of the nine cases, they were able to grow *B. influenzae* in pure culture, which they interpreted as a key indicator that the *bacillus* caused the disease.

However, not all researchers were able to isolate *B. influenza*. Failure to do so was put down to inadequate technique, as the bacteria were notoriously difficult to culture.[29] Arguments raged as both sides accused the other of professional incompetence. In the meantime, Pfeiffer himself remained silent.

Despite the high rate of infection, the spring and summer epidemics of 1918 were regarded as mild. While the influenza had made a massive impact on Allies and Germans alike, the majority of those infected had recovered. Some experts, however, were already predicting a second wave, which would prove deadlier than the last. Walter Fletcher believed that it was not a matter of whether there would be a recrudescence, but when, as did Fletcher's colleague, Major Greenwood.

Major Greenwood (Major being his forename, not an army rank) was the son of an East End doctor, and originally studied mathematics at University College, London, before training as a doctor at the London Hospital in Whitechapel. Already equipped with first-class skills in mathematics and medicine, Greenwood switched to the Lister Institute, where he was employed as a statistician. At the Lister Institute, Greenwood was inspired by Karl Pearson, whose *Grammar of Science* was to inspire a new generation of epidemiologists interested in the emerging discipline of biometrics.[30] Enlisting in the RAMC at the outbreak of war, Greenwood studied fatigue and industrial wastage for the Ministry of Munitions before turning his attention to the first wave of influenza in the summer of 1918.

Having been shocked by the high rate of hospitalization for influenza in the army, Greenwood plotted a graph showing the increase in cases and compared them with the onset of the Russian flu epidemic of 1889–90. During that epidemic, the first wave had occurred in the winter, not in the summer, but Greenwood observed that the outbreaks revealed near identical 'curves' showing a rapid increase followed by a steep decline, like an inverted V.[31] Judging by these results, Greenwood feared that the summer influenza epidemic indicated a second, more deadly wave, which would hit Britain in the autumn or winter of 1918. This period of the year, when resistance was at its lowest, was the worst possible time for respiratory diseases.

Although they did not work directly together, Fletcher shared Greenwood's fears that a second, more deadly wave of influenza was poised to hit Britain in the latter months of 1918. Fletcher subsequently commented that 'it is natural to expect secondary waves with great confidence and as the primary wave came in the early summer, it was not a bad guess that a secondary wave with its dangerous pneumonia would come at the approach of winter'. He added that the MRC would 'err on the side of caution' and prepare for a second wave, whether it came earlier or later.[32]

Unfortunately, the War Office did not share Fletcher's concerns. Despite the high rate of influenza in France and Flanders over the spring and summer, the army was more concerned about the daily realities of gangrene and sepsis, lice and trench fever than the prospect of another influenza epidemic. Nevertheless, Fletcher stuck to his guns. He urged Sir Arthur Newsholme to help investigate the cause of the summer outbreak in Britain and prevent further outbreaks later in year, writing that he would be grateful for any help investigating the epidemic. One solution, Fletcher suggested, would be to control the numbers travelling by public transport, which had to be playing a part in spreading influenza across the entire country. But Newsholme remained indifferent to Fletcher's pleas. In a speech of self-justification later that year, Newsholme conceded that public transport constituted 'prolific sources of infection' but maintained that, given the vital importance of the war effort, 'the vast army of workers must not be impeded by regulations as to overcrowding of vehicles in their efforts to go to work and to return home'.[33]

On 5 August 1918, Fletcher sent a memorandum to the *British Medical Journal* and *The Lancet* calling on pathologists and practitioners to prepare for a second epidemic. He asked for the results of the bacteriology research to be sent to the MRC. His aim was to ensure that laboratory and clinical work was well organized and centrally administered. But Fletcher was soon overtaken by events. Reports were already reaching the MRC that the dreaded second wave of influenza had been detected in France and at bases on the British mainland.

CHAPTER SEVEN

THE FANGS OF DEATH

⸺◆⸺

B Y SUMMER 1918, just as the Allies had begun to feel victory was within their grasp, Spanish flu succeeded where the Germany army had failed and effortlessly conquered Europe. The comforting routines of daily life were abandoned as the Spanish Lady strode across the continent. Trains were cancelled, businesses collapsed and trials went unheard as legal proceedings were suspended. The Kaiser himself was not immune. On 11 July, the *New York Times* reported that the Kaiser 'has fallen victim to the influenza which has been so prevalent in the German army . . . he had gone home from the French front because of an attack of the Spanish grippe'.[1] Kaiser Wilhelm's subjects suffered with him, at least 400,000 Germans dying of Spanish flu. As the disease raged through her adoptive country, Princess Evelyn Blücher, an Englishwoman married to a German aristocrat, witnessed 'the awful reality of influenza. Hardly a family in the country was spared.'[2]

'From our housekeeper at Krieblowitz I hear that the whole village is stricken with it, and the wretched people are lying about on the floors of their cottages in woeful heaps, shivering with fever and with no medication or any one [*sic*] to attend them.'[3]

In Hamburg, four hundred were dying each day and furniture vans had to carry the bodies to the cemetery. 'We are returning every day to the barbarism of the Middle Ages in every way,' wrote Princess Evelyn. 'I am often astonished that there are no religious fanatics nowadays to run through the streets, dressed in sackcloth and ashes, and calling on the people to repent their sins.'[4]

In Paris, 1,200 people died in one week. Elsewhere in France, 70,000 American troops had to be hospitalized, nearly a third of them dying. J. S. Wane, a Cambridge undergraduate who had signed up as an army clerk, found all the soldiers at the Normandy village of Goury sleeping in the open air, by order, because of the influenza epidemic.[5]

In August, Private A. J. Jamieson, 11th Battalion Royal Scots, was holed up in a small barn at Meteren, near the Belgian border:

Our signal section was occupying a small barn and due to move into the line on the day that illness struck. One after another, the occupants were carried out and meanwhile my head felt like a threshing machine. I wondered how many would be left to march off that night and resolved to stick it out as long as possible. Finally I joined 'A' company for the line and several times I staggered forward with my steel helmet catching the man in front in the small of the back. Ultimately, I lay down on a mattress in the cellar of a ruined farmhouse, checked that all my telephone connections were in order and knew nothing more until I was rudely shaken by the company commander who asked me if I knew that, for a soldier on duty sleeping at his post, the sentence was death. I explained my condition which he apparently understood and that was the end of it and of my Spanish 'flu.[6]

From Europe, the Spanish Lady had travelled remorselessly across the globe in four short months, crossing oceans and mountain ranges and infiltrating Scandinavia, Greece, Egypt and India. The first wave of influenza hit Bombay on 10 June 1918, when seven police sepoys (Indian soldiers serving under British orders), including one who worked the docks, were admitted to hospital suffering from a non-malarial fever.[7] Between 15 and 20 June, victims included dockyard workers, and the employees of a shipping firm, the Bombay Port Trust, the Hong Kong and Shanghai Bank, the telegraph, the mint and the Rachel Sassoon Mills.[8] Mortality rose and mass absenteeism became common in banks and offices. Health Officer J. A. Turned observed that Bombay in June was like a huge incubator, equipped with all that was necessary to cultivate infection: an overcrowded city with a large working-class population living in conditions which lent themselves to the spread of disease. From a daily mortality of 92 on 3 June, the figures rose to 230 by 3 July. According to *The Times of India*, 'nearly every house in Bombay has some of its inmates down with fever and every office is bewailing the absence of clerks'.[9]

Turner believed that the outbreak had originated with the crew of a ship that had docked in Bombay at the end of May, while the Indian government claimed that the sailors had caught Spanish flu in Bombay due to what it called the 'insanitary condition' of Indians.[10] Turner responded that the epidemic had been inevitable since 1915, as Bombay was a port of arrival and despatch for troops, and accused the Health Officer of Bombay Port of failing to report cases. The *Bombay Chronicle* argued that Bombay and indeed the whole of India had paid 'dearly' for this neglect, while *The Times of India* was outraged by the perceived failure of the Health Department, despite the *lakhs* (thousands) of rupees spent on it. Rumours also circulated that outbreaks of Spanish flu on military vessels had been suppressed.[10]

After a hospital ship arrived in Karachi on 20 June the majority of the patients developed Spanish flu within forty-eight hours. Again it is not clear whether the influenza had been brought with them or acquired in Karachi, but it is more likely that it was imported from outside. Although the outbreak of Spanish flu in Bombay in June lasted only four weeks, it took 1,600 lives and 'at least a million working days, an incalculable amount of discomfort, expense and inconvenience'.[11] The epidemic was confined to those working indoors, in offices and factories. The sickness rate in offices and mills was Europeans 25 per cent, Indians 33 per cent, and children 55 per cent. This last figure may appear surprising but at the time children were regularly employed in factories. Turner's description of the Spanish Lady is memorable. Whereas the causes of diseases such as cholera, smallpox and plague were known and their spread could be contained, Spanish flu came, he said, 'like a thief in the night, its onset rapid, and insidious'.[12]

Frederick Brittain of the Royal Army Medical Corps provided a snapshot of conditions in India when his hospital ship, the *Egypt*, arrived at Bombay, in August 1918. On Saturday 24 August, Brittain recorded: 'With Carter to Natunga Station and walked up to the sea front at Mahim. This part really seems like the India of the story books with its groves of beautiful banana trees and coconut palms, palm-thatched houses, etc.'[13] But this vision was swiftly dispelled when: 'We went on the beach at Mahim and walked along past a burning ghat where a body had just been burned. An Indian carried his bedstead down on his head, took it out into the sea and washed it. We thought how strange this would look at home!'[14]

From India, Spanish flu spread into Iran, then known as Persia. The disease, known to the Persians as '*bad-e nazleh*', arrived in

Persia at Bushehr, courtesy of the English and Indian soldiers stationed in Bushehr and Bandar-e Lengeh ports, then spread from Baghdad to Kermanshah in the west and Shiraz in the south. Although detailed information is scarce, the Spanish flu outbreak in Persia was estimated to have killed one million people, one-tenth of the country's population. The writer Mohammad Ali Jamalzadeh (1892–1997) described the appalling conditions in Shiraz: 'At the end of WWI, three lethal killers entered Shiraz; they were famine, cholera and the Spanish flu. Many people died and corpses were seen everywhere in the city. The Bazar and shops were closed. There was no doctor, no nurse, and no drug.'[15]

Influenza spread across the entire country, with rural areas more affected than urban regions. Ashair tribespeople, particularly the healthy men, died from it. The reported mortality rate in the nomadic Ghashghai tribe was as high as 30 per cent. In Shiraz, which had a population of 50,000, 5,000 died from Spanish flu. The mortality rate in Kermanshah was reported as 1 per cent, but in the villages as many as 20 per cent of the people were reported to have perished, a figure which seems exaggerated. In Tehran, during a three-month period, 50,000 people were reported to have died.[16]

In one respect, the mortality rate in Persia differed from that in other parts of the world. While in the majority of Spanish flu epidemics the victims were men and women aged between fifteen and forty-four, mortality rates in Persia were affected by other factors specific to the region such as famine, opium consumption, anaemia and malaria. While the total estimated deaths from the 1918 Spanish influenza epidemic in Persia was between 902,400 and 2,431,000, the real figure was probably somewhere between the two extremes.[17]

The Spanish Lady made a protracted and devastating visit to the African continent in August 1918, killing 50 million people over the course of six months and leaving a catastrophic effect on the demographic which lasted into successive generations. While North Africa, namely the Maghrib and Egypt, had already experienced the first, relatively mild wave of influenza and received some immunity, sub-Saharan Africa had not, and as a result found itself lethally exposed to the deadly second wave when infected ships arrived in Freetown, Sierra Leone, Cape Town, South Africa and Mombasa, Kenya. The South African experience of Spanish flu is the subject of a subsequent chapter of this book.

In Nairobi, East Africa, young Londoner Sidney Peirce 'got a nice packet of "Flu"' on 25 August, and felt 'rotten'.[18] The following day, he was 'Still in bed with the Flu, a little better. Aug 27th – Still in bed with the doings, still feel jolly bad. Aug 28th – Had a walkabout to-day.'[19]

Sidney, who had been sent to Africa to train a 'black army', suffered a second attack the following month. 'Sept 15th – Got another attack of Flu its [sic] pretty prevalent at Nairobi.'[20]

The unprecedented level of troop movements across the globe aided and abetted the Spanish Lady's campaign of destruction. Hundreds of thousands of US troops huddled together in overcrowded army camps before being herded into trains travelling to ports, then packed into battleships. In June 1918, 279,000 Americans sailed for Europe; in July, the number was 300,000; in August, 286,000. In total, 1.5 million American soldiers landed in Europe during the last six months of the war.[21]

American troops were just one contingent among the many different populations circulating the globe. Ships from New

Zealand refuelled in Sierra Leone, alongside British ships on their way to South Africa, India and Australia. Inevitably, Sierra Leone was soon riddled with Spanish flu. Allied ships headed towards Archangel through the White Sea in a bid to attack Germany from the rear, taking Spanish flu with them so that Russia too was soon engulfed. At Brest, France, five hundred men-of-war lay at anchor as 791,000 doughboys arrived at the Depot de la Marine to encounter the flu-ridden French soldiers. Worse was to come as ships arrived into American ports, bringing the deadly disease with them from Europe.[22]

On 22 July 1918, a depleted *City of Exeter* hobbled into Philadelphia from Liverpool. Among her passengers were twenty-seven Lascars and an English quartermaster 'so desperately ill with pneumonia that they had to be taken to a hospital immediately'.[23] On the same day, an Indian vessel, the *Somali*, 'steamed into the Gulf of St Lawrence and put 89 of her crew, ill with influenza, ashore at Grosse Island'.[24]

On 12 August, the Norwegian ship *Bergensfjord* docked in New York harbour carrying two hundred cases of influenza. Three had died at sea.[25] Eleven passengers were transferred to a hospital in Brooklyn. They were not placed in isolated wards. Health Commissioner Royal S. Copeland of New York City made the woefully over-confident announcement that the victims had pneumonia, not influenza, and claimed that Spanish flu rarely attacked the well-fed. 'You haven't heard of our doughboys getting it, have you? You bet you haven't, and you won't . . . No need for our people to worry over the matter.'[26]

On 27 August 1918, three sailors succumbed to Spanish flu on the Receiving Ship at Boston's Commonwealth Pier. This 'Receiving Ship' was not actually a ship but a massive floating barracks.[27] It was designed to hold around 3,700 men but some nights held around 7,000, so was 'grossly overcrowded' by the Navy's own admission.[28] The following day, eight new cases presented for treatment. The day after that, there were fifty-eight. On day four, eighty-one men fell ill; on day five, one hundred and six. One modern writer, Dennis Lehane, has compellingly recreated the chilling vision that met the eyes of onlookers when flu-stricken men were removed from their infected ship, describing their 'Pinched skulls and caved-in cheeks, their sweat-drenched hair and vomit-encrusted lips, they'd looked dead already.'[29] The deadly symptoms of heliotropic cyanosis were already present in three victims, who 'bore a blue tint to their flesh, mouths peeled back, eyes wide and glaring'.[30]

These Spanish flu cases overwhelmed the medical facilities at Commonwealth Pier, so fifty patients were transferred to Chelsea Naval Hospital, across the Bay. Physicians took blood samples and throat cultures and within forty-eight hours two of them had become infected. The most significant feature of this outbreak was the speed of onset. Within a matter of hours, perfectly healthy men were in a state of complete prostration. 'Fevers ran from 101° to 105°, and the sick complained of general weakness and severe aches in their muscles, joints, backs and heads. The sufferers commonly described themselves as feeling as if they "had been beaten all over with a club".'[31]

Within two weeks of the first case, 2,000 men of the First Naval District were critically ill with influenza. While the majority of patients recovered within a matter of days, a further 5 to 10 per cent developed severe pneumonia. 'As of September 11, 95 cases of influenza pneumonia had been or were being treated at Chelsea Naval Hospital. Thirty-five had died and another 15 or

20 were desperately ill. It seemed probable that the mortality rate for influenza pneumonia would be 60 to 70 percent.'[32] Autopsies revealed lung tissue sodden with fluid; and while pathologists expected to find Pfeiffer's *bacillus*, confirming to them that this was influenza, the *bacillus* was not always present. One physician at the hospital, Lieutenant Junior Grade J. J. Keegan, predicted that the disease 'promises to spread rapidly across the entire country, attacking between 30 and 40 percent of the population, and running an acute course in from four to six weeks in each community'.[33] He was right.

Despite this obvious public health emergency, it appeared as if military and civilian authorities were doing little to prevent the spread of Spanish flu. On 3 September, the first civilian casualty arrived at Boston City Hospital; instead of imposing strict quarantine, the city authorities permitted four thousand men to march through the streets of Boston in a freedom parade the very same day. As the American historian Alfred Crosby has observed, this did not win the war but it did spread the influenza epidemic.

On 4 September, the first cases of influenza appeared at the Navy Radio School at Harvard, in Cambridge. On 5 September, the state department of health released news of the epidemic to the newspapers. Doctor John S. Hitchcock warned the *Boston Globe* that 'unless precautions are taken the disease in all probability will spread to the civilian population of the city'.[34] But no precautions were taken, and a day later, on 6 September, thousands of sailors and civilians packed into a drill hall to celebrate the opening of a new building at the Radio School.

The first three official deaths from Spanish flu in Boston occurred on 8 September: one navy death, one merchant marine, and the first civilian death since early summer. A week later, on 11 September, the navy announced that the pandemic had killed twenty-six sailors in and around Boston, and the first flu cases were recognized among navy personnel in Rhode Island, Connecticut, Pennsylvania, Virginia, South Carolina, Florida and Illinois.[35] While concerned public health officials in Washington were telling reporters that they feared Spanish flu had arrived in the United States, a massive recruiting drive saw thirteen million men of precisely the ages most liable to die of Spanish influenza and its complications lined up all over the United States and crammed into city halls, post offices and school houses to register for the draft. It was a gala flag-waving affair everywhere, including Boston, where 96,000 registered and sneezed and coughed on one another.[36] The public health officials were wasting their breath. Meanwhile, three more victims dropped dead on the sidewalks of Quincy, Massachusetts.[37] The Spanish Lady was continuing her inexorable campaign against the United States.

On 8 September, Spanish flu appeared at Camp Devens, just four days after 1,400 fresh recruits had arrived from Massachusetts. Camp Devens, forty miles north of Boston, Massachusetts, was crammed to the rafters with over 45,000 men, preparing to ship out to France. On the same day, 2nd Lieutenant Alfred Tennyson had looked on as four of his men were threatened with a court martial for refusing to do the 'bear-crawl' during a training exercise.[38] Tennyson immediately realized that his men were sick and attempted to intercede on their behalf. Little did he know that they were the first victims of a Spanish flu epidemic that would rip through Camp Devens, killing 787 men. As soon as the extent of the epidemic became obvious, Dr Victor Vaughan, suffering from a bad cold, was summoned to do what he could for the stricken recruits.

'I went directly to the Surgeon General's office, where General Richard was officiating, as General Gorgas was in Europe,'[39] recalled Vaughan. 'Scarcely looking up from his papers, the general said, as I entered the door: "You will proceed immediately to Devens. The Spanish influenza has struck that camp." Then, laying aside his papers and looking into my suffused eyes, he said: "No, you will go home and go to bed." I took the next train for Camp Devens and arrived early the next morning.'[40]

On his very first day at Camp Devens, Vaughan saw sixty-three soldiers die. Recalling the traumatic scenes in his memoir, Vaughan wrote:

I see hundreds of young, stalwart men in the uniform of their country coming into the wards of the hospital in groups of ten or more. They are placed on the cots until every bed is full and yet others crowd in. The faces soon wear a bluish cast; a distressing cough brings up the blood-stained sputum. In the morning the dead bodies are stacked about the morgue like cord wood. This picture was painted on my memory cells at the division hospital, Camp Devens, in 1918, when the deadly influenza demonstrated the inferiority of human inventions in the destruction of human life. Such are the grewsome [sic] pictures exhibited by the revolving memory cylinders in the brain of an old epidemiologist as he sits in front of the burning logs on the hearth of his 'cottage in the woods.'[41]

Vaughan's most chilling discovery was that this new strain of flu, like war itself, killed 'the young, vigorous, robust adults . . . The husky male either made a speedy and rather abrupt recovery or was likely to die.'[42] As a result Vaughan, for all his medical qualifications, felt completely helpless: 'The saddest part of my life was when I witnessed the hundreds of deaths of the soldiers in the Army camps and did not know what to do. At that moment I decided never again to prate about the great achievements of medical science and to humbly admit our dense ignorance in this case.'[43]

The distressing scenes at Camp Devens shocked new doctors and hardened medics alike. One of Vaughan's colleagues, Dr Roy Grist, left a graphic description of this new influenza in a letter to a friend:

These men start with what appears to be an ordinary attack of La Grippe or Influenza, and when brought to the Hosp. [sic] they very rapidly develop the most vicious type of Pneumonia that has ever been seen . . . and a few hours later you can begin to see the Cyanosis extending from their ears and spreading all over the face, until it is hard to distinguish the colored men from the white. It is only a matter of a few hours then until death comes . . . It is horrible. One can stand it to see one, two or twenty men die, but to see these poor devils dropping like flies . . . We have been averaging about 100 deaths per day . . . Pneumonia means in about all cases death . . . We have lost an outrageous number of Nurses and Drs. It takes special trains to carry away the dead. For several days there were no coffins and the bodies piled up something fierce . . . It beats any sight they ever had in France after a battle. An extra long barracks has been vacated for the use of the Morgue, and it would make any man sit up and take notice to walk down the long lines of dead soldiers all dressed and laid out in double row.[44]

Working in these conditions was both depressing and exhausting, as Grist's closing remarks indicate: 'The men here are all good fellows but I get so damned sick of pneumonia we eat it live it sleep it and dream it to say nothing of breathing it 16 hours a day . . . Good By [*sic*] old Pal, God be with you till we meet again.'[45]

Grist's letter, with its testimony to the horrors of Spanish flu, was discovered among a cache of papers in an old trunk in 1979. We have no idea whether Dr Grist survived the war, or perished along with his patients; medical staff were among those who died at Camp Devens at the rate of 100 deaths a day.

When the veteran pathologist Dr William Welch arrived at Camp Devens, he confirmed that the cause of death in the majority of cases was lung failure. Autopsies revealed blue, swollen lungs filled with a bloody fluid. A calm and dignified man, who had witnessed many terrible sights, Welch was visibly shaken by the scenes that met his eyes. His young colleague, Dr Rufus Cole, later commented that 'it shocked me to find that the situation, momentarily at least, was too much even for Doctor Welch'.[46]

Welch, along with Vaughan and Cole, immediately informed General McCain that Camp Devens must go into quarantine, with no more troops arriving and leaving the camp. In addition, increased numbers of medical personnel must be drafted in as soon as possible. But McCain, with a war to win, 'had to delay and hedge on implementing and even ignore the meagre suggestions they did make'.[47]

It was left to Welch to vocalize the doctors' anxieties and the powerlessness of medical science in the face of this onslaught. Welch was not afraid to put his deepest fears into words: 'This must be some new kind of infection,' he said, and then, employing one of the few words in the medical lexicon that still has an aura of superstitious horror, 'or plague'.[48]

As Spanish flu ran unchecked across the United States and Europe, some patriots claimed that Spanish flu was actually a form of biological warfare, the natural successor to the mustard gas being used at the Front. It was feared that the Germans were to blame, having created a form of poison gas which had been released by U-boats onto the beaches of the United States. As thousands of Bostonians fell sick, rumours whirled as fast as the Spanish Lady. Outside the scientific constraints of the medical profession, one conspiracy theory held that German spies had deliberately seeded Boston Harbour with influenza-sprouting germs. On 17 September 1918, Lt Col. Philip Doane, head of the Health and Sanitation Section of the Emergency Fleet Corporation, opined that the epidemic had been started by Germans put ashore from U-boats.[49] 'It would be quite easy for one of these German agents to turn loose influenza germs in a theatre or some other place where large numbers of persons are assembled. The Germans have started epidemics in Europe, and there is no reason why they should be particularly gentle with America.'[50] Another wild rumour circulated that the Bayer brand of aspirin was impregnated with germs, because the Bayer patent was originally German. However ridiculous these allegations, the Public Health Service had to investigate. It was said that German spies had infiltrated the Army Medical Corps and spread Spanish flu through hypodermic shots, and that the spies had been discovered and executed by firing squad.[51] This was despite denials from Brigadier General Charles Richard, Surgeon General of the Army, who announced that 'There have been no medical officers or nurses or anyone else executed at camps in the United States.'[52] Despite this, some Americans continued to blame the Germans for Spanish flu, one declared: 'Let the curse be called the German plague. Let every child learn to associate what is accursed with the word German not in the spirit of hate but in the spirit of contempt born of the hateful truth which Germany has proved herself to be.'[53]

While no concrete evidence has been found to confirm these theories, historians such as Alfred Crosby suggested a more plausible explanation, namely that Spanish flu derived directly from the war itself, a man-made catastrophe created by a deadly combination of the poison gas and decomposing corpses created in No Man's Land:

> Wherever his armies met in Europe, man was creating chemical and biological cesspools in which any kind of disease might spawn. Never before had such quantities of explosives been expended, never before had so many men lived in such filth for so long, never before had so many human corpses been left to rot above ground, and never before had anything so fiendish as mustard gas been released into the atmosphere in large amounts.[54]

Victor Vaughan's response to the epidemic at Camp Devens was chilling. 'If the epidemic continues its mathematical rate of acceleration, civilization could easily disappear from the face of the earth,'[55] he feared.

CHAPTER EIGHT

LIKE FIGHTING WITH A GHOST

➤◆➤

I had a little bird
And its name was Enza
I opened the window and
In-flew-enza

THIS WAS THE rhyme the third-grade girls sang as they jumped rope in Miss Sykes' class in Dorchester, Boston. 'To our confident immortality, influenza seemed no threat at all, one more incident in the excitement of the war's climax,' recalled Francis Russell, just seven years old when Spanish flu hit Massachusetts. Like the children in Thomas Gray's poem, the little victims played, heedless of their impending doom.[1]

Initially, doctors and civic authorities were confident that the epidemic would be contained. On 13 September 1918, Surgeon General Rupert Blue of the United States Public Health Service (USPHS) gave a press interview, issuing guidance on how to recognize Spanish flu and recommending bed rest, good food, quinine and aspirin for patients.[2] The following day, the Public Health Service of Massachusetts telegraphed the national headquarters of the Red Cross for fifteen nurses to be rushed to Boston.[3] There were similar calls from elsewhere in New England in the following days. Despite these efforts the mortality rates increased day by day. On 26 September, 123 Bostonians died of influenza and 33 of pneumonia.[4] Overall, 50,000 cases were reported in Massachusetts. Governor Calvin Coolidge telegrammed President Wilson, the Mayor of Toronto, and the governors of Vermont, Maine and Rhode Island with the news that 'Our doctors and nurses are being thoroughly mobilized and worked to limit ... Many cases receive no attention whatever.'[5] Coolidge did not ask New Hampshire or Connecticut for assistance, 'because he knew they were nearly as badly off as Massachusetts'.[6]

By this point, Spanish flu had appeared at navy bases as far away from Boston as Louisiana, Puget Sound and San Francisco Bay, and in twenty army camps from Massachusetts to Georgia and as far west as Camp Lewis, Washington. Despite this sinister development, the city authorities insisted there was no cause for alarm. The *Boston Globe* proclaimed that the doctors had the Spanish flu 'pretty well in hand'[7] despite the fact that the Navy announced 163 new cases the same afternoon, with a Rear Admiral protesting that there was 'no reason to be alarmed'.[8]

Francis Russell's school in Dorchester, Boston, lay on the route to the New Calvary cemetery and from his classroom window Francis had a ringside view of the funerals. As the coffins piled up, the landowner, John 'Pigeye' Mulvey, pitched a circus tent alongside the chapel to hide them.

'The tent lay there white and billowing, like some grotesque autumn carnival among the withered leaves, with the somber line of vehicles trailing through New Calvary gate,' Francis recalled.[9] Caskets, buried too shallow, were rising out of the ground. From his classroom, as they followed the morning routine of multiplication tables,

We could hear the carriages passing outside, the clop of horses' hooves in the wet leaves . . . The plague stretched out its fingertips towards Miss Sykes. Trying as best she could to conceal it from us, she became sharp and tense-voiced. The rattle of the hacks had broken her nerve. In the afternoon the sun's rays would strike against the glass of a passing carriage, and reflect waveringly across the ceiling of our room, and we, distracted by light and sound, would crane toward the row of windows. 'Eyes front!' she would shriek at us. For the fear was on her.[10]

All the schools in Boston were closed in the first week of October 1918, as the authorities finally took action to stem the onslaught of the epidemic. This was a blessing as far as Francis was concerned:

For us it was pure joy in that abounding weather to be free of the third grade and the Palmer Method and the multiplication tables and Miss Sykes and her harmonica. The early mornings turned frosty, blackening the marigolds, but the afternoons were warm and sun-drenched and golden, heavy with cricket sounds, light as milkweed down. By Collins' Pond the witch hazel was in bloom, the lemon-yellow filaments crisscrossed against the bare branches, on the Hill, on such bright days, we lost ourselves in the immediacy of the timeless present, as free to wander as any coma of milkweed.[11]

Francis's idyllic memories of the fall contrast vividly with the grim reality of life in Massachusetts during the epidemic. When a Roman Catholic nurse on duty in Boston was asked why she had returned so late, she had replied: 'Well, the Mother had died, and there were four sick children in two rooms, and the man was fighting with his mother-in-law and throwing a pitcher at her head.'[12] 'The whole city is stricken,' wrote a nurse in Gloucester, Massachusetts. 'We were taken quite unawares.'[13]

Meanwhile, six-year-old John Delano was growing up in the Italian immigrant community in New Haven, Connecticut. 'Life to me was just lots of Italians living together. We all knew each other, we were always visiting, passing food around. We were just one big happy family. For every little affair – baptisms, birthdays, Communion – we had a party. It was always parties, parties, parties.'[14]

But Spanish flu soon changed all this. John lived down the block from an undertaker, and he began to witness coffins piling up on the sidewalk outside the morgue. As the piles of coffins rose, he and friends played on them, jumping from one to another: 'We thought – boy, this is great. It's like climbing the pyramids. Then one day, I slipped and fell and broke my nose on one of the coffins. My mother was very upset. She said, didn't I realize there were people in those boxes? People who had died? I couldn't understand that. Why had all these people died?'[15]

In Brockton, Massachusetts, 8,000 people, 20 per cent of the city's population, fell ill. Mayor William L. Gleason conducted an efficient holding operation, employing Boy Scouts to send messages and run errands, but despite this the infection spread. The chair of Brockton's Board of Health told one nurse that combating Spanish flu was like 'fighting with a ghost'.[16] One morning a young woman arrived at Brockton Hospital suffering from Spanish flu. Her lungs were already full of blood, and she was seven months pregnant.

'The baby was born prematurely and died at birth, but I did not dare tell the mother it had died,' recalled her nurse.[17]

'She kept begging me to see her baby . . . I assured her that he was fine and beautiful and she would hold him as soon as she was stronger. She had such a lovely look on her face as she talked about her son, and how happy her husband would be. It was an effort for her to talk as her lungs were filling . . . She died late that afternoon. I put the baby into her arms and fixed them so that they seemed only to be sleeping. And so the husband saw them when he came.'[18]

Young Francis Russell and his classmates, left to their own devices, made the most of their new-found freedom. One afternoon, Francis and his friend Eliot Dodds followed another boy, Everett Nudd, down towards the New Calvary cemetery. 'Want to come along?' Eliot asked. 'Want to come watch funerals? I do it every day.'[19] Francis had never attended a funeral, although he had seen many through his classroom windows, and he found himself unable to turn back.

We wandered down the main path past the brown and gray stone monuments, past carved crosses and sacred hearts and triumphant stone angels with impassive granite wings. Then the path ended at a dump, and Everett turned right through a thicket of ground oak and speckled alder, holding up his hand in warning. A funeral was going on directly below us. Around the raw earth of an open grave a group of mourners was huddled together like a flock of bedraggled starlings. The fumed oak coffin had been set beside the grave, and a priest in a biretta stood at its head, even as we looked down, making the sign of the cross over it. Then the others began to file past and some of them stopped to pick up a bit of earth which they scattered on the coffin. Just behind them two workmen appeared with ropes fastened in a sling. A heavy-built man with white hair and florid features stopped at the grave's edge, shook the damp clay from his fingers, then glanced up to see us peering through the alder bushes. 'Get out of here, you!' he shouted, his face turning scarlet. 'Get out!'[20]

The boys hid behind the bushes; Francis was desperate to get away but Everett tugged on Francis's shirt to make him stay. They had stumbled across a horrific sight. Exhausted gravediggers, hopelessly trying to keep up with the backlog, were dumping the corpses out of the coffins and re-using them. As the boys emerged beside another open grave,

A grave digger just climbed out and stood with his shovel beside him, lighting his pipe. He was an old Italian with a drooping mustache, wearing a shapeless felt hat with a turned-down brim. The grave digger started at us with shrewd, uncomprehending eyes, then took his pipe out of his mouth and spat again. 'Ah, you boys-a go-onna home,' he said thickly. 'You no playa here. Go-onna home.'[21]

Francis ran away home, but was never able to forget the experience:

Seeing the lights, thinking of the afternoon, in that bare instant I became aware of time. I knew then that life was not a perpetual present, and that even tomorrow would be part of the past, and

*that for all my days and years to come I too must one day die. I
pushed the relentless thought aside, knowing even as I did . . . I
should never again be wholly free of it.*[22]

John Delano, too, had his first taste of mortality at the hands of
the Spanish Lady.

*One day, my three best buddies didn't come out of their houses
in the morning. I realized no one in our neighborhood was
visiting each other. No one was passing around food, talking on
the street. Everyone was staying inside. Still, every morning, I
went to my buddies' houses. I knocked on the door and waited
for them to come out and play.*[23]

One morning, John knocked on the doors of his friends' houses
and waited for someone to come out. But nobody did. 'I didn't
know what was happening. Finally, my mother told me God had
taken them. My friends had gone to Heaven.'[24]

Down in New York, conditions were not as bad as they might
have been. Despite its role as the most important embarkation
port in the United States, New York did not suffer as gravely
as other American cities during the Spanish flu pandemic. As
we shall see in a subsequent chapter, that melancholy distinction
fell to Philadelphia. However, New York could not escape the
onslaught entirely. As a major port, it was subject to the disease
brought on board from foreign craft and from its own returning
servicemen. Also, Spanish flu was airborne: if it had not come
to New York via global military transportation, it reached New
Yorkers a dozen other ways: on the breath of returning soldiers
reunited with their families; from civilians travelling back and

forth the length and breadth of the country; and from civilians and military personnel gathering together for recruitment drives. On 12 October, President Wilson led 25,000 cheering New Yorkers down the 'Avenue of the Allies'[25] in a supreme example of 'stark raving patriotism'.[26] That same week, 2,100 New Yorkers died of influenza.[27]

On 19 September, the USS *Leviathan* returned to New York from Brest, France. Among her passengers was Assistant Secretary of the Navy Franklin Delano Roosevelt, who had developed influenza on the way home from an exhausting fact-finding mission to France. Eleanor Roosevelt received word through the Navy Department that Roosevelt had double pneumonia and they were to meet him on arrival with a doctor and an ambulance. According to Eleanor, 'the flu had been raging in Brest and Franklin and his party had attended a funeral in the rain. The ship on which they returned was a floating hospital. Men and officers died on the way home and were buried at sea.'[28] Among the passengers was Prince Axel of Denmark and his entourage, coming to the United States for a visit. 'When they felt the 'flu coming on they consulted no doctor but took to their berths with a quart of whisky [*sic*] each. In the course of a day or two, whether because of the efficacy of the whisky or because of their own resistance, they were practically recovered.'[29]

Roosevelt was so weak that he had to be carried off on a stretcher when the ship docked. 'An ambulance drove him to his mother's house, and four Navy orderlies carried him inside.'[30] It took Roosevelt a month to recover.

The Spanish Lady embraced the future president of the United States as enthusiastically as she flung her arms around the poor Chinese sailors who ended up sick in New York. Twenty-five Chinese sailors, suffering with flu, were taken from their ship to the Municipal Lodging House, which had been turned into an emergency hospital. To their horror, they were greeted by white masked figures in white robes, who spoke no Chinese. An interpreter had been found, but fled the scene when Spanish flu was mentioned. Fearing that they would be robbed, the sailors refused to take their clothes off, and afraid they would be poisoned, they refused to eat. Victims of mutual incomprehension, seventeen out of twenty-five sailors died.[31]

But the official mood remained buoyant. At the end of September 1918, the *Journal of the American Medical Association* claimed that Spanish influenza might sound unusual but this 'should not cause any greater importance to be attached to it, nor arouse any greater fear than would influenza without the new name'. The journal also maintained that Spanish flu had 'practically disappeared from the Allied troops'.[32]

Despite these claims, Bellevue Hospital, Manhattan, was swiftly overwhelmed with patients. People were dying in beds, on stretchers and in the corridors. In the paediatric wards, children were packed three to a bed. After the laundresses had panicked and fled from the basements, there was no clean linen to be had. Cleanliness, routine and discipline, the bedrock of hospital life, had disappeared.

Dorothy Deming, a student nurse during the pandemic, recalled: 'There were no more formal "doctors' rounds," neither for the attending physicians nor for the medical students. Doctors came and went at all hours, calling for a nurse only when giving an order or needing help. It was quite usual to see a haggard doctor come in long after midnight to make a last examination of his patient before staggering home to bed.'[33]

Another nurse was shocked by the difference between general nursing and the scenes which she encountered on a daily basis:

Until the epidemic, death had seemed kindly, coming to the very old, the incurably suffering or striking suddenly without the knowledge of its victims. Now, we saw death clutch cruelly and ruthlessly at vigorous, well-muscled young women in the prime of life. Flu dulled their resistance, choked their lungs, swamped their hearts . . . There was nothing but sadness and horror to this senseless waste of human life.

Many a morning after working hard over a patient, Dorothy [another Dorothy, Deming's friend] and I bore the grim task of trying to find words of comfort for dazed parents, husbands and children. One dawn – a glorious morning with rose-colored clouds above the gray buildings across the street – after a particularly sad death, I knew the tears I had been shedding inwardly must find outlet. I rushed to the linen closet, always our place of refuge, and there ahead of me was Dorothy, sobbing her heart out.[34]

Dorothy Deming took some consolation from the fact that she was 'doing her bit' for the war effort, a vital consideration at the time. It seemed to Dorothy that nursing in these conditions was the equivalent of being under fire, like 'our brothers in the Argonne'.[35] Despite this iron resolve, the noise coming from the wards was so loud that Dorothy could only sleep with the help of an eye mask fashioned from a black silk stocking, and her ears plugged with cotton wool.[36]

At Columbia Presbyterian Hospital in Washington Heights, Dr Albert Lamb recognized the fact that he was dealing with an unprecedented new disease, describing his incoming patients in graphic terms: 'They're blue as huckleberries and spitting blood.'[37] The by-now familiar stigmata of Spanish flu were adding a note of horror to the familiar symptoms of influenza: torrential nosebleeds, explosive haemorrhaging, air-hunger and cyanosis. Every hospital ward was a vision of hell.

But despite this horrific evidence, New York Public Health Commissioner Royal S. Copeland refused to take rudimentary measures such as closing schools and theatres, claiming that the epidemic was widespread but not serious. 'I'm keeping my theaters in as good condition as my wife keeps our home,'[38] he told reporters. 'And I can vouch that is perfectly sanitary.'[39] On the same day that Copeland made this speech, 354 New Yorkers died of influenza.[40]

The Spanish Lady made orphans of over 600 New York children. Among these was a little Jewish boy from Brooklyn named Michael Wind.

When my mother died of Spanish influenza, we were all gathered in one room, all six of us, from age two to age twelve. My father was sitting beside my mother's bed, head in his hands, sobbing bitterly. All my mother's friends were there, with tears of shock in their eyes. They were shouting at my father, asking why he hadn't called them, hadn't told them she was sick. She had been fine yesterday. How could this have happened?[41]

As Michael's father and five brothers and sisters wept together, Michael himself found it impossible to make sense of events. 'Looking at my mother, I could not relate to my loss. She looked like she was asleep.'[42]

The following morning, Michael and his two younger brothers were taken to the subway by their father. When he bought them all Hershey bars, Michael guessed something was wrong. He was right. They were on their way to the Brooklyn Hebrew Orphan Asylum.[43]

CHAPTER NINE

EYE OF THE STORM

———◆·◆———

N OWHERE DID THE spectre of death flap its wings more powerfully than above the city of Philadelphia. While Philadelphia, with its population of 1,700,000, was regarded as a largely healthy city in 1918, there were severe pockets of deprivation among its many immigrant communities, and it was also home to one of the oldest black ghettoes in the United States.[1] Historically, Philadelphia was a city where early death was taken for granted. Jack Fincher, screenwriter and one-time chief editor of *Life* magazine, whose uncle died of Spanish flu in October 1918, recalled:

> *My uncle's death was but one small, sad design in the vast tapestry of a fatally infectious disease as common to the fabric of American family life then as it is rare today. Times were so different then. Grown-ups and children were so quickly subtracted from the world by so many diseases that we no longer have to fear. My grandmother, for instance, died before* [my uncle]. *She sewed her tubercular sister's burial shroud and then died of the disease herself. Her youngest son was born tubercular. He died before his mother.*[2]

The 11th of September saw an outbreak of Spanish flu in the Naval Yard at Philadelphia, while Camp Dix in New Jersey and Camp Meade in Maryland fell victim on the 15th and 17th respectively. By 18 September, the Philadelphia Bureau of Health was issuing a warning about influenza, with a campaign about the dangers of spreading infection through coughing, sneezing and spitting. According to the *Philadelphia Inquirer*, 600 sailors were in hospital with flu and there were civilian cases as well.[3] On 21 September, the Bureau of Health made influenza a reportable disease, although doctors claimed it was unlikely that influenza would affect the civilian population.[4] Lieutenant Commander R. W. Plummer, medical aide to the commandant of the local naval district, told the public that naval and city officials were cooperating 'to confine this disease to its present limits, and in this we are sure to be successful'.[5] The doctors felt confident: on the same day that influenza was made a reportable disease in Philadelphia, Dr Paul A. Lewis, director of the laboratories of the Phipps Institute of Philadelphia, announced that he had isolated the cause of Spanish flu in the form of Pfeiffer's *bacillus*. According to the *Inquirer*, this 'armed the medical profession with absolute knowledge on which to base its campaign against this disease'.[6] Lewis's conclusion was only a local one, given the amount of research being conducted elsewhere into the causes of Spanish flu. It was also to have tragic consequences. In a buoyant mood, confident that a vaccine for Spanish flu was imminent, the city gave permission for a massive parade, the Fourth Liberty Loan Drive, on 28 September. Two hundred thousand people gathered at the start of the parade, which stretched through the city for twenty-three blocks.

Singing conductors and speakers were distributed among the marchers, and whenever the parade halted, they led the crowds in patriotic songs and harangued them to buy bonds. Women in mourning were plucked out of the crowd and used to advertise the purpose of the parade: 'This woman gave her all. What will you give?' Planes flew overhead and antiaircraft guns fired at them, the fuses carefully adjusted so that the shells would explode far below the aircraft.[7]

During each pause, the crowd was entreated, pressured, and harangued to buy bonds. Why buy bonds? Why send 'our darlings' to France? 'You have brought them into the soul-awakening experience of War for Principle. They must be kept there, equipped for this stupendous task, until the task is finished. And your support is the only thing that will do it.'[8]

Two faces in the crowd watching this parade were Susanna Turner and Columba Voltz. Susanna, seventeen years old, was a student at William Penn High School. 'We were so conscious of the war, of liberty. We marched and sang and saved our money for Liberty Bonds,' Susanna remembered.[9] Columba, aged just eight years old, recalled the parade as 'a marvelous singing fest, with huge posters of Uncle Sam bobbing through the crowd'.[10] Columba and her friend Katherine linked arms and sang, and spent their pennies on bonds. 'Katherine and I were happy,' Columba remembered, 'thinking we were helping the war effort.'[11]

A massive epidemic of Spanish flu exploded within a day of the parade. On October 1, 635 new cases were reported. Physicians were kept so busy that they didn't have time to file reports: the actual number of cases was likely to have been much higher. Dr A. A. Cairns of the Bureau of Health estimated 75,000 cases in Philadelphia between 11 September and the end of the month.[12]

At the Hog Island Shipyards 8 per cent of workers were laid off and so many riveting teams were broken up that the number of rivets driven on 3 October dropped from 86,000 to 11,000.[13] That night, all schools, churches and theatres in Philadelphia were ordered to be closed. On the same night, Dr B. F. Royer, Acting State Commissioner of Health for Pennsylvania, ordered all places of public amusement and saloons to be closed, while Surgeon General Blue recommended the same policy for the entire country. Although many towns and cities followed his advice, it did little to check the spread of the disease.

Anna Milani was just a little girl living in an Italian community in North Street, when tragedy struck. 'I remember it was a mild day and we were sitting outside on the steps. Around twilight, we heard screams. In that same house, the same family where the girl had died, an eighteen-month-old baby died. Someone told us there was an epidemic of Spanish influenza: *Influenza de la Spagnuolo*.'[14]

By the week ending 5 October, 700 Philadelphians had died of flu and pneumonia. The next week, 2,600 died, and over 4,500 died the following week. Doctors were rushed off their feet and were days behind in reporting deaths to the authorities. With hundreds of thousands estimated to be sick, patients overwhelmed the hospitals, arriving in limousines, horse carts and even wheelbarrows. To make matters worse, those whose job it was to treat the patients fell ill themselves. Hospitals had to struggle on with even less in the way of nurses and orderlies and cleaners. At the Philadelphia Hospital, forty nurses fell sick. Soon the authorities were pleading with anyone able bodied and willing to work to come forward. In North Philadelphia, Susanna Turner volunteered to help nurse Spanish flu victims:

I was seventeen years old and I thought I might like to be a nurse. So I went to our pastor and I asked what I could do. He told me to see Mrs Thomas (the wife of Ira Thomas who was the catcher for the Philadelphia Athletics, our city's baseball team) who was making masks in a little side room of the hospital. Mrs Thomas made me dip a mask in disinfectant outside the sickroom. Then I put it on and went in. I carried bed pans, helped the Sisters the best I could. People were so weak, they almost seemed dead.[15]

Every once in a while, I'd stiffen up and get scared and wonder if I was going to get the flu. But I was surviving. I just lived from day to day. I didn't think about the future.[16]

Essential services collapsed during the epidemic. Four hundred and eighty-seven police officers did not show up for work, while the Bureau of Child Hygiene was overwhelmed with hundreds of abandoned children. As they could not send the children to orphanages for fear of spreading the disease, they had to ask neighbours to take the children in. When 850 employees of the Pennsylvania Bell Telephone Company stayed away from work on 8 October, Bell was forced to take out a newspaper advertisement stating that the company could handle no 'other than absolutely necessary calls compelled by the epidemic or by war necessity'.[17] The following day, the Department of Health and charities authorized the company to deny service to anyone making unessential calls, which it did in a thousand cases.

Nurses witnessed scenes reminiscent of the original Black Death. In their distinctive white robes and gauze masks, they were followed by crowds desperate for help, or shunned out of fear. A nurse could start her day with a list of fifteen patients and end up seeing fifty. 'One nurse found a husband dead in the same room where his wife lay with newly born twins. It had been twenty-four hours since the death and the births, and the wife had no food but an apple which happened to lie within reach.'[18]

While civic leadership was patchy and inconsistent,[19] the Philadelphia Council of National Defense coordinated a campaign against the pandemic. This organization opened a Bureau of Information in the Strawbridge and Clothier department store on 10 October with a twenty-four-hour telephone helpline and ran an advertisement in the local papers: 'Influenza Sufferers, If you need Physicians, Nurses, Ambulances, Motor Vehicles, or any other service because of the epidemic, telephone "Filbert 100" and when the number answers, say: Influenza.'[20] The switchboard was immediately jammed. Bell Telephone Company doubled, then quadrupled, its lines. By 7 October, it was overwhelmed – 850 of the 'hello girls' were sick with flu.[21]

As always during epidemics, the poor were the most vulnerable. In the slum tenements, families who did not immediately succumb to Spanish flu starved when they lost their breadwinner parents, and had to rely on volunteers bringing supplies from the soup kitchens house to house. Mercifully, the Council for National Defense had plenty of vehicles. Over 400 vehicles from the Auto Committee of the Fourth Liberty Loan Drive were diverted to fight the epidemic, fifteen ambulances were available after 10 October, and dozens of private cars and even taxis were donated to drive doctors and nurses around.

But there was still a shortage of doctors, nurses and auxiliaries to carry out the work. Within days of the outbreak on 1 October, elderly doctors were being called out of retirement, while medical students suddenly found themselves shouldering the responsibilities of veteran physicians, working fifteen-hour days.

Charities and religious and political organizations were keen to help. Hundreds of teachers, unable to work since the schools had been closed, also volunteered; Archbishop Daugherty assigned 200 nurses from the Order of St Joseph to the emergency hospitals; Roman Catholic nuns worked at a Jewish hospital under the direction of a Doctor Cohen, while the St Vincent de Paul Society offered food, clothing and care, with its members prepared to dig graves if required.[22] Dozens of off-duty police officers from the Patrolmen's Benevolent Association acted as stretcher-bearers.[23] In South Philadelphia, where the epidemic was worse, hundreds of grocery stores closed to the public and distributed their goods to the poor and needy, and a fireman drove an old horse-drawn ambulance through the streets delivering aid and food.[24]

Until the Spanish Lady arrived in town, Columba Voltz had always loved the sound of bells from the nearby church. 'They rang jubilantly, joyfully, all the time. The bells were beautiful, and they gave me such joy.'[25] All this changed when Spanish flu hit the neighbourhood. Columba, who lived across the street from an undertaker's, watched coffins stacked up on the sidewalk.

> *The beautiful bells had stopped ringing. All day long, I watched coffins being carried into the church, accompanied by the low, sad, funeral bells: BONG, BONG, BONG. Only a few people were allowed into the church at a time and the service lasted only a few minutes, just long enough to bless the coffin. Then the casket would be carried out and another one would go in.*

All day long, the funeral bells tolled: BONG, BONG, BONG. Up and down the street, crepes were hanging on the doors of houses. I knew inside every one of those houses, someone was being laid out. I was very scared and depressed. I thought the world was coming to an end.[26]

The Philadelphia death rate spiralled, with 2,600 dead in the second week of October and 4,500 dying of flu and pneumonia in the third week. And then, in a horrific twist, Spanish flu hit the undertaking trade. 'On one occasion the Society for Organizing Charity called 25 undertakers before finding one able and willing to bury a member of a poor family.'[27] Bodies remained at home for days. Private undertaking firms were overwhelmed by the demand and some exploited the situation by raising their prices by as much as 600 per cent.[28] Complaints circulated that cemeteries charged families $15 for a burial, then made them dig the graves themselves. The Donohue family, who had run a small undertaking business since 1898, had to hire a security guard to mind their caskets. Michael Donohue, just a boy at the time, remembered:

Normally, stealing a casket would be inconceivable. It would be equated with grave robbing. But in October 1918, the influenza epidemic changed people's minds about what they would do, how they would act. People were desperate. They felt they had no alternative, there was no place for them to turn. These were nice people, people who wouldn't have done this otherwise. These were our neighbors, our friends, and for some of them, stealing a casket was the only way they could see to provide for their loved one.[29]

Philadelphia had just one city morgue, at 13th and Wood Streets, with space for just thirty-six bodies, normally sufficient for homicide victims or unknown 'John Does'. By the third week of October, it was struggling to cope with several hundred corpses, piled three deep in the corridors and in every room, covered with dirty blood-stained sheets.[30] The bodies were neither embalmed nor packed with ice, and soon emitted a nauseating stench. The doors, left open to allow air to circulate, stood open upon a scene from Hell. At one point, there were ten times as many bodies at the morgue as coffins.[31]

By 10 October, 500 bodies lay awaiting burial at the morgue and the undertakers, coffin makers and gravediggers were unable to keep pace with the demand. To cope with the sheer number of dead, the authorities opened an emergency morgue at a cold-storage plant on 20th and Cambridge Streets. Another five makeshift morgues would be opened before the epidemic was over.[32]

Collecting the bodies was another matter: while it was comparatively simple to remove bodies from Emergency Hospital Number One and take them to a cemetery, it was far more time consuming collecting the dead from homes and lodgings; on one occasion, six wagons and a motor truck drove around the city and collected 221 corpses between one and four days old.[33]

After 528 Philadelphians died in a single day, Father Joseph Corrigan, director of the city's Catholic Charities, organized a melancholy convoy of six horse-drawn wagons. Night and day, they combed alleys and back streets for the abandoned dead. Parish volunteers and theology students manned the grim march, carrying shovels and spades, lighting the way with kerosene lanterns.[34]

Little Harriet Ferrel lived in a poor black district. 'People were in a panic. Suffering. Crying. The Board of Health had issued a proclamation that anyone who died had to be left out for the wagons. But it was just too much to bear – having to put your loved one on the street for a truck to take them away.'[35]

Selma Epp's entire family succumbed to Spanish flu.

My parents went for help. They stood in line for hours outside Pennsylvania Hospital, but were turned away. So they came home and made up their own remedies, like castor oil, laxatives. My grandfather made wine. Nothing helped. Everyone in my family – my parents, my aunts and my brother Daniel – everyone up and down our block was sick. There were no medicines, no doctors, nothing people could do to heal themselves. My grandfather was very religious. He was an Orthodox Jew and he wore his tallith shawl and he prayed, hoping God would take away the illness. Everyone in our house grew weaker and weaker. Then Daniel died. My aunt saw the horse-drawn wagon coming down the street. The strongest person in our family carried Daniel's body to the sidewalk. Everyone was too weak to protest. There were no coffins in the wagon, just bodies piled up on top of each other. Daniel was two; he was just a little boy. They put his body in the wagon and took him away.[36]

Philadelphia's fifty embalmers were soon overwhelmed by demand, a problem partially solved by a resourceful undertaker, Mr H. S. Eckels of the Purple Cross undertakers' association. Mr Eckels asked the mayor of Philadelphia to contact the Secretary of War, who sent ten military embalmers.[37]

The shortage of coffins was another matter, with the cheapest ones sold out, leaving only the most expensive available, and in some cases marked up by unscrupulous undertakers. This problem was solved in Philadelphia by the Council of National Defense recruiting several local woodworking businesses to make extra coffins. These were distributed with strict instructions that they were only to be available for the burial of Philadelphians and that the undertaker could add no more than 20 per cent to the price.[38]

Faced with a shortage of gravediggers, the city authorities recruited navvies from the highways department and prisoners from the local jails. When the number of dead became so high that mere manpower was not enough, the Bureau of Highways lent a steam shovel to dig trenches in Potter's Field for the burial of the poor and unknown, their bodies tagged in case relatives appeared who would later want to remove them to family plots. Michael Donohue, whose family ran a small funeral home in West Philadelphia, recalled:

> *The cemeteries went to extraordinary lengths to help people, especially the Archdiocese of Philadelphia. In some cases, families had to dig the graves themselves, but it was either that or they weren't going to get the grave open. In order to maintain some level of humanity, the Archdiocese brought in a steam shovel to excavate section 42 of Holy Cross Cemetery – what became known as the 'trench.' The trench was the cemetery's way of expediting burials to help families, give people closure. They lined up the dead, one right after another, and did the committal prayers right there in the trench.[39]*

The Donohue family had one modern, motorized hearse engraved with the family name. It could not keep up with the sheer numbers of the dead. 'Everything was in panic, disarray. We were burying our neighbors, our friends, people we did business with, people we went to church with. The bodies never stopped coming. The sadness, the heartbreak went on and on, day after day.'[40]

Michael's family were particularly struck by the youth of the Spanish flu victims:

Usually a mortician sees people dying in their forties, their fifties, some older, some in their nineties. But in the fall of 1918, young people were dying: eighteen-year-olds, twenty-year-olds, thirty-year-olds, forty-year-olds. These were people who should not have died. Most of them were either first generation immigrants or right from their countries of origin: Ireland or Poland or Italy. These were people who came to the Promised Land. They came to start fresh, and when they got here, their lives were destroyed.[41]

The Donohue family had kept detailed ledgers dating back to 1898. But after the epidemic struck Philadelphia, the ledgers reflect the sheer chaos and havoc wreaked by Spanish flu.

Our ledger books are all handwritten and the ones from 1918 are written in the flowing fancy penmanship common in that era. In the early part of 1918, things are well documented. You can tell who a person was, who his parents were, his children. The book lists where he lived, what he died of, where the viewing and funeral were held, where he was buried. But when you get to October 1918, the ledgers become sloppy and confused; things are crossed out, scribbled in borders. Information is scant and all

out of chronological order – it's nearly impossible to keep track of
what's going on, it's just page and page of tragedy and turmoil.
Sometimes we got paid. Sometimes we didn't. Usually, we buried
people we knew. Other times, we buried strangers. One entry
reads: 'A girl.' Another says 'A Polish woman.' Another: 'A Polish
man and his baby.' Someone must have asked us to take care
of these people and it was just the decent thing to do. We had a
responsibility to make sure things were done in a proper, moral,
dignified manner. Scribbled at the bottom of the ledger, below
the entry for the 'girl,' is 'This girl was buried in the trench.' This
girl was our addition to the trench. I guess we had nowhere else
to put her.[42]

Meanwhile, Columba Voltz's parents had fallen sick and taken
to their beds. 'I was petrified. I was only eight. I didn't know
what to do. None of our relatives would come near us for fear of
getting sick. And all day long, those horrible funeral bells rang:
BONG, BONG, BONG. I heard them even in my sleep.'[43]

Eventually, a neighbour came to help out and nurse Columba's
stricken parents. Columba tried to help, 'I made mustard plasters
[a poultice of mustard seed inside a protective dressing, designed to
treat muscle pain] and put them on my parents' chests. I brought
lemonade, ran errands.'[44] Columba went on gazing out of the
window, watching the ceaseless tide of funerals winding their way
in and out of the parish church. But then her teeth started to chatter,
her head ached, she felt feverish and dizzy. She got into bed and:

All I heard was those horrible bells: BONG, BONG, BONG. I was
terrified. I was too afraid even to move. I lay very still, almost
without breathing. All day long, I heard those funeral bells. I

was sure I was going to die. I was sure they were going to put me
inside a coffin, and carry me inside the church. I was sure those
horrible bells were going to ring for me.[45]

Little Harriet Ferrel had fallen sick, too, alongside her father, brother, sister, aunt, uncle and cousin. Harriet's mother had to nurse all of them: 'Our family doctor, Dr. Milton White, came by. He told my mother she didn't need to feed me anymore, because I wasn't going to live. He said if I did live, I would be blind.'[46]

In North Street, Anna Milani fell sick, along with her brothers and sisters:

The pain was awful. I remember the terrible, terrible headache,
the pain all over my body, in my legs, my stomach, my chest. We
were all very, very sick. Our father made us drink chamomile
tea. Our mother made plasters out of flour. She couldn't afford
mustard plasters, so she heated up flour, put it in a warm cloth,
and put it on our chests.[47]

Life became harsh in the City of Brotherly Love, and Susanna Turner saw her neighbourhood torn apart by Spanish flu. 'Neighbors weren't helping neighbors. No one was taking any chances. People became selfish. We lost our spirit of charity. Fear just withered the hearts of people.'[48]

Meanwhile, Anna Milani's favourite brother, two-year-old Harry, was getting worse. A neighbour brought a doctor to the house, who diagnosed double pneumonia.

I was like a second mother to Harry. When Harry got sick,
he called for me all the time. Even though I was sick, I was

always beside him. I would cuddle and pet him; I couldn't do anything else. Harry had big, beautiful eyes, but his face got so thin, his eyes bulged out. He was in so much pain. We were all in so much pain.[49]

In another district of Philadelphia, Mrs Ferrel was ignoring medical advice to withhold food from her little daughter. 'You know how mothers are. No mother listens when someone tells her not to feed her child. She does what she has to do for her children, and doesn't listen to anyone else, and that's what my mother did for me.'[50]

For Susanna Turner, working in the parish hospital alongside the nuns, the epidemic allowed her to prove her worth as a nurse. When Susanna asked after one patient, a pregnant woman, Francis the messenger boy said that she had died. '"Where is she?" I asked. Francis said, "In the back room of the school." So we walked down the hall and I said, "Francis, I think I hear a noise in there." We went in. She was alive. The nuns called the ambulance. The woman was taken to a hospital where she delivered her child.'[51]

Anna Milani, sick herself, was caring for her little brother when her mother told her to get some sleep.

My mother said I'd been up too long taking care of Harry. I should rest. While I was lying down, Harry died. My mother came to get me. She was crying, holding my baby sister and crying. She said Harry had opened his eyes – his head rolled back and forth – and he said, 'Nanina.' My name was Nanina in Italian. Harry died with my name in his mouth.

There were no embalmers, so my parents covered Harry with ice. There were no coffins, just boxes painted white. My parents

*put Harry in a box. My mother wanted him dressed in white –
it had to be white. So she dressed him in a little white suit and
put him in the box. You'd think he was sleeping. We all said a
little prayer. The priest came over and blessed him. I remember
my mother putting in a white piece of cloth over his face; then
they closed the box. They put Harry in a little wagon, drawn
by a horse. Only my father and uncle were allowed to go to the
cemetery. When they got there, two soldiers lowered Harry into
a hole.*[52]

CHAPTER TEN

A Winding Sheet and
a Wooden Box

A FTER MAKING A catastrophic impact on America's Eastern
Seaboard, the Spanish Lady returned to the Midwest,
attacking the military and civilians alike. Valiant efforts to
halt her progress floundered for lack of sufficient medical staff.
With so many doctors and nurses away in the army, 'all the
organizational machinery in the world could not make up for the
cold fact that there weren't enough nurses to care for all the men,
women, and children who would need them so desperately in the
coming weeks'.[1]

When influenza struck the Great Lakes Naval Training Station
at Illinois, thirty miles north of Chicago, on 11 September, 2,600
sailors went sick within the week. Josie Mabel Brown was among
the nurses summoned to Great Lakes to cope with the epidemic.

Josie, who had graduated from nursing school just a few
months after the United States entered the war, had already been
called up. At this period, newly graduated registered nurses were
obliged to serve in the military. 'I had to go,'[2] Josie recalled.
'There was no choice about it. When my paper came back, it
said, "You are in the Navy now. Do not leave Saint Louis; do not
change your address; do not change your telephone number."'[3]

Josie's actual call-up was dramatic:

One day, I was at the theater and suddenly the screen went blank. Then a message appeared across the screen: 'Would Josie M. Brown please report to the ticket office?' I went back and there was a Western Union boy with a telegram from the Bureau of Medicine and Surgery in Washington, DC. It said, 'You are called to duty. Do you have enough money to travel?' and 'When is the earliest date that you can travel?' And I wired back, 'I have money. I can pay my way.' About forty-five minutes later a reply came back. 'Proceed to Great Lakes, Illinois. Keep strict account of your expenses. Do not pay over $1.50 for your meals or over 50¢ for tips. You will be reimbursed.'[4]

Josie boarded an old Pullman train to Chicago. 'I went right through our town and saw the light in the window that mother put there. I got to Chicago in the morning. When someone opened a paper in front of me I saw "6,000 in the hospital have Spanish Influenza in Great Lakes, Illinois." I said, "Oh, that's where I'm going. What is Spanish Influenza?"'[5]

Josie soon found out. After arriving at Great Lakes Naval Training Station, she was given a meal of roast pork and apple sauce and then went on duty for the first time. Josie was appalled by the sight that met her eyes.

My supervisor took me to a ward that was supposedly caring for 42 patients. There was a man lying on the bed dying and one was lying on the floor. Another man was on a stretcher waiting for the fellow on the bed to die. We would wrap him in a winding sheet because he had stopped breathing. I don't know whether he

was dead or not, but we wrapped him in a winding sheet and left
nothing but the big toe on the left foot out with a shipping tag on
it to tell the man's rank, his nearest of kin, and hometown. And
the ambulance carried four litters. It would bring us four live
ones and take out four dead ones.[6]

The morgues were overflowing, packed almost to the ceiling with
bodies stacked one on top of another as the morticians worked
day and night. 'You could never turn around without seeing a big
red truck being loaded with caskets for the train station so the
bodies could be sent home.'[7]

Little attempt was made to treat the patients.

We didn't have time to treat them. We didn't take temperatures;
we didn't even have time to take blood pressure. We would give
them a little hot whiskey toddy; that's about all we had time to
do. They would have terrific nosebleeds with it. Sometimes the
blood would just shoot across the room. You had to get out of the
way or someone's nose would bleed all over you.[8]

Some were delirious and some had their lungs punctured.
Then their bodies would fill with air. You would feel somebody
and he would be bubbles. You would see them with bubbles all
through their arms.[9]

There was worse to come. 'When their lungs collapsed, air was
trapped beneath their skin. As we rolled the dead in winding
sheets, their bodies crackled – an awful crackling noise which
sounded like Rice Crispies [*sic*] when you pour milk over them.'[10]

Working sixteen-hour days, Josie was little more than an
intermediary between the ambulance and the morgue. Even

as she slept, Josie seemed to hear the trucks reversing into the morgue, collecting the dead. As to the numbers of the dead, Josie had no idea of the final total. 'They died by the thousands. There were 173,000 men at Great Lakes at the time, and 6,000 were in the hospitals at the height of the epidemic. I suppose no one knows how many died. They just lost track of them.'[11]

Back in Chicago, a young man nicknamed 'Diz' lied about his age and enlisted as an ambulance driver with the Red Cross. Ignoring his father's desperate pleas, young Diz took himself off to the Red Cross Ambulance Corps Training Facility on Chicago's South Side and was soon learning how to drive and repair cars and trucks. When Diz himself was struck down by influenza like so many healthy young men, his father's fears had been realized. Sent home and nursed by his mother, Diz survived, to become the world's most successful animator under his full name of Walt Disney.[12]

As thousands of theatres closed across the country, an up-and-coming vaudeville act named the Marx Brothers had worked up a show. Entitled *The Street Cinderella*, the production had a score by Gus Kahn and Egbert Van Alstyne, but Groucho Marx had little faith in the enterprise. Living up to his name, Groucho later commented that his brother Chico had 'hired six dancers out of a five-and-dime store, and gave them each ten dollars. They were overpaid.'[13] *The Street Cinderella* might have prospered but for Spanish flu. In a strange twist on the concept of flu prevention, 'vaudeville theaters were only allowed to be half full – members of the audience had to leave the seat on either side empty so that they would not breathe on one another. To further protect themselves many wore surgical masks, so that even when they laughed the sound was muffled.'[14] As a result,

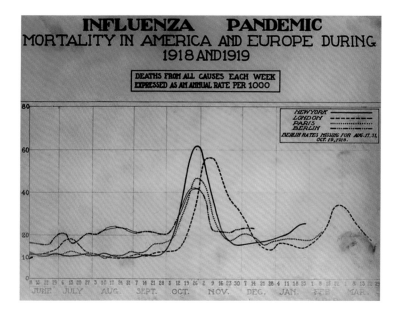

INFLUENZA PANDEMIC
MORTALITY IN AMERICA AND EUROPE DURING
1918 AND 1919

DEATHS FROM ALL CAUSES EACH WEEK
EXPRESSED AS AN ANNUAL RATE PER 1000

NEW YORK
LONDON
PARIS
BERLIN
BERLIN RATES MISSING FOR AUG. 17, 31,
OCT. 19, 1918.

ABOVE: 'Death Chart' showing the infamous first and second waves of Spanish flu in 1918 and 1919.

BELOW: Camp Funston, Fort Riley, suffered one of the first epidemics in April 1918.

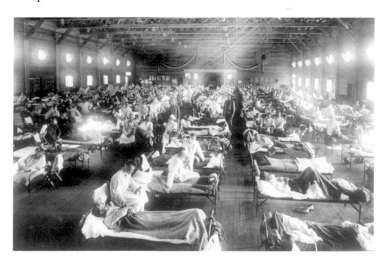

PLATE 3.—This illustrates another type of the cyanosis, in which the colour of the lips and ears arrests attention in contrast to the relative pallor of the face. The patient may yet live for twelve hours or more.

Influenza-Crazed He Slays His Family

By International News Service

CHICAGO, Oct. 22.—Crazed by influenza, Peter Marrazzo, a laborer here, last night blotted out his entire family of wife and four children, cutting their throats with a razor. The entire family had been suffering from the malady for a week.

After killing wife and children, Marrazzo attempted self-destruction by cutting his own throat. He is at the Bridewell hospital today in a serious condition. The children ranged in age from the baby, six months old, to a little girl of five years.

ABOVE: Medical textbook showing a patient suffering from the deadly symptoms of 'heliotrope' cyanosis.

LEFT: Extract from the *Los Angeles Evening Herald*, 22 October 1918. Family slayings became a tragic consequence of panic over Spanish flu.

ABOVE: The ill-fated transport ship the USS *Leviathan* in camouflage, September 1918.

BELOW: An AEF hospital in France. The first wave of Spanish flu hit the Allies in April 1918.

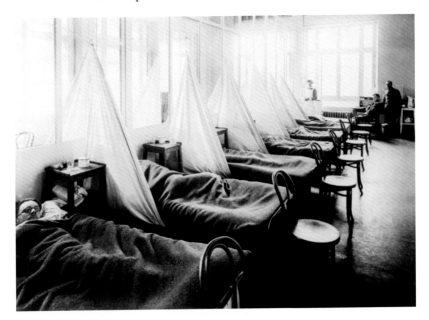

LEFT: An early victim: Mrs Rose Selfridge, wife of Selfridge's founder Gordon Selfridge.

RIGHT: Katherine Anne Porter, Spanish flu survivor and Pulitzer Prize winner.

LEFT: Flying ace William Leefe Robinson VC survived being shot down by the Red Baron but succumbed to Spanish flu.

BELOW: Norwegian artist Edvard Munch painted his 'Self Portrait with the Spanish Flu' in 1919.

ABOVE: 'Don't Spit!' poster at the Naval Aircraft Factory in Philadelphia, warning the public to avoid infection.

BELOW: Advertisement for 'Sanitas Fumigator' for the treatment of influenza.

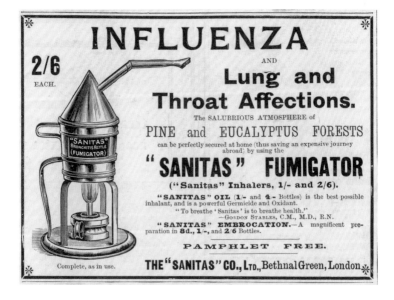

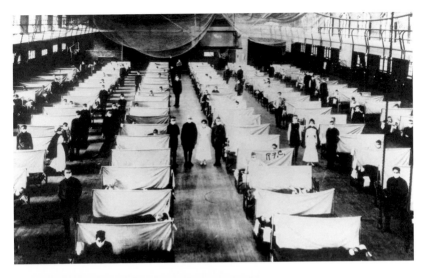

ABOVE: A school's gymnasium in America is converted into a flu ward due to overcrowding at the hospitals.

LEFT: Cartoonist William Heath-Robinson's response to the open-air treatment, as published in the *Bystander*, 16 April 1919.

ABOVE: Troops at Camp Dix gargling with salt water to prevent infection from Spanish flu, 24 September 1918.

BELOW: 'Suck a tablet whenever you enter a crowded germ-laden place' advised Formamint.

Why catch their Influenza?

YOU need not! Just carry Formamint with you and suck these delicious tablets whenever you are in danger of being infected by other people.

"Suck at least four or five a day"—so says Dr. Hopkirk in his standard work "Influenza"—for "in Formamint we possess the best means of preventing the infective processes which, if neglected, may lead to serious complications."

Seeing that such complications often lead to Pneumonia, Bronchitis, and other dangerous diseases, it is surely worth while to protect yourself by this safe, certain, and inexpensive means. Protect the children, too, for their delicate little organisms are very exposed to germ attack, especially during school-epidemics. Be careful, however, not to confuse Formamint with so-called formalin tablets, but see that it bears the name of the sole manufacturers: Genatosan, Limited (British Purchasers of Sanatogen Co.), 12, Chenies Street, London, W.C.1. (Chairman: The Viscountess Rhondda.)

"Attack the germs before they attack you!"

Though genuine Formamint is scarce your chemist can still obtain it for you at the pre-war price—2/3 per bottle. Order it to-day.

Formamint
THE GERM KILLING THROAT TABLET

The Street Cinderella 'could be chalked up as another victim of flu, succumbing in Michigan to bad reviews and empty houses'.[15]

As the epidemic intensified, the windy city witnessed similar tragic scenes to the ones that had blighted Boston, New York and Philadelphia. October the 17th 1918 swiftly became known as 'Black Thursday' when 381 people died and 1,200 fell sick. The city ran out of hearses, and trolley buses, draped in black, were used to collect the bodies. In an even more desperate bid to halt the spread of Spanish flu, funerals were banned. The civic authorities declared that:

> *There shall be no public funerals held in Chicago over any body dead from any disease or cause whatsoever. No wakes or public gatherings of any kind shall be held in connection with these bodies. No one except adult relatives and friends not to exceed ten persons in addition to the undertaker, undertaker's assistants, minister, and necessary drivers shall be permitted to attend any funeral. No dead body shall be taken into any church or chapel for funeral services in connection with such body.*[16]

While Chicago Health Commissioner Dr John Dill Robertson ordered the police to 'arrest thousands, if necessary, to stop sneezing in public!' there was one small grain of comfort: Reverend J. P. Brushingham of Chicago's Morals Commission noted that during October the crime rate in Chicago had dropped by 43 per cent. There was no protection against insanity, alas. Chicago resident Peter Marrazo, a recent immigrant, became convinced that his family was doomed and barricaded his wife and four children inside their apartment, shouting: 'I'll cure them in my own way!' Then he slashed their throats. It was subsequently revealed that none of them had actually been suffering from Spanish flu.[17]

Up in Alaska, Governor Thomas Riggs, Jr, learned of the pandemic raging in the 'Outside' and imposed strict quarantine regulations. Travel into the Alaskan interior was restricted, US marshals were posted at ports, trail heads and river mouths, and schools, churches, theatres and pool halls were shut down.[18] At Fairbanks, quarantine stations were guarded by marshals, and citizens underwent regular health checks, with those who passed their inspections issued with armbands. The frontier town of Shaktoolik, out in the wilderness, took a more traditional approach. Guards were paid at the rate of four deer a month, while anyone who violated quarantine was fined in firewood, which had to be delivered up to the community, 'sawed, split and piled'.[19]

Despite these precautions, Spanish flu broke through the sanity cordons, spreading along the coast of Alaska and into the interior. Half the white population of Nome succumbed to influenza, with Superintendent of Education Walter Shields becoming one of the first victims; the native population was practically annihilated.[20] Spanish flu cut a swathe through Nome's Iñupiat Eskimo population, killing 176 out of 300.[21] According to the Arctic explorer Vilhjalmur Stefansson, the Iñupiat had reacted to the news of Spanish flu by panicking and running from cabin to cabin, spreading disease. Entire families, too sick to keep their fires going, froze to death. When one group of native Alaskans were taken to hospital, they became convinced they had been condemned to a death-house and hanged themselves. Stefansson himself suffered bereavement during the epidemic, losing five of his guides, including the legendary musher, Split-the-Wind.[22]

In a desperate attempt to control the outbreak, Governor Riggs ordered the native Alaskans to stay inside their cabins and avoid public gatherings, a diktat which flew in the face of their traditional values. The Iñupiat people were convivial, generous and had a culture characterized by communal living. Isolation was to them a form of living death. They were also considered to be fatalistic, responding to the epidemic in a markedly different fashion from the white settlers. One schoolteacher wrote that:

They refused to help themselves but preferred to sit on the floor and wait to die. I did everything for them; furnished wood and water, split kindling, made shavings, built fires, cooked food and delivered it to them, and even acted as undertaker and hearse driver. Apparently the native had no regard but rather fear for their dead. Frequently I had to rescue corpses from the dogs which began to eat them.[23]

Across Alaska, village after village fell to influenza. Too sick to hunt, many native Alaskans resorted to killing and eating their sled dogs, while in Hamilton the dogs started eating the people.

Given the isolated nature of the remote Alaskan communities, the swift trajectory of Spanish flu seems inexplicable. At this point, before the Armistice, Alaska could not blame the epidemic on returning soldiers or big social gatherings. Tragically, the explanation lies with the one service that promised it would always get through: the postal service. And, like the US mail, the Spanish Lady always got through, even where others had failed.

North of the border, the first documented case of Spanish flu in the civilian population of Canada was reported at Victoriaville, on 8 September 1918.[24] Within a month, the disease controlled the entire country from coast to coast. By the end of 1918, 50,000 Canadians had died of Spanish flu.[25]

The Spanish Lady arrived in Winnipeg, capital of Manitoba, on 30 September 1918, travelling west on a troop train containing sick soldiers. Within four days of arrival, two of the soldiers had died, along with a local railway worker, Winnipeg's first civilian casualty. The civic authorities were hopeful that the influenza infection would soon pass, but by 12 October the *Manitoba Free Press* was telling its readers that 'All schools, churches, theatres [*sic*] dance halls, and other public places in Winnipeg and suburbs will be closed for an indefinite period at midnight tonight as a precautionary measure against the spreading epidemic of Spanish "flu," of which 12 new cases were reported in the city yesterday.'[26]

Despite these valiant efforts on the part of the city fathers, Spanish flu raged through Winnipeg and its suburbs and, by 31 October, 2,162 cases had been reported. Just as in the United States, medical interventions were thwarted by a shortage of doctors and trained nurses. Out on the prairies, small towns in Manitoba, Saskatchewan and Alberta attempted to quarantine themselves through isolation, but this did not stop the Spanish Lady's inexorable progress across Canada. The infection arrived in the remote Hudson's Bay Trading Company outpost of Norway House, Keewatin, on 4 December 1918, courtesy of a dog team carrying the mail packet from Crow Lake, which was already badly infected.[27] This region of Canada was notable for harsh conditions at the best of times. Locals eked out a hunter-gatherer existence, subsisting on food hunted and foraged from the bush, while basic supplements such as flour, tea and sugar were traded in return for furs from the Hudson's Bay Company stores. They had little laid by in the way of food, and when Spanish flu struck in the dead of winter, families starved. Harry Everett, who grew up in Berens River, Manitoba, recalled the Spanish flu vividly in his memoir:

My first recollection is being on a hammock like swing and seeing beds all around the room and one woman reaching down inside her blouse in front and bringing out her small purse and giving it to my Dad. This was during the Spanish Flue [sic] *Epidemic. My Dad was the only one that was not sick and was pretty well alone for a number of days making the rounds to different houses to see that they had enough wood inside to keep the fires going and to take any bodies that were in the house . . . They said if the sick that died had stayed in the house where it was warm* [sic]. *They went out too soon and got cold and had a relapse.*[28]

Desperate to find food for their families, many recovering victims got up too soon and developed secondary pneumonia. In an additional complication, their constitutions were already compromised by tuberculosis, which was rampant among the Canadian indigenous people at the time.

Reverend Henry Gordon described conditions when Spanish flu hit the Grenfell Mission in Cartwright, Labrador.

It has struck the place like a cyclone, two days after the Mail boat had left. After dinner I went on a tour of inspection among the houses, and was simply appalled at what I found. Whole houses lay inanimate all over their kitchen floors, unable to even feed themselves or look after the fire . . . I think there were just four persons in the place who were sound . . . A feeling of intense resentment at the callousness of the authorities, who sent us the

139

disease by the Mail-boat, and then left us to sink or swim, filled one's heart almost to the exclusion of all else. The helplessness of the poor people was what struck to the heart . . . It was very upsetting, people crying, children dying everywhere.[29]

The frozen ground of a northern winter made it impossible to bury the victims of Spanish flu, and locals devised ingenious solutions for keeping the bodies away from ravenous dogs. Some corpses were wrapped in sheets and placed on rooftops, creating a vista of ghostly shrouds until they could be buried in the spring.[30] At Norway House, bodies were stacked like firewood in a cabin until they could be buried. One eyewitness recalled:

There were so many people, you know, they can't bury them all . . . when they all gathered and they were buried in a box. They just threw the bodies in a box, I don't know how many in that box. And they had big cranes you know and they put those bodies together and there's a lot of people and children . . . they have an awful time, difficult time, to gather all the people and to bury them. Though some of these people were kept in the cabin until after, they didn't have much lumber to use for coffins, and they just buried them like that in a bag.[31]

Parish registers from the Christian mission at Norway House suggest that some 183 deaths per 1,000 population occurred during the 1918–19 epidemic, a sevenfold increase in deaths compared with the two decades on either side; approximately one-fifth of the adult population over the age of twenty perished in this epidemic.[32] Nathaniel Queskekapow, a Cree elder, not even born at the time, was well informed about the epidemic, his knowledge handed down from his predecessors. Interviewed by researchers around 2002, at the age of seventy-two, Nathaniel said: 'It was very strong on the south side and the people were just, somebody was walking over there and somebody dropped, just like a shot. Even the children, they, about 10-year old, [sic] they just fell down and died. Like that. They don't, you don't bother anybody, just fall right down.'[33]

Meanwhile, back in the United States, the Spanish Lady hurtled west, harvesting corpses as she went. Camp Funston, the site of an earlier outbreak back in February 1918, received a second onslaught of influenza in October, when the 29th Field Artillery was devastated by a further epidemic, leading to 14,000 cases and 861 deaths by the end of the month.[34]

By this time, First Lieutenant Elizabeth Harding was an experienced senior nurse who had already dealt with over '800 cases of mumps, measles, smallpox, diphtheria, and every conceivable contagious disease'.[35] When Harding left Fort Riley in October 1918, for duty in the Office of the Surgeon General, the second wave of influenza had just struck.

The day I left there were over 5,000 patients. Barracks were opened at Camp Funston to accommodate the sick. Several nurses died, I am not certain, but it seems to me at least sixteen. The nurses who had been on duty at Fort Riley stood up very well, but nurses who were rushed in for the emergency were hard hit, and arrived sick.[36]

Sergeant Charles L. Johnston, writing home to his wife from the camp infirmary, left a vivid picture of conditions at Camp Funston.

It's about 3 a.m. and all the poor old boys are resting very well. I am sure some nurse, believe me. I have been working nights for about three days now, from 7 to 7 and fight the flies the whole day long while trying to sleep. I thought I was getting along on very little sleep when I was home, but this has the world cheated . . . there are between 6 and 7,000 cases in the camp. I never did know that a sick fellow was so hard to wait on before. These birds almost chase you to death after water or pills or something else all the time.[37]

When he wasn't waiting on his patients hand and foot, Sergeant Johnston was occupied with replacing the covers as the men kicked them off during a high fever, and administering 'sponge baths to run down the temperature. Each of our men has about 20 patients, so you see we are pretty busy rookies.'[38]

Over in Lincoln, Illinois, ten-year-old William Maxwell had been enjoying an idyllic childhood. William, who would grow up to become a famous author and a fiction editor at the *New Yorker* magazine, later composed a haunting memoir of his childhood experiences of the Spanish flu epidemic. When America had entered the war, William's mother had volunteered for the war effort and he remembered her dressed in white, with her head wrapped in a tea towel with a red cross on it, rolling bandages. It was a way of helping, but at this point the war seemed a long way off. So did the epidemic of Spanish flu. 'We heard stories, lots of stories. We heard about what was happening in Boston, but people didn't want to believe they could be healthy in the morning and dead by nightfall.'[39]

When Mrs Maxwell fell pregnant, the family decided that she would give birth at the large city hospital in Bloomington, just over thirty miles away. William and his brother were duly packed off to stay with their aunt and uncle – strict, churchgoing people – in their big gloomy house. 'My aunt and uncle were narrow minded . . . my brother and I were very uncomfortable being in their house. I can best suggest the quality of the house by saying in the living room there was a large framed photograph of my grandfather in his coffin.'[40]

William fell sick that very day. A skinny little boy, normally with a massive appetite, he couldn't touch the big turkey dinner his aunt laid out in front of him. After touching his forehead, William's aunt took him upstairs and put him to bed in his uncle's office, a bleak room containing little more than a desk and a filing cabinet. At this point, time became a blur. William slept and slept, awoken at times to be given pills. 'I remember being awakened at intervals during the night and day. If it was night, my aunt would be in a nightgown with her hair in a braid down her back, holding a pill out to me and a glass of water. At other times, it was my uncle.'[41]

Delirious or not, William could still hear everything that was going on, as his room was at the top of the stairs and he could hear the telephone. William learned that his mother was still in hospital in Bloomington, and that the baby had been born. 'One day I overheard my aunt say the dreadful phrase, "She's doing as well as can be expected." I've never heard that used except in circumstances where the worst was about to happen.'[42]

On the third day after the baby was born, William's father rang.

I heard the telephone conversation from my room. I heard her say, 'Will, oh, no,' and then, 'If you want me to.' She came into my room and took me into my grandmother's room. I sat on my grandmother's lap. My aunt brought my brother into the room. She tried to tell us what had happened, but tears ran down her face, so she didn't need to tell me. I knew that the worst that could happen had happened. My mother was marvelous and when she died the shine went out of everything.[43]

CHAPTER ELEVEN

THE SPANISH LADY GOES TO WASHINGTON

WHEN LOUIS BROWNLOW, City Commissioner for Washington, DC, was informed that forty patients had been admitted to one hospital with '*la grippe*' on 2 October, he took instant action. Brownlow knew that 202 Bostonians had died of influenza the day before; he was anxious to prevent a similar epidemic in Washington. Commissioner Brownlow shut down Washington, DC, closing schools, theatres, pool halls and bars. Medical centres were opened in empty schools and an emergency hospital in a store on F Street, supervised by Dr James P. Leake, an epidemiologist.[1] With no shortage of resources in wealthy Washington, Model T Fords and chauffeur-driven limousines were pressed into service as ambulances. Brownlow, with his two fellow commissioners already sick, took responsibility for the city, as Dr Noble P. Barnes of the American Therapeutic Society publicly declared: 'Persons at large sneezing and coughing should be treated as a dangerous menace to the community, properly fined, imprisoned, and compelled to wear masks until they are educated out of the "Gesundheit!" and "God Bless You" rot.'[2] The Red Cross distributed gauze face masks, and advertisements warned the public:

Obey the laws
And wear the gauze
Protect your jaws
From septic paws.[3]

But the Spanish Lady was not so easily defeated. The sick-list swiftly rose to over ten thousand. Hundreds of police officers and trolley drivers fell ill. So many firemen were sick that the capital's Fire Marshall feared 'the whole city'd burn to the ground if a fire ever got started'.[4] The Federal government was paralysed and the courts went into recess. At Herbert Hoover's Food Administration, half the employees went off sick. Congress closed its public galleries and at the State Department staff were 'aired' for twenty minutes every day, taken outside and instructed to breathe deeply. As he studied Washington's mortality figures at the Vital Statistics Bureau, a clerk named W. E. Turton collapsed and died.[5] The *Washington Evening Star* ran a regular column entitled 'Prominent People Who Have Died of Influenza'.

One famous person who refused to die of influenza or even entertain the notion of falling victim to the disease was humourist James Thurber. Writing a letter in reply to a concerned friend on 15 October 1918, Thurber described the mood in Washington in his typically irreverent style: 'All one sees here is nurses & hearses and all he hears is curses and worse. And such a heroic thing to pass out with, Influenza!' Dying of influenza in these times of brave, poetical deaths . . . I'd just as soon go with house-maid's KNEE.'[6] Thurber maintained he was in 'chipper' condition, with the correct psychological attitude towards all flu. 'The influx of Enza will have to select a clever rapier and twist an adroit write [*sic*] to pink me, altho' I am in the pink of condition.'[7]

Eleanor Roosevelt, who had returned to Washington with Franklin and their family, witnessed the horror at first-hand:

As soon as we returned to Washington the 'flu epidemic, which had been raging in various parts of the country, struck us with full force. The city was fearfully overcrowded, the departments had had to expand and take on great numbers of clerical workers. New bureaus had been set up, girls were living two and three to a room all over the city, and when the 'flu hit there were naturally not enough hospitals to accommodate those who were stricken. The Red Cross organized temporary hospitals in every available building, and those of us who could were asked to bring food to these various units, which often had no kitchen space at all.

Before I knew it, all my five children and my husband were down with the 'flu, and three of the servants. We succeeded in getting one trained nurse from New York . . . this nurse was put in charge of Elliott [aged eight years old] *who had double pneumonia. My husband was moved into a little room next to mine, and John, the baby, had his crib in my bedroom, for he had bronchial pneumonia. There was little difference between day and night for me, and Dr Hardin, who worked as hard as he possibly could every minute of the time, came in once or twice a day and looked over all my patients. He remarked that we were lucky that some of us were still on our feet, for he had families with nobody able to stand up.*[8]

Despite the constant anxiety for her own family, Eleanor tried to take the opportunity to do some good in Washington: 'If all the children were asleep I went in the car and visited the Red Cross unit I had been assigned to supply and tried to say a word of cheer to the poor girls lying in the long rows of beds.'[9]

Six-year-old Bill Sardo, whose family ran a small funeral parlour, was surrounded by death. Caskets were stacked in the living room, the dining room and along the hallways. Bill himself was roped in to build caskets in the basement morgue. 'I was constantly afraid. I would walk through rows and rows of caskets, seeing names, people I knew. Entire families were dying. The dead were everywhere.'[10]

Commissioner Brownlow's draconian response to the epidemic saved lives. Working with Dr H. S. Mustard, a public health service epidemiologist and specialist in malaria control, Brownlow declared Washington a 'sanitary zone' and divided the city into four self-contained districts. A new law made it a crime to knowingly transmit influenza, and it was also a crime to go out in public when sick. Fines for doing so started at $50.

Despite this, Washington's hospitals were swamped. At George Washington University Hospital, every single nurse went down with influenza. At Garfield Hospital and the emergency hospital at Leake, staff were overwhelmed, with patients spilling out into the corridors. 'The only way we could find room for the sick was to have undertakers waiting at the back door, ready to remove bodies as fast as people died. The living came in one door and the dead went out the other.'[11]

At Camp Humphreys near Washington, 5,000 men were sick with influenza and the chief medical officer, Lieutenant Colonel Charles E. Doerr, had died. Despite this, Brownlow insisted that fifty soldiers were sent from Camp Humphreys to Washington to dig graves. This was in spite of the fact that there were no coffins to be had for love or money, with unscrupulous undertakers pushing up their prices. One Washington official commented: 'Charging high prices for coffins in this direful time is nothing short of ghoulish in spirit and unpatriotic to the point of treason.'[12] Brownlow proved himself not above theft. When he heard that two cartloads of coffins destined for Pittsburgh were in the Potomac freight yards, Brownlow hijacked the shipment, and had them redirected to the playground of Central High School, where they were placed under armed guard.

One afternoon, Commissioner Brownlow, nursing his wife who was sick with flu, answered the telephone to hear a woman sobbing and saying she shared a room with three other girls. Two were already dead and the third dying. She was the only one left. Brownlow called the police and asked them to go and visit the woman. A few hours later, a police sergeant rang back and told Brownlow: 'Four girls dead.'[13]

In another part of Washington, a volunteer nurse knocked on a door and heard a voice rasp: 'Come in.' She walked into the room where, to her horror, she found the only creature left alive: a pet parrot.[14]

Congress itself was not spared. US Congressman Jacob Meeker, forty, was taken to the Jewish Hospital on 14 October after being 'stricken' with influenza at a hotel. Meeker married his secretary in a small private ceremony, with bride, groom, judge and witnesses all wearing masks, and died just seven hours later.[15]

As Commissioner Louis Brownlow and Dr Mustard both fell victim to influenza, young Bill Sardo was drafted in to help at his father's funeral parlour. The house was stacked with coffins.

When grieving relatives came to see their loved one, my father would tell me, 'Go up to the second floor, and in the third row of the living room or the fourth row of the dining room you'll find a body. Take these people there.' So I would lead them through the house, past all the other bodies, to where their beloved was resting.[16]

Years later, Bill Sardo could not recall the events of October 1918 without a shudder.

From the moment I got up in the morning to when I went to bed at night, I felt a constant sense of fear. We wore gauze masks. We were afraid to kiss each other, to eat with each other, to have contact of any kind. We had no family life, no school life, no church life, no community life. Fear tore people apart.[17]

In North Carolina, news of the epidemic spread more slowly. Seven-year-old Dan Tonkel worked in the yard goods department of his father's clothing store. To Dan's surprise and shock, he found that suddenly the farmer's market and the local movie theatre had been shut and schools had closed. At first, Dan was excited when the schools closed, but then he was pressed into service by his father, who needed him to help run the business because all his employees were sick.

From then on I went to work with him. We had to shut down the whole second floor of the store – ladies ready-to-wear and our big millinery department – which was a momentous decision. Business was very, very sparse.

Then my father told me already three of his eight employees had died. He told me, 'Miss Leah will not be coming back.' I said,

'Why not?' He said, 'Because Leah died.' Miss Leah was the first of his employees to die.

I was old enough to understand what death was. I suddenly realized what was happening, that many of our good friends and people who loved us were going to die.[18]

The experience left Dan with little faith in the medical profession. It seemed that there was nothing doctors could do to help, or to prevent the relentless progress of the Spanish Lady with her trail of death. 'The medical world did not know how to handle the disease. Doctors didn't have any medicines or vaccines. And since doctors didn't have the cure-all in their little black satchel, there was very little they could do.'[19]

But the doctors did try. Civilian practitioners, mostly old or dragged out of retirement, struggled valiantly to save the lives of their patients. Over in Ashville, North Carolina, future novelist Thomas Wolfe witnessed the local doctor's attempts to save his brother's life as the community gathered round to try to save their son.

Thomas Wolfe's *Look Homeward, Angel* contains one of the most explicit descriptions of Spanish flu in modern literature, based on the experiences of Wolfe's brother, Benjamin Harrison Wolfe, who was just twenty-five. While Wolfe's language may strike the reader as a slice of Southern Gothic, overblown and grotesque, then so was Spanish flu.

Wolfe's protagonist, Eugene Gant, a thinly veiled version of the author himself, had escaped his stifling small-town life in North Carolina when a letter arrived from his mother telling him that Spanish flu had made inroads in his home town: 'Everyone has had it, and you never know who's going to be next,' she wrote. 'It seems to get the big strong ones first. Mr. Hanby, the Methodist minister, died last week. Pneumonia set in. He was a fine healthy man in the prime of life.'[20]

Eugene heard nothing more for several weeks but then, one rainy evening, he was summoned home with the news that his brother, Ben, was desperately ill with pneumonia of both lungs. Returning to the family home, a grim small-town lodging house, Eugene witnessed a horrific vision of Ben gasping for breath like an enormous insect on a naturalist's table, 'fighting, while they looked at him, to save with his poor wasted body the life that no one could save for him. It was monstrous, brutal.'[21]

After the family had spent the night on tenterhooks, nervously tiptoeing outside the sickroom door, Ben's condition seemed to improve. But he went downhill again in the afternoon, and attempts to administer oxygen were unsuccessful. When the nurse tried to place the cone over Ben's face, he 'fought it away tigerishly'.[22]

The Gant family prepared themselves for the end, all hoping that Ben would pass peacefully. But at the last moment Ben rallied, and in one final surge of life there was a glimpse of the old Ben, the character, the town rebel. 'Ben drew upon the air in a long and powerful respiration; his gray eyes opened, and . . . he passed instantly, scornful and unafraid, as he had lived, into the shades of death.'[23]

CHAPTER TWELVE

'YOU CAN'T DO ANYTHING FOR FLU'

A S THE SPANISH Lady continued her campaign of global terror, food and pharmaceutical manufacturers seized on the commercial potential of the epidemic. Respectable proprietary brands such as Oxo and Milton, Jeyes' Fluid and Black & White Whisky, bought advertising space alongside quacks and snake oil salesmen, all keen to persuade a desperate public to purchase their wares. Alongside over-the-counter products, frightened families also turned to folk remedies, traditional and reassuring cures familiar to their heritage, whether this be onions, asafoetida (a foetid-smelling herb historically used for chest complaints) or opium. As the mortality rates soared, so too did the willingness to try something, anything, to save themselves and their loved ones from a horrible death. And while attempts to develop a vaccine against Spanish flu floundered, doctors pioneered other methods to care for its victims, from the 'rooftop cure' where patients were exposed to the elements, to an experiment with potassium permanganate on British public schoolboys.

From the apparently innocuous first wave during the early spring of 1918, to the escalating second wave of Spanish flu that gripped the world in the later months of the year, daily newspapers carried an increasing number of advertisements for influenza-related remedies as drug companies played on the anxieties of readers and reaped the benefits. From *The Times* of London to the *Washington Post*, page after page was filled with dozens of advertisements for preventive measures and over-the-counter remedies. 'Influenza!' proclaimed an advert extolling the virtues of Formamint lozenges. 'Suck a tablet whenever you enter a crowded germ-laden place.'

Another advertisement announced that 'as Spanish Influenza is an exaggerated form of Grip', readers should take Laxative Bromo Quinine in larger doses than usual, as a preventive measure. For those who had already succumbed, Hill's Cascara Quinine Bromide promised relief, as did Dr Jones's Liniment, previously and mysteriously known as 'Beaver Oil' and intended to provide relief from coughing and catarrh. Demand for Vick's VapoRub, still popular today, was drummed up by press adverts warning of imminent shortages:

DRUGGISTS!! PLEASE NOTE VICK'S VAPORUB OVERSOLD DUE TO PRESENT EPIDEMIC.

Ely's Crème Balm, which 'may prevent Spanish influenza when applied in the nostrils', appears to have been a copycat product, while more traditional remedies were available in the form of Lydia E. Pinkham's famous Herb Medicine and Hale's Honey of Horehound and Tar.

With the threat of the Spanish Lady looming large, familiar household products became suddenly endowed with magical powers. While readers of the *Nottingham Journal* were wisely informed that 'OXO appreciably compensates for the shortage of meat',[1] another, more elaborate advert declared that Oxo 'fortifies the System against Influenza Infection'. According to a testimonial obtained 'from a Doctor',

A cupful of OXO two or three times a day will prove an immense service as a protective measure. Its invigorating and nourishing properties are most rapidly absorbed into the blood, and thus the system is reinforced to resist the attacks of the malady. It will be apparent that a strong healthy person will escape contagion when the ill-nourished one will fall a victim, consequently, one's aim must be the maintenance of strength.

The benefit to the community of a concentrated Fluid Beef like OXO is greater than ever in the present day; it increases nutrition and maintains vitality in the system, and thus an effective resistance is established against the attacks of the influenza organism.[2]

If Oxo did not appeal, Horlick's Malted Milk was recommended as THE diet 'During and After Influenza'.[3]

Americans were informed that it was their patriotic duty to 'Eat More Onions!' as part of a 'Patriotic Drive Against the "Flu."' One placard proclaimed:

An onion car arrived today
Labelled red, white and blue
Eat onions, plenty, every day
And keep away the 'Flu.'[4]

An American mother took this suggestion to extremes, and fed her sick daughter syrup made from onions before wrapping her in onions from head to toe. Fortunately, the outcome was successful and the child survived.[5]

While the actual nature of the Spanish flu organism still awaited discovery, doctors and laymen alike knew that treatment should focus on the avoidance of germs and microbes. As a result, contemporary newspaper adverts revealed a compulsive obsession with personal and domestic hygiene. As Spanish flu made inroads into the British midlands, the *Nottingham Journal* carried an advertisement for Gossages' Purified Carbolic Soap, 9d per pound, recommended on 'Doctors' Orders' to clean floors, wash-tub, bath and toilet. 'It disinfects as it cleanses. Use it for all purposes.' Readers were also reminded that 'no house is safe without Milton' (the sterilizing solution).[6] At Repton, a boys' boarding school in Derbyshire, the school doctor experimented by administering tobacco snuff to the boys and spraying their throats with a solution of potassium permanganate, an inorganic chemical compound used as an antiseptic, with apparently successful results: the rate of infection was low.[7]

Conventional medical advice for the treatment of influenza included morphine, atropine, aspirin, strychnine, belladonna, chloroform, quinine and, disturbingly, kerosene, which was administered on a sugar lump. Alongside these, folk remedies thrived. If a product from the drugstore failed to alleviate the symptoms, many patients and their families turned to more traditional methods. One popular remedy in South Africa was to place a block of camphor in a bag and tie it around the patient's neck. One eight-year-old girl, who was taking no chances, announced that she was wearing a camphor bag around her neck 'to keep off the Germans'.[8] The practice was so widespread that, over half a century later, an elderly South African lady in a nursing home, who had survived the 1918 outbreak, refused inoculation against the 1969 epidemic of Hong Kong flu. 'Not for me,' she maintained. 'I still have my camphor bag.'[9]

In North Carolina, young Dan Tonkel had taken to wearing a bag of asafoetida around his neck, in the belief that the stinking extract would protect him. 'It smelled to high heaven,' he recalled.[10] 'People thought the smell would kill germs. So we all wore a bag of asafetida and smelled like rotten flesh.'[11] In Philadelphia, Harriet Ferrel was rubbed with tree bark and sulphur, and forced to drink herbal teas and take drops of turpentine and kerosene on a lump of sugar. Harriet was also subjected to the asafoetida treatment but was philosophical: 'We smelled awful, but it was okay, because everyone smelled bad.'[12] Robert Grave's 'Welsh gypsy' housemaid had an even more unusual form of protection, consisting of 'the leg of a lizard tied in a bag around her neck'.[13] It was clearly successful as she was the only person in the Graves household who did not develop Spanish flu. In South Africa, a traditional cure for the '*longpest*' consisted of placing a recently killed animal on the patient's chest.[14]

The success of traditional remedies owed much to the placebo effect, although it was not always possible to follow up the results. In Meadow, Utah, William Reay was appointed Health Officer and spent his time riding from house to house and farm to farm checking up on families to see who was sick and needed help. One morning, accompanied by the city Marshal, George Bushnell, Reay rode out to check up on a group of Pahvant Indians, members of the Ute tribe, camped six miles out of town at the edge of a canyon.[15] Influenza had hit the camp and Reay and Bushnell were horrified to discover that the Indians were observing their traditional custom of sitting around the dead bodies and singing them to the Happy Hunting Grounds.[16] Reay and Bushnell moved the bodies to separate tents, which they sewed up until the bodies could be buried. Then they turned their attention to the living.

'The Indians were moaning, "Medicine, medicine, medicine." The Medicine Man was sick. Reay and Bushnell asked the Chief (who was so sick he could hardly talk) if they could bring up some medicine from Meadow.'[17]

Meadow's only doctor was also sick with influenza, so Reay went to visit the local 'wise woman', Aunt Martha Adams, who gave him some herbs, including horehound, a herb used to create expectorant and a traditional remedy for fever. Reay took these home and stewed them up in the five-gallon wash boiler, adding other items, including bacon – as it was believed that wrapping a rasher of bacon around the neck would cure a sore throat – and anything else he thought might help. 'And we cooked it up and it smelled like medicine and it tasted like medicine and put in a lot of honey so it would taste good,' remembered Reay's son, Lee. 'Then we bottled it and put a label on it, "The Influenza Medicine." It wasn't real medicine, of course, but it made people feel better, because they thought it was medicine.'[18]

The medicine was taken up to the camp, and young Lee watched from a safe distance as the Indians drank it and the men dug graves. Lee and his father never knew whether or not the medicine had made a difference. As soon as they were well enough to travel, the Pahvant Indians took down their tents and went away. 'They were afraid, and they just left,' said Lee. 'I don't know where they went.'[19]

In the Deep South, other traditional remedies were popular. In Louisiana, the superintendent of a Methodist hospital recommended a quilt made of wormwood, sandwiched between layers of flannel and dipped in hot vinegar and placed on the patient's chest,[20] while some residents of New Orleans turned to voodoo and bought charms against Spanish flu. These consisted of 'anything from a white chicken's feather to an ace of diamonds for the left shoe'.[21] Other voodoo remedies included performing a spell three times a day while rubbing vinegar over the face and palms: 'Sour, sour, vinegar – Keep the sickness off'n me.'[22]

Whiskey had always been a traditional remedy for colds and influenza, and whiskey prices soared in the United States during the epidemic. In Denmark and Canada, alcohol was only available by prescription, while in Poland brandy was regarded as highly medicinal. One brave soul in Nova Scotia recommended fourteen straight gins in quick succession as a cure for Spanish flu.[23] The result of this experiment was unknown; if the patient had survived he had doubtless forgotten the proceedings entirely.

In Britain, the Royal College of Physicians stated that 'Alcohol Invites Disaster', a conclusion which was ignored by many.[24] The barman at London's Savoy Hotel created a new cocktail, based on whisky and rum, and christened it 'the Corpse Reviver!'[25] while John Frewer, a soldier from Wisbech, Cambridgeshire, credited his recovery to whiskey:

As a last resource [the doctor] *asked my mother whether I drank whisky as, if I was not accustomed to it, it might have a shock effect on my body and cause the turning point. That night I had a half tumbler of whisky and in a very few minutes was bleeding black blood from my mouth and nostrils. From that time I made slow but steady progress.*[26]

In the universal panic of the Spanish flu epidemic, many believed that the air itself was poisonous. One woman in Citerno, Italy, sealed up her house so effectively that she died of suffocation.[27] Lee Reay of Meadow, Utah, recalled one family who sealed their house up. They plugged keyholes, sealed the windows and even closed the dapper on the stove.[28]

Roy Brinkley's father, a sharecropper in Max Meadows, Virginia, decided that fresh air could be fatal during the epidemic and sealed up his wife and four children in one room. The family spent seven days sitting around the wood-burning stove until it caught fire. As his family fled the house and took refuge in the vegetable patch, Brinkley was convinced that the fresh air would kill them. For the rest of his life, Roy remembered a sudden rush of fresh air and the sight of cabbages, as big as wash tubs. But, once outside, the entire family soon recovered.[29]

Many doctors believed that far from being deadly, fresh air was vital to a patient's recovery, blowing away the foetid contagion of the sick room. When a doctor in Halifax, Yorkshire, smashed a window with a rolling pin, he reported that his gasping patients immediately began to recover. In Alberta, Canada, one doctor treated his patients in tents and they all recovered. At the Ospedale Maggiore in Milan, patients treated in the courtyard for lack of space recovered more quickly than their peers.[30] In London, Dr Leonard Hill of the London Hospital recommended that everyone should sleep in the open air, convinced that cool air increased circulation and helped rid the body of toxins.[31]

A controversial approach at the Roosevelt Hospital in New York saw children placed on the roof to get the benefit of fresh air. Protected from the wind by screens, they were put to bed with hot water bottles.[32] While the general public regarded this treatment as outrageous, six hospitals in Massachusetts followed the Roosevelt's example. At the beginning of October 1918, Dr Louis Croke of Boston set up a therapeutic community on Corey Hill. The patients were nursed in tents, warmed with hot bricks wrapped in newspaper, and the nursing staff improvised masks by stuffing sieves with newspaper. The results appeared to be successful: only 35 patients out of 351 died, compared with the hospitals in Boston, where half the influenza patients perished.[33]

In London, Dr William Byam, who had been researching trench fever, was called back to England to treat influenza patients at a hospital in Hampstead. The wards were filling up with patients, while the mortuary was stacked to the ceiling with bodies, as there was no wood available to make coffins. Many victims had died of pneumonia, exhibiting the characteristic blue-purple colour of cyanosis. When yet another patient arrived and developed 'the dreaded form of pneumonia' and cyanosis he too was not expected to live. According to Byam, the staff had 'not seen a case of "blue" pneumonia recover.'[34] In addition, the patient was a heavy drinker. Byam persuaded the man's estranged wife to visit, although she did so reluctantly, having avoided him for twenty years and having no intention of 'letting him get hold of her again'.[35] Byam had to convince the patient's wife that her husband was as good as dead before she would condescend to visit the hospital.

When the patient's wife arrived, she found her estranged husband had turned a deep purple and had breathing difficulties and a weak pulse. In order to supply the patient with oxygen, Byam inserted two hollow needles into the skin of his chest and connected them to a large oxygen cylinder. That night, the nurse on duty fell asleep, probably exhausted by the demands of her patients, while the lingering effects of dental anaesthetic may also have been to blame. Whatever the cause, the nurse must have slumped forward onto the valve regulating oxygen flow, because when she came to, the oxygen cylinder was completely empty. As for the patient, he

> Closely resembled a fully-inflated balloon. His skin was tensely distended with oxygen; even his eyelids were inflated and so swollen that it was impossible to open them even with the finger. Pressure applied to any portion of the body produced a sensation of crackling such as might have been felt had the finger been pressing on a lemon sponge pudding. There was no concealing what had happened and in lachrymose mood nurse [sic] made her report to the Sister in charge of the floor.[36]

The condition the needles had produced was 'surgical emphysema' caused by air, or in this particular case, oxygen, in the subcutaneous tissues. Remarkably, the patient survived and was discharged soon afterwards. Byam concluded that the delivery of oxygen under pressure had released it into the patient's bloodstream. The only person left unsatisfied by the entire episode was the patient's estranged wife, who was not impressed by the fact that her estranged husband was still alive and accused Byam of lying to her.

CHAPTER THIRTEEN

'NATIVE DAUGHTER DIES'

⎯⎯◆⎯⎯

S AN FRANCISCO IN 1918 was a small city of some 550,000 souls, many of whom were members of the recent immigrant population, particularly Italians and Chinese. When the Spanish Lady appeared menacingly on the skyline on 21 September, Dr William Hassler, chief of San Francisco's Board of Health, responded by imposing quarantine restrictions at the Yerba Buena Island Naval Training Station and other Bay Area naval installations.

Hassler was a familiar and well-respected public figure. Following the 1906 earthquake, he had set up a births and deaths registry on the porch of his own house. Along with Surgeon General Rupert Blue he had steered San Francisco through several epidemics of bubonic plague in Chinatown. But on this occasion, Hassler wavered. Instead of imposing sanitary precautions on the city, Hassler expressed doubt that Spanish flu would actually reach San Francisco, citing the city's 'ideal climate' as protection against the disease.[1] Any discussion of further quarantines or closing the schools and theatres was postponed. Instead, on 28 September, the Fourth Liberty Loan Drive saw 10,000 people parade down Market Street displaying an effigy of Kaiser Wilhelm in an open coffin. There was community singing for 25,000 people and silent screen star Mary Pickford addressed thousands at a rally at the Bethlehem Shipbuilding Corporation.[2] On 6 October, 150,000 people attended a rally at Golden Gate Park, and a few days later French tenor Lucien Muratore stood on the steps of the *San Francisco Chronicle* and sang 'The Star-Spangled Banner' and 'La Marseillaise' to a crowd of 50,000 people. The national anthem was disrupted by the wail of an ambulance and the crowds parted to let it through. This was an ominous sign. A week later, San Francisco was engulfed by an epidemic of Spanish flu.[3]

When the epidemic became obvious, Hassler efficiently mobilized civic resources. Citizens were told to wear masks and the city was divided into districts, each with their own resources. Nevertheless, Hassler was appalled by some of the sights he witnessed. In Chinatown, he saw influenza victims languishing on the streets, suspicious of western medicine and refusing official help. Hassler felt he could do little more than advise the wealthier San Franciscans to keep their Asian servants at home, away from the infection in Chinatown.

Soon, San Francisco was at full stretch. Dental students took on the role of doctors; schoolteachers turned into laundresses; police trucks served as ambulances and policemen collected bodies. With the entire staff of the coroner's office off with influenza, a fireman was running the morgue. San Franciscans lobbied Mayor Rolph to pump water from the Pacific into the streets, to keep them continuously washed down. The mayor's response was that 'You might as well sit out and watch the changes of the moon.'[4]

Hassler was particularly adamant about the value of masks, declaring that 'every person appearing on the public streets [or] in any public place . . . shall wear a mask or covering except when partaking of meals'.[5] Mayor Rolph echoed Hassler with this stern warning: 'Whomever leaves his mask behind, dies.'[6] The San Francisco Chronicle soon got behind the campaign, advising that 'The man who wears no mask will likely become isolated, suspected, and regarded as a slacker. Like a man of means without a Liberty Loan button, he'll be shy of friends.'[7]

By October 1918, masks had become an enduring symbol of the Spanish influenza epidemic, adding a surreal quality to the photographs of the period. Images of masked people going about their daily business, from police officers directing traffic to typists absorbed in office work, from children playing to pet animals, resemble stills from an old science fiction movie.

First worn by doctors and nurses, masks were made of surgical gauze fastened behind the head with tapes. They were of little practical value as the virus itself passed easily through the thin fabric. While a layer of fabric might have absorbed the water droplets in which the virus was carried, it would have to be a great deal thicker, and more cumbersome; and such masks would only have succeeded if worn at all times, indoors and out, with goggles to protect the eyes.

Eye-catching but totally ineffective, the masks proved universally popular, despite their ineffectiveness. Dr H. S. Mustard of Washington, DC expressed his scepticism when he referred to masks as 'an absurdity, a menace when worn by the civilian population, military or naval class'.[8]

While the Red Cross gave out thousands of masks for free, manufacturers were quick to foist masks on the gullible public. Woods Hutchinson, a New York-based physician who travelled the country in the autumn of 1918 espousing the virtues of the face mask as a means of preventing the spread of influenza, told newspaper readers in late October, as a way of enticing fashion-conscious women to don masks, that masks had been effective in the East, and that 'chiffon veils for women and children have been as satisfactory as the common gauze masks'.[9] As supplies of gauze masks ran low, the chairman of the San Francisco chapter of the American Red Cross suggested that women craft flu masks from linen.

The *San Francisco Chronicle* described some city residents as wearing masks ranging from standard surgical gauze to creations resembling nosebags, from the Turkish-inspired muslin yashmak veil to flimsy chiffon coverings draped lazily across the mouth and nose.[10] Some wore 'fearsome looking machines like extended muzzles' on their faces as they walked the streets and shopped in downtown stores.[11]

Dr William Hassler himself resorted to an elaborate mask, comically described by the *San Francisco Chronicle*: 'The snout extends partially, like the helmets affected by the French knights at the period of Agincourt, but it is not so protrusive as the metal muzzles. Furthermore, it is sheathed outside in gauze like the common or garden mask more usually adopted by the public.'[12] The three most popular styles were the 'Agincourt', like Hassler's; the square 'Ravioli', favoured by policemen; and the veil, which was particularly popular with young women.[13]

The majority of San Franciscans were content to wear masks, particularly as it showed one was 'doing one's bit', an important consideration during wartime. While the vast majority of San Franciscans followed the mask order, police arrested 110 people on 27 October alone for failure to either wear or keep their masks properly adjusted. They were each charged with 'disturbing the peace', and the majority given a $5 fine, with the money to go to the Red Cross. Arrests continued in the following days, with the majority receiving small fines and a few being sentenced to a few days in jail. Enforcement soon became an issue. As the city chief of police later told reporters, if too many residents were arrested and jailed for the offence, he would soon run out of space in his cells. As the number of arrests mounted, the city jail did indeed become crowded, and judges worked long into the evenings and on Sundays to clear the backlog of cases.[14]

For some, wearing a mask was simply a nuisance, and if they believed they could get away without donning one in public they tried. Others may simply have been among those unfortunate enough to be caught during a momentary lapse or when they thought no one would notice. This was especially the case for commuters who passed through San Francisco, many of whom were caught with their masks dangling from their chins while they enjoyed a morning pipe on the ferry. To ensure that there could be no excuses, the Red Cross set up a stand at the ferry terminal to sell masks to those who did not have them for their commute.[15]

While most residents caught without a mask were simply forgetful or minor transgressors, some harboured deep resentment over being forced to wear a mask in public. One woman, a downtown attorney, argued that the mask ordinance was 'absolutely unconstitutional' because it was not legally enacted, and that as a result every police officer who had arrested an unmasked citizen was personally liable.

An extreme example of the consequences of refusing to wear a mask was captured in the *San Francisco Chronicle* on 28 October 1918:

REFUSES TO DON INFLUENZA MASK;
SHOT BY OFFICER

While scores of passers-by scurried for cover, H. D. Miller, a deputy health officer, shot and severely wounded James Wisser, a horseshoer, in front of a downtown drug-store early today, following Wisser's refusal to don an influenza mask.

According to the police, Miller shot in the air when Wisser first refused his request. Wisser closed in on him and in the succeeding affray was shot in the arm and the leg. Wisser was taken to the central emergency hospital, where he was placed under arrest for failure to comply with Miller's order.[16]

The anonymity conferred by masks was a godsend to criminals. One night Mr W. S. Tickner, a taxi driver, picked up three masked men who proceeded to rob him at gunpoint, dump him by the side of the road and drive, their identities concealed by their masks.[17]

HAVING INFLICTED EPIDEMIC sickness upon San Francisco, the Spanish Lady headed down the coast, drawn by the bright lights of Hollywood. Among her victims was a beautiful young film actress, Myrtle Gonzalez, veteran of seventy-eight silent movies, who had starred in *The Girl of Lost Lake* to great acclaim. Myrtle had retired from acting after her marriage to a young army officer, Allen Watt, a former assistant director at Universal, and tried to live with him at his base in Washington. However, despite the fact that she was regularly cast as the outdoor type, Myrtle proved too fragile for life in a military camp and had retreated to her parental home in Los Angeles before the epidemic broke out. On 22 October 1918, Myrtle succumbed to Spanish flu at her parents' home, aged just twenty-seven.[18]

Another film star, Lillian Gish, was more fortunate. Lillian developed Spanish flu on the way home from a costume fitting in the closing days of October 1918. Lillian had been trying on costumes for D. W. Griffith's melodrama *Broken Blossoms*, in which the twenty-four-year-old actress had been cast as the physically abused twelve-year-old daughter of a boxer. Although she was wealthy enough to afford two doctors and two nurses, Lillian's condition still gave sufficient cause for concern for her mother to telegraph home:

THINK SHE WILL RECOVER RAPIDLY AS WE TOOK CARE OF IT IN TIME HER FEVER HAS GONE DOWN FROM HUNDRED FOUR TO HUNDRED TWO IF SHE GETS WORSE WILL LET YOU KNOW.[19]

According to Lillian herself, who recovered just as the bells were ringing out to celebrate the Armistice, the only drawback of the flu was the legacy of unattractive nightwear. 'The only disagreeable factor was that it left me with flannel nightgowns,' she told fans. 'Have to wear them all winter – horrible.'[20]

Lillian's brush with death had at least conferred one advantage. Being twenty-four years old and tall, Lillian had queried Griffith's wisdom in casting her as a twelve-year-old child. Griffith duly raised the character's age to fifteen, but by the time filming rolled around, Lillian had lost so much weight from influenza that she looked appropriately waif-like.

Meanwhile, further up the Pacific coast in Seattle, the McCarthys were planning to head back east with their four small children. Mary, their seven-year-old daughter, would later become a famous author and described the devastating consequences of this journey in her memoir, *Memories of a Catholic Girlhood*. The subsequent tragic sequence of events began at the end of October 1918, a timetable of grief recorded in the *Seattle Post-Intelligencer*: 'Mr. and Mrs. McCarthy, with their four young children, left Seattle on October 30 for Minneapolis, where they were to make their future home.'[21]

The party that departed from Seattle on the evening of 30 October 1918, aboard the Northern Pacific's *North Coast Limited*, consisted of Tessa and Roy McCarthy, their children Mary, six, Kevin, four, Preston, three and Sheridan, one. Also travelling with them were Roy McCarthy's brother and sister-in-law, budding millionaire Harry McCarthy and his lovely young wife, Zula. Harry and Zula had travelled from Minneapolis to Seattle to help with the move. Tess and Roy's house at 934 22nd Avenue (now 22nd Avenue E) had been sold, and the family spent their last days in Seattle with Harry and Zula at the New Washington Hotel, the grandest hotel in the city.

Roy McCarthy, charming but feckless, was keen to make the trip home to Minneapolis to see one of his brothers, Louis McCarthy, who was due home on leave from the aviation service. Roy's family were also keen to get him home, as a means of controlling his improvident nature and constant appeals for financial help. Conditions could not have been worse: not only was Spanish flu raging across the United States but Roy was an invalid, and the prospect of a long train journey with four small children was scarcely ideal. Mary McCarthy later recalled that the atmosphere in their hotel suite had been decidedly sombre the night before departure, with Aunt Zula and the baby already sick.

Despite their reservations, the McCarthy family boarded the train on Wednesday, 30 October 1918. With the other members of their party lying sick in their sleeping compartments, Mary and her father gazed out at the awesome landscape of the Rocky Mountains. As Roy McCarthy regaled his daughter with tales of rocks hurtling down and crushing passing trains, Mary's teeth began to chatter. At first, she thought it was from fear; but she was in fact developing the symptoms of Spanish flu. As members of their party fell sick, the conductor threatened to put the McCarthys off the train at a tiny station in the middle of a North Dakota prairie. Roy McCarthy responded by pulling a gun on him.

At Minneapolis, the family were met by stretchers, a wheelchair, distraught officials and Mary's grandparents, and had to be carried off the train one by one. A week later, this headline appeared in the *Seattle Post-Intelligencer*:

NATIVE DAUGHTER DIES

Mrs. McCarthy died on last Wednesday and her husband on the following day. The children are recovering. Mr. and Mrs. Preston, informed of the serious condition of their daughter, left Seattle for Minneapolis last Wednesday, but Mrs. McCarthy died before they arrived.[22]

Tessa McCarthy was just twenty-nine years old; Roy was thirty-nine.

Their children, meantime, were taken in by their grandmother and nursed 'during those fatal weeks of the influenza epidemic, when no hospital beds were to be had and people went about with masks or stayed shut up in their houses, and the awful fear of contagion paralyzed all services and made each man an enemy to his neighbor'.[23]

Several weeks later, they 'awoke to reality in the sewing-room ... to an atmosphere of castor oil, rectal thermometers, cross nurses and efficiency'.[24] Told that their parents had been taken to hospital, it was further weeks still before the children learned that their mother and father were dead. Indeed, this development came to be regarded by Mary's grandmother as something of a social gaffe: 'Our father had put us beyond the pale by dying suddenly of influenza and taking our young mother with him, a defection that was remarked on with horror and grief commingled, as though our mother had been a pretty secretary with whom he had wantonly absconded into the irresponsible paradise of the hereafter.'[25]

In Denver, Colorado, Katherine Anne Porter was a reporter on the *Rocky Mountain News*, a big regional daily with a large circulation. At twenty-eight years old and newly divorced, Katherine struggled to survive on $20 a week, living on coffee and doughnuts so she could save her money for clothes.[26] Katherine was also a heavy smoker, a habit which enabled her to fit into the dresses she loved, but ruined her health.[27] When Spanish flu hit Denver in the first week of October 1918, Katherine was living in a rooming house at 1510 York Street. Katherine's landlady threatened to throw her out when she came down with influenza, but with the hospitals overflowing, there was nowhere to go. Katherine was fortunate enough to find a bed when her friends appealed to her physician, head of the local emergency committee.[28]

Even then, it seemed as if help would come too late. Katherine had been running a fever of 105° for nine days when she was admitted to the county hospital. Gay Porter Holloway, Katherine's sister, rushed up to Denver and telephoned their other sister, Kitty, every day. Both girls expected Katherine to die at any moment, and her family planned her funeral while colleagues at the *Rocky Mountain News* typeset her obituary.[29] Meanwhile, the delirious Katherine hovered between life and death, swinging in and out of consciousness and suffering from terrifying hallucinations.

One Sunday afternoon, with the doctors convinced nothing more could be done, Katherine was left behind the screens to die.[30] As Gay telephoned their sister Kitty to say that she was having a special Mass said for Katherine, a group of young interns examined Katherine and decided to give her an experimental shot of strychnine, as a last resort. Miraculously, Katherine's temperature dropped and an overjoyed Gay rang Kitty to say that Katherine was going to live.

Recovery was far from a simple process. Writing about the experience later in *Pale Horse, Pale Rider*, Katherine recalled 'a terrible compelling pain running through her veins like heavy fire, the stench of corruption filled her nostrils, the sweetish sickening smell of rotting flesh and pus'; 'she opened her eyes and saw pale light through a coarse white cloth over her face, knew that the smell of death was in her own body and struggled to lift her head'.[31]

Katherine's convalescence lasted for months. Her hair turned white, then fell out (she tied bandanas around her head until her hair grew back); the first time she tried to sit up she fell out of bed and broke her arm; she had phlebitis (an inflamed vein close to the surface of the skin caused by a blood clot) in one leg and was told she would never walk again. But Katherine was determined, and after six months she took her first steps since her illness.

The experience of surviving Spanish flu had a profound effect on Katherine. For the rest of her life, she would view her ordeal as an epiphany, a reminder she needed that she should pursue her destiny and had been spared for some special purpose:

> *It just simply divided my life, cut across it like that. So that everything before that was just getting ready, and after that I was in some strange way altered ... It was, I think, the fact that I really had participated in death, that I knew what death was, and had almost experienced it. I had what the Christians call the 'beatific vision,' and the Greeks called the 'happy day,' the happy vision just before death. Now if you have had that, and survived it, come back from it, you are no longer like other people, and there's no deceiving yourself that you are. But you see, I did: I made the mistake of thinking that I was quite like anyone else, of trying to live like other people. It took me a long time to realize that that simply wasn't true, that I had my own needs and that I had to live like me.*[32]

Katherine's recognition that she had no choice but to be her own woman and live life on her own terms led to great success. A Pulitizer Prize winner, Katherine later recorded her own experiences of Spanish flu in the short story 'Pale Horse, Pale Rider'.

CHAPTER FOURTEEN

THE FATAL VOYAGE

ON 29 SEPTEMBER 1918, the USS *Leviathan* transport ship was preparing to leave Hoboken, New Jersey, to sail to Brest, France. The vessel, along with other ships, was due to ferry around 100,000 troops across the Atlantic to France during October. On her ninth voyage to France, the *Leviathan* would carry troops from ten different army organizations, including nurses and combat replacements.

The USS *Leviathan*, operating as an American troopship in 1918, began life in Hamburg in 1914, where she was launched as the *Vaterland*, the pride of the German passenger fleet. When the USA entered the war in 1917, the *Vaterland* was resting at anchor in New York. As her German captain was unwilling to scupper her, the *Vaterland* became 'the most gigantic Prisoner of War the world has ever known'.[1] She was seized by US Customs officials in the early morning of 6 April 1917, and turned over to the Shipping Board to be manned and operated. After nearly three years in dry dock at Hoboken, she was finally turned over to the Navy Department on 25 July 1917, regularly commissioned as a Naval vessel and assigned to transport duty under the command of Vice-Admiral Albert Cleaves, US Navy, Commander of the Cruiser and Transport Force, United States Atlantic Fleet, and renamed the USS *Leviathan*.

When she was seized, the old *Vaterland* had been packed with luxury goods, glassware, silverware and vintage wines, which were immediately impounded by Customs. In the process, an eighty-piece gold coffee service, designed for the Kaiser, mysteriously disappeared without trace.[2] By September 1918, pampered socialites in jewels and furs had been replaced by a crew of the United States Navy, consisting of fifty officers and over one thousand men. Although the ship had been stripped and painted with striped 'Dazzle' camouflage to deceive the spying eyes of the U-boats, she retained the remnants of a happier life before she had come down in the world: a swimming pool with Roman decorations, and first-class salons glittering with mirrors and furnished with carpets and chairs covered in rose-coloured brocade.[3] But needs must when the devil drives. The dining hall had been converted into a mess hall for the troops, the swimming pool had become a baggage room, and the baggage room itself had turned into a brig (ship's prison) and a 'powder magazine' (gunpowder store). The once-majestic ballroom and theatre had been converted into a hospital, while the gymnasium on 'A' deck became an isolation ward for contagious cases and the former ship's doctor's office was to serve as a sick call station and dispensary for troops and crew.[4]

For the transports to France, ten thousand doughboys would be crammed onto the *Leviathan*'s fourteen, self-contained decks. Nobody could forget that there was a war on when they saw the three giant smokestacks, one of them a ventilator, rearing proudly. Their slight backward slant and the wicked-looking guns that thrust themselves from unexpected places below gave a fleeting impression of a crouching lion with flattened ears and bared teeth.[5] Like many a beauty fallen upon hard times, there was a hint of tragedy about the *Leviathan*, evident in her piercing siren. 'At nightfall and in the dusk of early morning the iron throat of the big prisoner sends forth such a wail as wrings the soul. It dies away and rises again from its own echo like the mourning cry of a world bereaved.'[6] On her first day out, the ship's log noted that 'A carrier pigeon, w-7463, fluttered through the air and dropped dead on C deck.'[7] An omen, perhaps, of what was to come.

The USS *Leviathan* was now the biggest ship in the world – the officer of the watch covered twelve miles in his nightly rounds[8] – and also one of the fastest, tearing through the water at 22 knots and usually travelling without an escort as it was believed she was too fast for the U-boats unless directly in their path.[9] The doughboys jokingly referred to her as the Levi Nathan, but she already had a tragic past. Several passengers and crew had died of influenza on the *Leviathan*'s previous voyage back from Brest, France, in September and had been buried at sea. Among those taken ill on that journey was the young Franklin D. Roosevelt, who had barely escaped with his life. Now, the *Leviathan* lay at anchor at Hoboken, New York, preparing for her ninth voyage to France. The following troops were on board:

Troops, 9,366; 57th Pioneer Infantry; September Auto Replacements Drafts from Camps McArthur, Humphreys, Hancock and Jackson; Medical Replacement, No. 73; 401st Pontoon Train; 467th Pontoon Train; 468th Pontoon Train; Water Tank Train No. 302; 323rd Field Signal Battalion; Base Hospitals No. 60 and 62; Female; Debarking and Billet Party 31st Div.; Major General Leroy S. Lyon, C. G. 31st Div.[10]

The only complete unit was the 57th Pioneer Infantry from Vermont. On the night of 27 September 1918, the men of the 57th began an hour's march from Camp Merritt, New Jersey, to the Alpine Landing, where ferries waited to take them down the Hudson to the *Leviathan*. But that night the march took far longer. Soon after the journey began, the column halted. Men suffering from the symptoms of Spanish flu were falling out of the ranks, unable to keep up.[11] While the most sensible course of action would have been to abandon the march and get back to quarters, this was not an option. The army and the schedules of the *Leviathan* were inflexible: they waited for no man, healthy or sick. After a break to allow the struggling men to catch up, the march resumed. But some men lay where they had fallen; others struggled to their feet and even jettisoned items of kit so that they could keep up. The soldiers were followed by trucks and ambulances, which picked up men as they fell and took them back to the camp hospital. It is not known how many men were lost on this march.[12]

The majority of the 57th made it to Alpine Landing and then endured a cold wet two-hour ferry trip down river. This was followed by final inspections on the pier at Hoboken – during which more soldiers collapsed – and coffee and rolls from the Red Cross, their first food in hours.[13] The men climbed the gangplank and then boarded the *Leviathan*, where they had their first sleep for twenty-four hours, a period of hardship guaranteed to challenge any soldier's immune system and break down his resistance to flu and pneumonia.[14]

The *Leviathan* left port on the afternoon of 29 September and before the ship even sailed, another 120 men fell sick. 'Many men and several nurses were obliged to leave the ship just before we cast off our lines,' stated the ship's log. 'While the embarkation troops were lined up on the big pier some of the men dropped helpless on the dock. We were informed that a number of men had fallen by the wayside, limp and listless, on their march from the camp to the scene of Transportation.'[15]

Despite this setback, the *Leviathan* eventually set sail with over 2,000 crew men and around 10,000 army personnel, including 200 nurses. 'Under clear skies we steamed slowly through the big harbor filled with shipping and proceeded straight to sea, stopping only to drop our pilot, Capt. McLaughlin, of the Sandy Hook Pilot Association and who always piloted the *Leviathan* in and out of New York Harbor.'[16] The ship's log indicated the crew's forebodings: 'everyone felt that we would have a distressing time going over'.[17]

Although the United States was in the grip of the Spanish flu epidemic, the army still insisted that there was no reason for alarm. On 4 October, while the *Leviathan* was at sea, Brigadier General Francis A. Winter of the American Expeditionary Force told the press that everything was under control and there was no reason to fear an epidemic. 'About 50 deaths only have occurred at sea since we first began to transport troops,' he claimed, eager to maintain morale by assuaging fears.[18]

The *Leviathan* was overcrowded, although not as overcrowded as on previous voyages, when she had carried 11,000 soldiers. The ship originally had a capacity of 6,800 passengers, but this capacity had been increased by over half. The US government referred to this process as 'intensive loading' rather than the 50 per cent overload it really was.[19] Conditions were cramped, with the men confined to quarters, huge steel rooms each holding 400 bunks. There was nothing for them to do apart from lie on their bunks or play cards, and the portholes,[20] painted deep black, were clamped tight shut at night to avoid the enemy submarines spotting light shining from them.[21]

Rules and prohibitions were precise and strictly enforced. A lighted cigarette upon a dark deck high in the air might be seen a half a mile at sea, enabling an enemy submarine to radio a lookout warning to another 'sub' lying in wait ahead. Those pests of the deep generally worked in pairs. To show how strict the blackout regulations were, one man was court martialled and sent to prison, an officer was court martialled and reduced, and an army chaplain, who was assisting the chaplain of the ship in administering to the dying, was threatened with court martial because he had opened a porthole slightly in response to a dying soldier's request for air.[22] As a consequence of the blackout regulations, life on the *Leviathan* was spent, for the most part, in conditions of near darkness.

As if to add further degrees of hellishness, the ineffectual ventilation system made little impact on the reek of sweat, and the noise levels in the all-steel structure approached pandemonium, with thousands of footsteps and shouts and cries echoing back and forth throughout the steel walls, stairs and passageways.[23]

And then the nightmare was unleashed. Despite the fact that 120 sick men had been removed from the *Leviathan* before sailing, Spanish flu symptoms manifested themselves within less than twenty-four hours of leaving New York harbour. To deter the spread of the disease, the troops were quarantined, sent to mess in separate groups at mealtimes to avoid the risk of infection, and confined to quarters. At first, they meekly accepted this ruling in the belief that the quarantine was keeping them safe.[24]

Soon every bunk in the sick bay was occupied and other men were lying sick in regular quarters. They were all marked with the deadly symptoms of the Spanish Lady: coughing, shivering, delirium and haemorrhaging. The nurses began to fall sick too. Colonel Gibson, Commander of the 57th Pioneer Infantry Regiment, recalled that:

The ship was packed. Conditions were such that the influenza could breed and multiply with extraordinary swiftness. The number of sick increased rapidly. Washington was apprised of the situation, but the call for men for the Allied armies was so great that we must go on at any cost. Doctors and nurses were stricken. Every available doctor and nurse was utilized to the limit of endurance.[25]

By the end of the first day, 700 troops were sick and the *Leviathan* was undergoing a full-blown epidemic. The horrific truth became apparent: the Spanish Lady had boarded the vessel with the doughboys and nurses bound for France. There was an urgent need to separate the sick men from the healthy to stop the disease spreading. Arrangements were made to put the overflow patients from the sick bay into 200 bunks in F Room, Section 3, port side. Within minutes, F Room was filled with sick men from the decks. Next, the healthy men of E Room, Section 2, starboard side, surrendered their bunks to the sick and were sent down to H-8. This room had been previously condemned as unfit for human habitation as it was poorly ventilated. By 3 October, the port side of E Room, Section 2, which held 463 bunks, had been commandeered for the sick and the occupants were sent off to find space in the ship wherever they could. In a grim game of musical chairs, three sick soldiers evicted four healthy men. The top bunk of the four-bunk stack could not be used by the sick, as the nurses were unable to climb up and the sick could not climb down.[26] During this horrific voyage the army nurses were described by the ship's historian as 'ministering angels during that dreadful scourge. They were brave American girls who had left home and comfort in order to undergo peril and sacrifice abroad.'[27]

The number of sick increased, with a high proportion of patients developing pneumonia. There was no room on the *Leviathan* for 2,000 sick and recovering men, and no way to care for such a high number of patients. Those doctors and nurses who had not succumbed themselves devised a system of separating the sick from the very sick. All patients were discharged from the sick bays and sent back to their units the minute their temperatures dropped to 99°.

It was impossible to determine just how many men were sick. Many remained in their bunks, unable to move and seek help. Rough seas made sea sickness an additional complication. Young men who had never experienced sea sickness before presented themselves to the sick bay and were admitted by inexperienced medics. Meanwhile, a stream of men with genuine flu symptoms were turned away for lack of space, and, so delirious that they were unable to find their way back to their own quarters, they simply laid themselves down on the deck. Others walked into the sick bay unchallenged and occupied any empty bunks they could find.

Conditions deteriorated by the hour. Chief Army Surgeon Colonel Decker was the only man on board with the military experience to solve this logistical problem, but the colonel fell ill himself on 1 October. Two other doctors also fell ill and remained in their cabins for the rest of the voyage, while 30 of the 200 army nurses also succumbed to flu. This left just eleven doctors in charge of an increasingly nightmarish situation.[28]

Over on another troopship, the *Briton*, which was travelling four days ahead of the *Leviathan*, Private Robert James Wallace experienced similar conditions. After several days at sea, Private Wallace woke up feeling 'utterly miserable' and reported to the medical officer, who took his temperature and ordered him to gather his blanket and equipment and make up a bed on deck.[29] When Private Wallace objected that it was cold and windy on deck, the medical officer retorted: 'Suit yourself. You have a temperature of 103°. You are sick. If you want to go below and infect all of them down there, go ahead!'[30]

Private Wallace walked out in the gale to join the others on deck, spread his blanket and wrapped himself up in his greatcoat, put on his hat and went to sleep. Although conditions were scarcely ideal, the open deck was at least fully ventilated. Private Wallace drifted in and out of consciousness, dreaming of a great rope of coloured silk, which he must not climb down, because to do so would be desertion. Waves swept across the deck, soaking the blankets of the sick. One night, Private Wallace's mess kit rattled away forever across the pitching deck. The following morning, he discovered that his cap and puttees had been swept away, too.[31]

Every morning, orderlies appeared on deck to check on the patients and carry away those who had died during the night. The sight of the dead men being taken away was a matter for 'sober conjecture' among the living. One morning, Private Wallace was picked up and carried below decks to a luxurious first-class salon, where private passengers had been entertained in the long-lost days before the war. The ghosts of pleasures past lingered on in the brocade-covered sofas and soft warm carpets. Private Wallace still had to sleep on the floor, but at least the carpets were comfortable and he was fed several times a day. One night, a nurse appeared, and asked with an English accent whether he was having a hard time. She brought Private Wallace a warm drink, and even washed his feet for him, peeling off the socks that were glued to his feet after twelve days. Private Wallace remembered this nurse with gratitude half a century later. 'That gentle washing of my feet with her soft soapy hands engraved a memory in my mind I shall record in Heaven when I get there.'[32]

Conditions in the salon were more salubrious than out on deck but this did not guarantee recovery. One night, a fellow patient cried out for water, but Private Wallace was too ill to get it for him. He called to a medic, and fell asleep. The man cried out again, and again Private Wallace called for water on his behalf: and again, he fell asleep. This happened many times until the other man whispered: 'Don't bother any more, I won't need it.' In the morning, the medics arrived at last, and found the man 'where he had rolled in some final, dim, instinctual effort to gain protection, under the settee. They carried him out for the burial detail.'[33]

Meanwhile, back on the *Leviathan*, conditions were deteriorating further. The troop compartments were crammed with sick and dying men, the air rank and foetid due to the ineffectual ventilation system. Without daily cleansing, these quarters swiftly became pigsties. To make matters worse, morale was low. The men, who came from ten separate units, were draftees, with no habit of obedience to a single commander or army discipline. The *Leviathan* was alone at sea, without an escort, with Spanish flu knocking men flat by the score every hour and with the almost palpable spectre of the Spanish Lady stalking through the ship. As the vessel sailed on across the Atlantic the prospect of being torpedoed by a U-boat must have been positively welcome. Below decks, scenes resembled the aftermath of a battle. Colonel Gibson later described:

> Scenes which cannot be visualised by anyone who has not actually seen them. Pools of blood from severe nasal haemorrhages of many patients were scattered throughout the compartments, and the attendants were powerless to escape tracking through the mess, because of the narrow passages between the bunks. The decks became wet and slippery, groans and cries of the terrified added to the confusion of the applicants clamouring for treatment, and altogether a true inferno reigned supreme.[34]

CHAPTER FIFTEEN

SHIP OF DEATH

THE FIRST DEATH from Spanish flu on the USS *Leviathan* was at 6:08 p.m. on 2 October, when Private Howard Colbert, 11th Battalion, 55th Infantry, was declared dead of lobar pneumonia.[1] 'He was a sailor who did duty in the Hospital Corps. He told the chaplain that he did not want to die because of the great need of his help at home.'[2] On the same morning, galvanized into action by this fatality, the army officers ordered healthy soldiers to go down into the holds and clean out the troop compartments and bring out the sick. In an act of mutiny, the troops refused to obey. 'No threat could be made which filled the men with greater fear than the pestilence loose below.'[3] But someone had to clean up before the *Leviathan* became a floating charnel house. Despite tradition, which dictated that the army and navy were separate entities, the 'bluejackets' or sailors were ordered below decks to clean up, a task which, to their eternal credit, they performed.[4] Without doubt, their actions halted the progress of the disease. There were no further mutinies among the men: horrified by the impact of Spanish flu, they belatedly recognized that anarchy would make conditions even worse.

From 2 October, not a day passed without a death. Three men died after Private Colbert, then seven, and then ten on succeeding days. The *Leviathan*'s war diary revealed a new horror: 'Total deaths to date, 21. Small force of embalmers impossible to keep up with rate of dying . . . Total dead to date, 45. Impossible to embalm bodies fast enough. Signs of decomposing in some of them.'[5] There was nowhere to store the dead: the morgue was already being used to nurse the living.

Initially, the deaths were carefully recorded in the *Leviathan*'s log, with details of the victim's rank and cause of death: '12.45 PM. Thompson, Earl, Pvt 4252473, company unknown, died on board . . . 3.35 PM Pvt O Reeder died on board of lobar pneumonia . . .'[6] But by the time the *Leviathan* was a week out of New York, the deaths were so numerous that the officer no longer bothered to add 'died on board'. There were so many deaths that he was simply recording a name and a time. Two names at 2.00 a.m.; another two at 2.02 a.m.; two more at 2.15 a.m.[7]

Identification of the sick and the dead proved impossible. The sick were too ill to say who they were and although they had all been issued with dog-tags on a chain around their necks, the tags had not yet been engraved with the owner's name, rank and number. This meant that the names of those who died and those who survived on the *Leviathan* would never be accurately recorded.[8]

Burials at sea soon became expediencies. Traditionally, burial at sea was a time-honoured ritual, carried out with great solemnity and dignity. But this was soon forgotten in the ongoing horror of the *Leviathan*'s Spanish flu epidemic. The urgent concern was to get the diseased and decomposing bodies off the ship as soon as possible. One sailor recalled watching similar proceedings on the *President Grant* from the deck of his own ship, the *Wilhelmina*. Time after time, after a few muttered prayers, the ship's colours were dipped and the plank tipped the shrouded corpses into the sea. 'I was near to tears, and there was tightening around my throat. It was death, death in one of its worst forms, to be consigned nameless to the sea.'[9]

On 7 October, thirty-one more soldiers died, and the *Leviathan* finally entered the port of Brest. The ship's log recorded the grim death toll: 'Upon our arrival in Brest we had on board 96 dead soldiers and three sailors.'[10] The healthy and all but the sickest disembarked at once, and 969 patients were removed and taken to army hospitals. The army nurses, who had saved countless lives by putting their own at risk, wept as they walked ashore and 'bade the sailors an affectionate goodbye'.[11] As the historian of the *Leviathan* concluded, 'surely they have earned a place in Heaven'.[12]

Of those who died on board the *Leviathan*, fifty-eight were buried in France, thirty-three were repatriated to the United States and seven were buried at sea in the war zone. The ship departed from Brest after three days, and on the following morning at sunrise, 'after an imposing prayer by the chaplain, the flag was half-masted, taps were sounded, three volleys fired and the coffins containing the bodies of the dead soldiers were lowered gently into the sea'. The ship was speeding at 21 knots, as the crew feared the imminent arrival of enemy submarines.[13]

After 'seven days of mostly fair weather and without trouble from submarines',[14] the *Leviathan* returned to New York. The ship's log concluded, with evident relief: 'we docked in New York on the morning of 16 October. It was a nerve-racking voyage and we were all greatly relieved that the trip was over.'[15]

There are no clear records of the numbers who died on the *Leviathan*'s ninth voyage to France. While the ship's Deck Log lists seventy deaths, the *Leviathan*'s War Diary gives the figure as seventy-six. *The History of the USS Leviathan*, written by crew members after the war, states that seventy-six soldiers and three sailors died during the crossing, but in another place it states that the numbers were between ninety-six and three. This confusion may arise from the fact that the chroniclers of the *Leviathan* were writing about the round trip from France to the United States and back again; or the deaths could simply have been mis-recorded as a consequence of the 'inferno' epidemic that raged through the ship.[16]

Whatever the true figure, the dying did not stop when the *Leviathan* put into port at Brest. Around 280 sick soldiers were still on board on 8 October, and 14 of them died that day. Dozens of soldiers who had escaped dying at sea went ashore to die on land. Those who could walk were expected to make the four-mile journey to the army camp at Pontanezan on foot, during a violent storm.[17] When they arrived at the camp, the barracks was not ready to receive them, and the camp hospital was full. Lieutenant Commander W. Chambers of the United States Navy Medical Corps was already horribly familiar with this situation. In the previous month, 1,700 cases of Spanish flu had arrived in Brest; the death rate of flu and pneumonia cases coming off the troopships was already 10 per cent higher than among those ashore. Chambers ordered the local military hospital to create more space in their wards, and the YMCA transformed their hut, initially designed as a club for the doughboys, into a seventy-five-bed hospital.[18] Aid stations along the route were staffed with orderlies, and the YMCA and Knights of Columbus ambulances followed the marching column, collecting the men as they fell. Six hundred men, too sick to walk, were picked up on the night of 7 October. Three hundred and seventy were convalescent, 150 were still sick with flu and 80 had pneumonia. Four who collapsed during the march were dead. Over the following days, hundreds of the men who came over on the *Leviathan* died.[19] Out of the 57th Infantry alone, 123 died at Kerhuon Hospital, 40 at Base Hospital Number 23 and several at Naval Hospital Number 5 and the hospital at Landernau. Nearly 200 of the flu victims of the 57th were buried at Lambezellec, overlooking the ocean.[20]

The tragedy of the *Leviathan* illustrated the way in which a troopship could become a liability to the Allies. The vessel, and ships like her, were no more than floating incubators for a virus, which erupted once it hit dry land. The most extreme example was the RMS *Olympic*, which arrived at Southampton, England, on the night of 21 September after a six-day voyage. The *Olympic*, a sister ship of the doomed *Titanic*, carried 5,600 men, of whom 450 had shown symptoms of flu while at sea, though only one died. By 4:00 p.m. on 29 September the flu cases among the passengers had risen. A third of the entire number of troops travelling on the *Olympic* – 1,947 people – had been admitted to hospital and 140 had died.[21]

Private Wallace survived his dose of Spanish flu and sailed into Liverpool on the *Briton*, staggering ashore to join his regiment, the 319th Engineers.[22] As the men gathered in a desultory fashion, unsure of quite what to do, the sergeant standing next to Private Wallace swayed under the weight of his pack, keeled over and fell to the ground. A group of officers hurried across and one exclaimed in shock: 'He's dead!'[23]

Private Wallace and the 319th took a train to the Liverpool suburb of Knotty Ash. From there they were to march to the

American camp. An army truck picked up the baggage of the sick detail, which Private Wallace had joined. It was raining heavily and the water was pouring down his neck. From time to time, men collapsed. Eventually, Captain Edward B. Pollister of the 319th found the sick detail and procured a truck to carry his men to the camp.[24] After a wet, draughty night by a tent flap, wracked with pain from the secondary ear infection caused by the flu virus, Private Wallace asked a supply sergeant for a new cap and puttees, and was told to go to hell.[25] Realizing that he had survived Spanish flu on the *Briton* only to face dying in Liverpool, Private Wallace promptly went AWOL. Heading for the cookhouse, he was taken in by a sympathetic Italian-American cook, who fed him and looked after him until he recovered.[26] Returning to camp, Private Wallace faced no disciplinary action; he had not even been missed in the chaos of the epidemic. Going AWOL had saved his life, but Private Wallace was left with the distinctive stamp of the Spanish Lady, which it took a long time to eradicate: his hair had turned white, and then fallen out.[27]

Back in Washington, the generals began to realize that the losses experienced by the American Expeditionary Force crossing to France were unacceptable. Spanish flu was already enough of a problem in France without the Allies importing it from America. It was understood that one factor was overcrowding, and by the time the Armistice was declared on 11 November, troopship capacity has been reduced by 30 per cent.[28] The generals also conceded that it was madness to send troops across the North Atlantic in the autumn with little more than one blanket and no overcoat. A greater effort was made to inspect the health of troops before they sailed, and some were issued with throat sprays and face masks. Troops on the *Olympic* and the *Henderson* spent their entire voyage to France wearing masks, although the effectiveness of these was debatable.[29] It was also recommended that only units that had already experienced the influenza epidemic be sent overseas, on the grounds that these units had developed some degree of immunity. But ultimately, few of these precautions made an impact: despite all attempts to contain her, the Spanish Lady remained a terrifying and implacable enemy.

The *Leviathan* was not the worst example of influenza on a troopship. In the same period, 97 soldiers out of 5,000 perished on the *President Grant*. When General March declared, in a speech, that every soldier who had died on his way to France had still played his part in the war, the statement brought little comfort to their families.[30]

CHAPTER SIXTEEN

'LIKE A THIEF IN THE NIGHT'

A T 3.30 ON the morning of 1 October 1918, Driver W. E. Hill was hoisting a cage full of black miners to the surface at the East Rand Proprietary Mine in Witwatersrand Basin, South Africa. Suddenly, as Hill sat before his controls, he became 'powerless to act', with 'a multitude of lights exploding before his eyes'.[1] As Hill sat paralysed, the cage went on being raised until it hit the top of the headgear and plummeted back to earth from a height of 100 feet. It smashed onto the collar of the shaft, killing twenty of its occupants and injuring eight.

The cause of this tragedy was not exhaustion or intoxication. Hill had suffered a sudden and devastating onset of Spanish flu. Mercifully, the official inquiry into the accident did not find Hill to have been 'criminally neglectful, but in view of the shock to his nervous system and owing also to the lack of knowledge of the possible after-effects of Spanish influenza on a person who has contracted the malady',[2] it felt he should not resume his job for at least a month, and then only if the mine's medical inspector certified him fit to do so.

Hill's dreadful experience came after the Prevention of Accidents on Mines Committee had recommended that workers operating lifting equipment should report any unusual symptoms at once. The advice had been issued too late for the twenty miners who died in the accident, but it did at least indicate that Spanish flu was being taken seriously in one region of South Africa.

The first reference to Spanish flu in South Africa appeared on 9 September 1918, when a mild form of the disease manifested itself in Durban.[3] It appeared in the gold mines of the Rand around about 18 September, but was not considered serious. But by 27 September, 14,000 mineworkers had been reported as suffering from influenza, predominantly black workers although the report included 100 white men. It had already been noted that the black workers were particularly vulnerable to pneumonia.[4]

Initially, Spanish flu had caused little alarm among the South African medical profession. Influenza was regarded as a routine scourge, seldom fatal unless patients were already compromised by extreme youth, extreme age or pre-existing conditions. Dr E. Oliver Ashe, a distinguished Kimberley doctor, felt more than capable of dealing with an outbreak:

> Having worked through epidemics in London (Whitechapel), Sheffield, and Maidstone nearly 30 years ago, I thought I knew what epidemic influenza meant, and when rumors of an impending outbreak began, I merely looked forward to a few weeks of extra hard work, with a rather heavy death-rate amongst the old, the feeble, and the alcoholic, though the majority of the cases would be mild.[5]

At first the influenza made little impact. Deaths were rare and recovery swift. The news agency Reuters declared that the outbreak was 'not seriously regarded' and would only 'produce temporary inconvenience without serious loss; in view of the fact that such a very large number of people have been affected, the fact that there has been only one death must be considered to be reassuring'.[6]

As a consequence, the Union was totally unprepared for the epidemic of Spanish flu unleashed in September 1918. The medical profession and public health officials had remained ignorant of the epidemic in other parts of the world, as influenza was not a notifiable disease. There had been no official warnings that ships coming to the Union might be carrying the disease, and there had been little news of the epidemic in Europe because of the war. Those press reports and medical journals that did refer to Spanish flu suggested that it was highly infectious but low in mortality. The region had no idea of the impending catastrophe.

Cape Town had already experienced the first, comparatively mild, wave of Spanish flu in July 1918, providing the population with some immunity. But the lethal strain of influenza that hit Cape Town in September 1918 was in a different league.

On 13 September, a troopship named the *Jaroslav* arrived in Cape Town from Sierra Leone, bringing with her some 1,300 South African Native Labour Corps (SANLC) troops home from Europe to be demobilized, including forty-three cases of influenza.[7] Thirteen men were still ill when the ship docked in Cape Town, one of whom died that night. As a result, those suffering from influenza were sent to No. 7 Military Hospital, Woodstock, and the remainder quarantined at Rosebank Camp.[8] When none of these men developed symptoms, they were permitted to leave for home on 16 and 17 September. The very next day, influenza broke out among the staff at Rosebank, the transport unit that had carried the troops there, and among the hospital staff. On 19 September, more cases appeared among men from a second troopship, the *Veronej*, which had also called at Freetown, Sierra

Leone.[9] The troops were quarantined, as before, and only those who were flu-free were permitted to travel home. But, despite all these precautions, Spanish flu and pneumonia deaths were exceeding 160 a day in Cape Town by 6 October.[10]

When the connection between the outbreak and the arrival of the *Jaroslav* and the *Veronej* in Cape Town became public knowledge, the newspapers were the first to claim that the troopships had brought the disease, with the *Cape Times* claiming that the Department of Health's officials were 'gravely lacking in a sense of their duty to the public',[11] and *De Burger* accusing the Department of gross negligence.[12]

Cape Town offered perfect conditions for a deadly epidemic. It had a population of over 270,000, including thousands of servicemen in addition to white, black and Cape Coloured citizens (the Cape Coloureds, as they describe themselves, are an indigenous ethnic group with mixed African and European heritage). Influenza flourished in the filthy tenements and slums of District Six and the Malay Quarter. Spanish flu was still not a notifiable disease, meaning there were no official reports, but by 1 October the *Cape Argus* was claiming that 'it may almost be said that every other household is affected'.[13] But few were prepared to consider Spanish flu as a serious threat to life, even when John Smith, a twenty-year-old Cape Coloured brush maker from District Six, died on 30 September.[14]

'It was regarded as quite a joke', recalled a woman then at the University of Cape Town. 'She's gone down with Spanish flu. What's the fuss about?' her friends asked when she contracted it.[15] At the Opera House, a cough in the audience provided the actor on stage with an excellent opportunity to ad-lib, 'Ha, Spanish flu, I presume?' The remark brought the house down.[16]

But within days, that joke wasn't funny any more. A wave of deaths among the Coloured community, and reports of victims lying dead and dying in the streets of District Six and the Malay Quarter, changed the public mood. As doctors and nurses struggled to care for their patients, pharmacists enjoyed a boom period, staying open all hours to supply the crowds with the quinine, aspirin and patent medicines now advertised in the newspapers. On Sunday 6 October, one doctor's secretary wrote in her diary: 'Nothing but phones and doorbells going all day. Influenza Epidemic [sic] in full swing. Felt pretty beastly myself.'[17] A city doctor observed, 'It is not safe for me to put my nose out of doors – I am mobbed wherever I go.'[18]

Cape Town became a ghost town as shops, banks and businesses stayed shut for lack of a workforce; schools closed and the law courts were suspended; there were no deliveries of groceries, or fresh bread.

'It is doubtful if the Tivoli theater was ever so empty on a Saturday night,' remarked one audience member on 5 October, 'which shows how big a hold this new form of influenza has taken upon the social life of Cape Town.'[19]

Another survivor recalled that the impact of Spanish flu 'was like a blind coming down',[20] while another journalist described the mood perfectly when he quoted 'holy writ' by declaring that the scourge had arrived in Cape Town 'like a thief in the night'.[21]

On Monday 7 October, with the newspaper's 'Deaths' section already nearly a column long, the *Cape Times* devoted its first leader to the epidemic, instead of the war.[22] The same day, the *Star*'s Cape Town correspondent reported 'Cape Town at the moment is a stricken city',[23] while a *Cape Argus* columnist noted the tragic fact that so many victims of Spanish flu were young and healthy: 'Death has stalked from its vantage ground in these crowded rooms and seized our youngest and strongest in their immaculate surroundings.'[24]

While Cape Town's civic authorities occupied themselves with an executive committee to combat the epidemic, many individuals threw themselves into relief work to overcome their own grief. Young Mr A. van Oord, a clerk, heard that one of his closest friends had died, 'a big well-built chap, of my own age, 20'.[25] Van Oord was so deeply shocked that he felt, 'it did not matter to me now in the least if I got the flu and died too. In fact I even hoped I would!'[26] Van Oord put in extra-long hours registering deaths at the Woodstock Police Station, hoping that he might catch influenza and die too, but 'despite the constant stream of coughing and deeply saddened, tearful people standing before and around me in that small room and stricken area, I did not even sneeze.'[27]

Meanwhile, the mortality rates crept upwards. Between 8 October and 13 October deaths from Spanish flu and its complications rose to more than 300 per day, and the week's total was a horrifying 2,404. The *Cape Argus* called it 'the blackest week in the history of Cape Town',[28] and described a 'sense of calamity engendered by the terrible mortality',[29] while years later a flu survivor remembered how in Fresnaye, 'All the house blinds were kept down on hearing of a death in the neighborhood, and bewildered children were awe-inspired by elders talking in subdued tones in an atmosphere of gloom.'[30] As rumours swirled about who had actually died, Morris Alexander, a local MP, was astonished to receive a phone call from the editor of the *Cape Times* enquiring as to the time of his own funeral.[31]

Doctors soon became as nervous as laymen about the consequences of this deadly outbreak. When a close friend asked the distinguished Dr F. C. Willmot whether Cape Town was going to be wiped out, Willmot replied: 'I will tell you what I would not tell any other man in the Union, for the first time in my life I am panicky, and believe we are.'[32]

By 12 October, Adderley and St George's Street were 'almost deserted even in the middle of the day ... Cape Town is like a city of mourning ... and nothing is talked of or thought about other than Influenza.'[33] A little girl walking through the city centre at this time recalled 'deathly silent streets which were really frightening',[34] while the veteran politician, John X. Merriman, noted in his diary on 17 October, 'Cape Town very empty & forlorn.'[35] As people dropped down dead in the streets, one twenty-one-year-old student at the University of Cape Town recalled that 'Cape Town was a veritable city of the dead.'[36]

In scenes reminiscent of London's Great Plague of 1665, carts circulated every morning, picking up the dead and taking them away to the cemeteries. Convicts, recruited with the promise of remission, piled up body after body, and occasionally the tarpaulin slipped to reveal arms and legs, tagged with labels. One eyewitness wrote: 'I actually saw the wagons going round, a bell ringing as they went, whilst the drivers called "Bring out your dead!" Just as one reads in accounts of the Black Plague, and at which one has so often shuddered.'[37]

With every undertaker in Cape Town overstretched, many families had to convey the bodies of their loved ones to the cemetery themselves. When cars and taxis were not available, they resorted to carrying them on traditional biers (carts or trolleys upon which the coffin is placed), or even pushing them to the graveside on wheelbarrows. The inevitable shortage of coffins that came as a consequence of the epidemic meant that many corpses were buried in nothing more than a blanket.

As Spanish flu fanned outwards across the peninsula, native Africans became the inevitable victims. Mine workers returning home from the Rand died on the road or in the veldt or bushland as they travelled on foot. One farmer in the Graskop district, a gold-mining camp in Mpumalanga province, reported that it was quite common 'to come across natives all along the road just left to die'.[38] This farmer had seen 'gangs of natives fleeing in terror from a sick boy lying in the road',[39] and recalled that 'if an ailing native is unable to proceed farther he is simply abandoned by his friends or brothers who may happen to have been accompanying him'.[40]

Dying miners were carried off packed trains, 'while conditions in the Black coaches must have been horrific. On one such train the ticket-collector refused to enter these carriages "because there was so much illness there." When another passenger went in, he found "it was a ghastly mess."'[41] *De Burger*'s Pietersburg correspondent wrote that the corpses of black men could be seen lying along the tracks of the train to Messina.[42] Conditions became so bad that, in the middle of October, hospital coaches were attached to trains carrying large numbers of black men to or from the Rand.

Spanish flu had a devastating impact on the South African mining industry. 'The influenza has indeed played havoc with the profits and makes one very anxious about the future',[43] admitted Sir Lionel Phillips, chairman of Central Mining, in a private letter to the President of the Chamber of Mines. 'One thing after another appears to arise to prey upon the gold mines.'[44] Losses were experienced at a financial level, with seventeen of the forty-eight mines on the Rand reporting a net loss for the month of November 1918. While this had serious repercussions for the mine owners, their attitude towards the workforce appears callous in the extreme.

Spanish flu proved even more destructive when it hit the diamond fields of Kimberley, carried by railway passengers from Cape Town. With its defective sanitation, poor housing and overcrowding, Kimberley was a magnet for disease, and Spanish flu flourished in the overcrowded jail, military camp, black neighbourhoods and the De Beers' compounds. As the general manager of De Beers told the subsequent Influenza Epidemic Commission: 'With conditions existing as they did previous to the epidemic it was not surprising that when the epidemic started conditions for its spread were all in its favor.'[45]

Initially, doctors and public officials regarded the outbreak as 'trifling', and 'nothing to worry about provided ordinary precautions were taken'.[46] But as the disease spread through Kimberley, the distinctive symptoms of Spanish flu became manifest. In addition to the 'crackling sounds from the lungs, bloody expectoration, a furry coating of the tongue, heliotrope tingeing of the skin, bleeding from nose or mouth',[47] and diarrhoea and vomiting, there was a distinctive odour, 'like very musty straw, the unforgettable smell of the 1918 influenza', one survivor recalled, 'so pungent, it just came into your nostrils with a bang'.[48] Many doctors came to the conclusion that this was not influenza at all, but something far more sinister. One doctor in Kimberley decided that he was looking at a new strain of pneumonia. He 'had seen cases with gangrene of the feet and fingers', he told the Influenza Epidemic Commission, 'and one did not get gangrene with influenza or ordinary pneumonia'.[49] Other expert opinion echoed previous theories that plague might be responsible for the devastating epidemic. Dr Alexander Edington, the prominent bacteriologist at the head of Grey's Hospital, Pietermaritzburg, claimed that the causative agent was related to plague, while Dr W. Purvis Beattie stated in the *Cape Times* that the epidemic was in fact pneumonic plague and that he was notifying the authorities to this effect.

The public embraced the plague theory. 'In God's name, when are you going to cease talking piffle about "influenza"?' demanded an exasperated reader of the *Star*. 'Influenza does not turn a corpse black but pneumonic plague does.'[50] Many Afrikaners agreed with this diagnosis, while the biblical connotations of plague were irresistible to many Christians, who regarded the epidemic as a form of divine punishment for immorality. South African president General Louis Botha even claimed the epidemic was a punishment for the lack of unity between English and Afrikaners. 'This visitation will prove to be one of the means sent by God in order to sober us by punishment; to clear out misunderstanding, so that everything may lead along the road of greater affection, tolerance, co-operation, and a truly united national existence in matters spiritual as well as political.'[51] Botha himself became a victim of Spanish flu the following year, dying on 27 August 1919.

Other theories as to the aetiology of the disease echoed those circulating in Europe and the United States. The *Cape Times* maintained 'that Spanish influenza may be directly traced to the use of poison gas by the Germans',[52] while others shared the widespread belief that Spanish flu originated from scores of rotting bodies left to decompose on the battlefields. This theory was widespread, and even in the remoter parts of Manyikaland, Southern Rhodesia, local *ngangas*, or witch doctors, were convinced that 'So many were killed in the great war of the white people that the blood of the dead had caused this great sickness.'[53]

The Spanish Lady went by a new name in South Africa. Afrikaners called the disease *longpest*, reflecting the view that this pestilence was not influenza at all, but a form of plague. Among the black population, names for Spanish flu included *mbethalala* and *driedagsiekte*, or 'that which smites' and 'the thing that strikes you down and sends you to sleep'.[54] In one district, where African natives were the first victims, the disease was dubbed *Kaffersiekte* or 'black man's sickness', while in another, where whites died first, the black Africans christened the disease 'white man's sickness'.[55] But whatever name they gave it, the meaning was clear. This was no ordinary influenza and it spread terror across the Union. Horrifying stories circulated to the effect that victims fell into comas indistinguishable from death, with 'corpses' reviving to life on their way to the cemetery;[56] bodies turned black and decomposed within hours, and the mystery disease was also killing birds, pigs and baboons.[57] This 'plague' was said to have been borne in on a dark rain, and meat exposed to the atmosphere turned black.[58]

At Dutoitspan, another diamond mine, operations were halted on 30 September because of the large number of men laid up, as numerous cases appeared among Kimberley's white population. As life in the town ground to a halt, the De Beers Company suspended work at its mines amidst rumours of an appalling number of deaths in its compounds. 'No one realizes what is lying there', a nurse told her family when she returned from helping out at Dutoitspan.[59]

Almost a quarter of the 11,445 black employees died within a month, and the death toll did not fall below 100 per day between 5 October and 14 October. On 8, 9 and 10 October it rose to over 300 per day. Soon all three compound hospitals were overflowing, with mattresses out on the verandas to accommodate more patients. Part of the side walls were removed at Wesselton Compound Hospital to improve ventilation and St John Ambulance nurses of the De Beers Corps had to be called in to supplement the nursing staff.[60] When pneumonia set in and the death toll climbed, De Beers realized it had to cease work in all its mines. Conditions had become horrific, with men dropping dead in their tracks, hospital floors covered with dying patients and corpses piled on top of each other awaiting removal. One doctor said that he had seen 'horrible things happen in the war, but nothing so terrible as the way that the natives died from influenza in the compounds'.[61] On 6 October, the General Manager, Alpheus Williams, withdrew the St John nurses (of which his wife was a member) when he saw that if he left them there any longer, 'owing to the terrible death rate everyone would have contracted the disease'.[62] Days later De Beers stopped burying their dead in the local cemetery and began using a site on their own property instead.

Workers who had not yet been affected by the flu soon realized that if they wanted to stay alive, they had better leave the compound death trap quickly. From 8 October some requested permission to leave, saying they would rather die at home and wanted to look after their families.[63] For a week, De Beers officials tried to dissuade them, but increasing numbers of miners begged to leave, their ranks swelled by survivors. As the De Beers management debated its options, the miners announced that they had decided to leave, and if De Beers did not agree they would break out of the compound, 'even if fired upon'.[64] De Beers gave way, and repatriation began on 18 October. Over 5,000 survivors went home, the majority by rail, over the following two and a half weeks. Provision was made for any who fell ill on the journey, although De Beers tried to ensure that no one even suspected of being ill was allowed to embark.

Horrified by the death toll in its compounds, especially as this compared so unfavourably with other mines in the country, the De Beers management realized that improvements were imperative; they could not afford the risk of another devastating epidemic like the Spanish flu. Amid general applause, the chairman promised the Annual General Meeting in December 1918 that 'no expense will be spared to make the Compounds, if possible, more comfortable and healthy for the natives than those occupied previous to the Epidemic'.[65] But there was no mention of improving conditions underground.

CHAPTER SEVENTEEN

The Dying Fall

———

B Y THE AUTUMN of 1918, few Allied families had reason to celebrate, despite encouraging news from the Front. Across the globe, they had lost loved ones either to the Spanish Lady or to the war. It was against this backdrop that the Spanish Lady played out her death march, killing without compunction. She did not discriminate between statesmen, painters, soldiers, poets, writers or brides.

On 11 September 1918, British Prime Minister David Lloyd George arrived in Manchester to receive the Freedom of the City, the greatest honour that a city can confer. Although Lloyd George was raised in Wales, he had been born in Chorlton-on-Medlock in Manchester and the city was understandably proud of its famous son. As his open-topped carriage drove through Manchester, Lloyd George received a hero's welcome from soldiers home on leave and munitions girls, lining the Piccadilly and Deansgate areas and creating such 'turmoil in the streets', according to the *Manchester Guardian*, that it took over an hour to reach Albert Square.[1] During this journey, Lloyd George was soaked in a shower of Manchester's ubiquitous rain.

The following day, Lloyd George made a powerful speech about the war at his Freedom of the City ceremony. Although he reassured his audience that 'nothing but heart failure'[2] could prevent a British victory, it soon became obvious that the Prime Minister was not in the best of health. One spectator who shared the platform with him recorded that Lloyd George was 'long' and 'not in his best form'. But at the time his words seem to have had a powerful impact.[3]

After the ceremony, Lloyd George attended a civic lunch at the Midland Hotel, where he delivered another, shorter speech, praising the exploits of the Manchester regiment and other Lancashire units. By the time evening had arrived, with the prospect of giving yet another speech at a dinner at the Reform Club, the Prime Minister felt too ill to go on. He took to his bed and all the plans for his visit had to be cancelled. Lloyd George would spend the next nine days in his bedroom at Manchester Town Hall. His room was at the front of the building, and he later recalled looking out at the statue of John Bright, 'dripping with constant rain'.[4]

As the eminent ear, nose and throat specialist Sir William Milligan was summoned to supervise Lloyd George's care, his aides battled to suppress news of the illness. The fact that the Prime Minister of Great Britain had influenza would have alarmed the public and provided a morale boost to the enemy. Bulletins were issued to the press but these gave no indication of the gravity of Prime Minister's condition. The public were informed that Lloyd George had caught a chill, caused by the rain the previous day. There was no mention of the alarming possibility that he had contracted the same lethal strain of Spanish flu that had appeared in Manchester during the previous summer, infecting 100,000 Mancunians and killing 322.

When Lloyd George's condition deteriorated, Sir William Milligan decided to take the risk and announce that the Prime Minister had influenza. While the traffic was diverted from Albert

Square, so that Lloyd George would not be troubled by the sound of the trams, the press downplayed the gravity of the situation.

Maurice Hankey, Secretary of the War Cabinet, later confided that the Prime Minister had been 'very seriously ill' and that his valet, Newnham, had said it was 'touch and go'.[5] According to one biographer, Lloyd George 'seems to have been acutely, perhaps critically, ill at a time of mounting crisis in the world, when he needed to be in full vigour to tackle a situation that took him by surprise'.[6]

By 21 September, Lloyd George had recovered sufficiently to travel back to London, accompanied by Sir William Milligan and wearing a ventilator. After a brief stop at 10 Downing Street, the Prime Minister was taken to Danny Park, his country retreat in West Sussex, for a working convalescence. Despite being a man of great energy and drive, Lloyd George was almost broken by Spanish flu.

'I am crawling upward but have not yet recovered strength,' he wrote to his wife, Margaret. 'Unfortunately – or fortunately – things are moving so rapidly I cannot keep off affairs of State. Someone here every day.'[7] By the end of September, he was still cancelling public meetings on medical advice and when he travelled to France on 4 October, Milligan insisted on accompanying him.

'I am off by the 8 train from Charing X,' he wrote to Margaret. 'My temperature is still very low & my pulse too feeble . . . I had my first Cabinet yesterday & it tired me so that I am not yet fit for much work. It is a pity that the Paris journey could not be put off until next week . . . I propose staying at Versailles . . . more reposeful than a Paris hotel.'[8]

As Lloyd George's biographer has stated, his recovery was remarkable in the circumstances.[9,10] Had Great Britain lost her war leader to Spanish flu at this juncture, the blow to national morale would have been crippling.

Another famous leader almost perished at the hands of the Spanish Lady on 2 October 1918. Following the death of his daughter-in-law and her young son from influenza, the forty-nine-year-old Mahatma Gandhi began to show symptoms of the disease. Spanish flu also raged in the Sabarmati Ashram, Ahmedabad, where Gandhi had retreated for meditation and prayer.[11] By the time Gandhi had been admitted to hospital in Bombay awaiting an operation for boils and suffering from dysentery, he was refusing all treatment. Unlike the majority of patients, Gandhi had resigned himself to his imminent death.

'My heart is at peace,' Gandhi wrote to his son, Harilal, who was still struggling to come to terms with the death of his wife and little son. 'And so I do not find the going at all difficult.'[12] Gandhi's doctors were persistent in their efforts to keep him alive, however, and so were his supporters. 'Mr Gandhi's life does not belong to him – it belongs to India', proclaimed the weekly *Praja Bandhu* magazine.[13]

Gandhi was eventually coaxed into drinking goat's milk. This was in violation of his religious beliefs, but Gandhi recovered and even recommended his treatment to others: 'Even after we feel that we have recovered, we must continue to take complete rest in bed and have only easily digestible liquid food. So early as on the third day after the fever has subsided many persons resume their work and their usual diet. The result is a relapse and quite often a fatal relapse.'[14]

Gandhi survived, but India had been stricken by a 'national calamity' according to the Sanitary Commissioner for Government of India.[15] Typically of Spanish flu, the disease was fatal among the ten to forty age group, and more women died than men. In total, around 17 million people died of Spanish flu between June and December 1918. Bombay suffered terribly. Between 10 September and 10 November 1918, the total mortality was 20,258.[16] This was made worse by the failure of the south-west monsoon and resultant crop failure. As a consequence, Bombay had to cope with an influx of migrants from districts suffering from 'scarcity and dearness of food'. In Ahmedabad, 3,527 died, the highest mortality being among the lower castes, who were both 'poor and underprivileged'.[17]

Bombay's sanitary commissioner, while adopting the fatalistic attitude that influenza could not to be stopped by public health measures, nevertheless recommended sleeping in the open air, away from ill-ventilated homes, and using disinfectant. *The Times of India* advised readers to gargle with permanganate of potash and seek hospitalization for pneumonia.[18] When the hospitals ran out of beds, schools were requisitioned. There was a general feeling among the Indians that the government could have done more, and that the majority of the officials had stayed in the hills, and abandoned the population to their fate. Food shortages caused by the famine and a contaminated water supply scarcely helped matters, and the colonial administration was criticized for its apathy, allowing 'sixty *lakhs* of people to die of influenza like rats without succor'.[19] In Calcutta, the scenes were equally grim. The Associated Press reported that the Hooghly River was 'choked with bodies', and 'streets and lanes of India's cities are littered with the dead. Hospitals are so choked, it is impossible to remove the dead to make room for the dying. Burning ghats and burial grounds are literally piled with corpses.'[20]

In Britain, Sir Hubert Parry, best known for his scoring of William Blake's poem *Jerusalem*, became a victim of Spanish flu on 17 October 1918. In honour of his creative significance, Parry was buried in St Paul's Cathedral, London. To be pre-deceased by one's son was no longer uncommon, a legacy of the war which killed so many young men. But Sir Arthur Conan Doyle, creator of Sherlock Holmes, suffered a particularly painful bereavement. When his son, Kingsley, had been injured at the Battle of the Somme in 1916, it seemed as if he would survive once he had recovered from his wounds. But, cruelly, Spanish flu attacked Kingsley in his weakened state and he died on 28 October 1918. Already fascinated by spiritualism, Sir Arthur turned to this popular new belief system to make sense of his devastating loss.

Meanwhile, the Spanish Lady's killing spree continued, cutting down the famous and the unknown alike. VAD Vera Brittain, now back in London, struggled to cope with her exhausting duties during the 'ferocious' epidemic. In Nottingham, young Katherine Wade Dalton was married at St Mary's church in the Lace Market district on 23 October 1918. Just one week later, the newly-wed returned to St Mary's for her own funeral, after falling victim to Spanish flu. Katherine's heartbroken husband and family installed a stained-glass window at the church as a memorial.[21] In the same city, the Victoria Baths swimming pool was drained and turned into a temporary morgue when the local council ran out of places to store the dead.[22] By the week ending 16 November 1918, Nottingham had recorded the highest death rate in the country: 60,000.[23]

On 26 October, in London, pacifist campaigner Caroline Playne noted: 'Influenza very bad in places. People did not seem cheered at the prospect of peace. In trains and trams the depression shown on travellers' faces was very noticeable and talk was all about specially sad cases of death from influenza. A sense of dread is very general.'[24]

Four days later, later, Caroline wrote that 'The London correspondent of the *Manchester Guardian* 30 October, says that people in general are scared about the influenza. They besiege doctors' surgeries and chemists' shops.'[25]

Matters were not improved by the fact that Spanish flu represented a threat to law and order due to the shortage of police officers, with civil unrest a real possibility. On 1 November 1918, *The Times* reported: '1,445 members of the Metropolitan Police Force and 130 members of the London Fire Brigade on the sick-list with influenza. During the twenty-four hours ending at seven o'clock yesterday morning forty-four persons were stricken with sudden illness in the London streets and were removed to hospitals in the LCC ambulances.'[26] Lady Diana Manners, 'the most beautiful woman in England',[27] wrote to her fiancé, Duff Cooper, who was serving with the Grenadier Guards: 'This pneumonia plague is ferocious. Lovely Pamela Greer, *née* Fitzgerald dead in three days.'[28] Pamela Greer was just one of the society beauties falling victim to the Spanish Lady. Mrs Dubosc Taylor, described by *Tatler* magazine as 'one of the most beautiful women in Society',[29] and who had turned her house in Portland Square into a hospital, perished as a result of Spanish flu. Survivors included Miss Lavender Sloane-Stanley, who had been serving as a VAD, and Lady Victoria Brady, only daughter of the Earl of Limerick.[30]

In central London, Dr Basil Hood was struggling to stay in control of his hospital, Marylebone Infirmary. At this period, Marylebone was a poor district of London with a high level of depravation, and Hood's unpublished memoirs provide a devastating insight into conditions as Spanish flu raged throughout Marylebone like wildfire.

'I have refused no case ever,' Hood confided, 'remembering what would be their state, in this area of undernourished and overworked poor. I considered our results were good, considering all things. Of course, cases of influenza/pneumonia if they came from our slum area arrived [sic] with a bad prognosis – inevitably.'[31]

Within a few days of receiving some 200 patients from Paddington Infirmary, by way of sick soldiers there, the great and awful influenza epidemic fell upon us under which the place literally reeled. All training and indeed every part of training went by the board, whilst the staff fought like heroes to feed the patients, scramble as best they could through the most elementary nursing and keep the delirious in bed. Each day the difficulties became more pronounced as the patients increased and the nurses decreased, coming down like ninepins themselves. In total, nine of these gallant girls lost their lives in this never-to-be-forgotten epidemic. I can see some of them now literally fighting to save their friends and then going down and dying themselves.[32]

Hood requested that, in any subsequent citations, the names of his colleagues remain anonymous to protect the sensibilities of their relatives. As a result, Hood's colleagues remain unnamed in these extracts.

At the end of October we lost our first nurse with pneumonia and then on 7th November I had to report the deaths of 4 more nurses, the last having only been with us 4 days . . . One nurse especially I remember, nursing Sister X, in a side ward. Nothing that I could do or say had the slightest effect . . . she was just consumed with a burning desire to save her if she could. In the end they both perished, the nurse a charming little Irish girl devoted to her work. I can see her now, buttonholing me in the passage, 'did I think Sister was a little better?' 'was she doing well?' 'was there anything more she could do?' With never a moment's thought of herself. It was a real blow when she was laid to rest and not least to me. I have never really got over that time and no wonder.[33]

Hood's memoirs also illustrate the stark reality of the symptoms of Spanish flu:

One poor nurse I remember with a terribly acute influenza/ pneumonia. She could not stay in bed and insisted on being propped up against the wall by her bed until she was finally drowned in her profuse, thin blood-stained sputum constantly bubbling froth.

I knew she was doomed and that her end was near so we did as she desired in making her as comfortable as possible. This epidemic was certainly the worst and most distressing of my professional life. In the first week of December 1918 the total patients reached 779 in one day, the nursing staff total under 100.[34]

The epidemic inevitably took its toll on the medical staff, Hood included:

Towards the end of November the incidence among the nursing staff began to diminish . . . and the worst being apparently over

LEFT: Americans were encouraged to 'Eat More Onions!' to keep Spanish flu at bay.

BELOW: Factory workers in Brisbane, Australia, 1919.

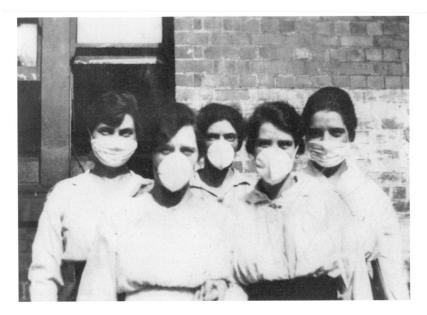

ABOVE: A family in Dublin, California, along with their cat, demonstrate the importance of flu masks.

BELOW: Seattle police in masks add a surreal touch to this photograph.

ABOVE: Safety at work: a typist in her flu mask, New York, 1918.

BELOW: 'Obey the laws!' A couple in their masks.

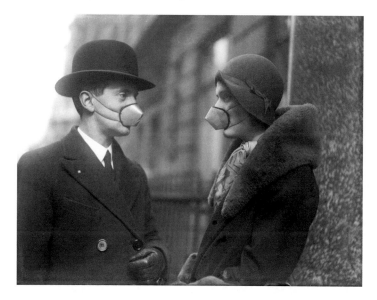

LEFT: A customized flu mask sets off a young man's straw boater.

RIGHT: A sentimental view of an influenza patient, as printed in the French magazine *La Vie Parisienne*, November 1918.

LE COMBLE DE LA GUIGNE

AVOIR LA GRIPPE LE JOUR DE LA VICTOIRE

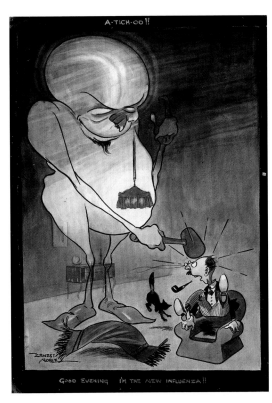

LEFT: 'Out to get you!' A British cartoon by E. Noble of the 'Flu Monster', c. 1918.

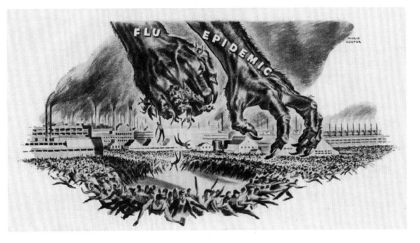

ABOVE: A nightmare memory of the Spanish flu from a Dixie Cups advertising campaign, 1920.

LEFT: The songbook cover of 'Happy' Klark's dance hit 'The Influenza Blues'.

RIGHT: Spanish flu was often mistaken for *La Grippe*, which could affect even those who were in good health.

Die spanische Krankheit

(Zeichnung von Wilhelm Schulz)

Der Friedensengel: „Und dieses scheußliche Frauenzimmer hat überall Zutritt!"

ABOVE: Wilhelm Schulz's cartoon in the German satirical magazine *Simplicissimus* shows the Angel of Peace being overtaken by a cat-faced 'Spanish Lady', September 1918.

LEFT: Postcard showing a memorial to the victims of Camp Funston. Harry A. Harding (seen here) designed the monument.

ABOVE: The Influenza Pandemic Window from the Johannes Schreiter windows at the Medical Library, the Royal London Hospital, Whitechapel.

> ... I <u>collapsed</u>. I had been finding it increasingly difficult to get
> about the place – we had no lift that could be used by us when
> going from floor to floor – they were too slow in the work – as
> some 15 or 16 hours a day was required of me as well as night
> calls all the work had to be done at top speed and the stress and
> distress all coming at the end of 4½ years of war finally proved too
> much for me so that at the end of November I became incapable
> of continuing and was given 3 months' sick leave. I could barely
> stand and always when possible against a wall![35]

Hood survived the war, and left his unpublished notes to posterity
as a fascinating insight into conditions at a London hospital
during the Spanish flu epidemic.

In Vienna, Austria, an extremely gifted but scandal-prone
young painter, Egon Schiele, was supporting his wife, Edith,
through her first pregnancy. Schiele, whose obsession with
under-age girls had led to a criminal prosecution for seducing
a girl beneath the age of consent, had finally settled down and
devoted himself to his work. Schiele was a magnificently gifted
artist, with 'an exceptional graphic ability and an unusual
feeling for colour . . . and he employed these gifts like a virtuoso
in order to depict a small number of constantly reappearing,
dreadfully distorted and frightening figures, or in landscapes
which, seen as though from the bird's-eye view, also have
something grimacing and caricatured about them . . .'[36] But
he also had a weak constitution, no match for the consuming
monster of Spanish flu.

On 27 October, Schiele wrote to his mother: 'Nine days ago
Edith caught Spanish influenza and inflammation of the lung
followed. She is also six months pregnant. The illness is extremely

grave and has put her life in danger – I am already preparing myself for the worst since she is permanently short of breath.'[37]

Schiele already had a strong sense of mortality, reflected in his work, and a 'penchant for deathbed sketches'.[38] When Schiele's mentor, the symbolist painter Gustav Klimt, had developed Spanish flu, following a stroke in February 1918, Schiele had sketched him on his deathbed. Schiele sketched Edith as she lay dying on 27 October. In a stark but tender drawing, Edith stares out of the page, with sad haunted eyes. She died the following day.

Schiele did everything in his power to avoid getting infected. But he had a weak constitution and died on 31 October 1918 at his mother-in-law's house on the Hietzinger Hauptstrasse.[39] 'The war is over,' he said as he died, 'and I must go. My paintings shall be shown in all the museums of the world.'[40]

Obituaries focused on the irony of Schiele's death.

Not only had he died not long after the Secession exhibition had made his name a household word, at the point where he was clearly soon to become the richest and most celebrated painter in Vienna. He had also died at the same moment as the old Imperial Austria had passed away, the 'Expressionist painter [who] was one of the greatest hopes of our young art world.' He was still only twenty-eight.[41]

In the first days of November 1918, Swiss-born novelist Blaise Cendrars witnessed 'the incineration of plague-ridden bodies piled up in the fields and sprinkled with petrol, since the city had run out of coffins', on the outskirts of Paris.[42] When Cendrars arrived in Paris, he encountered the celebrated Modernist poet

Guillaume Apollinaire (1880–1918), who was recovering from a gunshot wound to the head, having survived 'combat, a head wound, trepanning, and military medicine'.[43] The two men lunched in Montparnasse and spoke of 'the subject of the day, the epidemic of Spanish flu which had more victims than did the war.'[44] Five days later, Cendrars passed the concierge of Apollinaire's building, who told him that his friend had caught Spanish flu. Cendrars hurried inside, where he met Apollinaire's wife Jacqueline. She too was ill, but not as bad as her husband, who had turned black. Cendrars rushed to get a doctor, who said it was too late to help Apollinaire. The following evening, Saturday 9 November, he died.

Cendrars wrote an extraordinary account of Apollinaire's funeral, which reads like a state funeral crossed with a black comedy. Proceedings began in a conventional fashion, with a traditional Roman Catholic funeral:

> *The final absolution having been given, the casket of Apollinaire left the church of St Thomas Aquinas, draped in a flag, Guillaume's lieutenant's helmet on the tricolore, among the flowers and wreaths. A guard of honour, a squad of soldiers, arms at their sides, led the slow convoy, the family behind the carriage, his mother, his wife, in their mourning veils, poor Jacqueline, who had escaped the epidemic which had taken Guillaume, but who was still weak.*[45]

These in turn were followed by Apollinaire's most intimate friends, including Max Jacob and Pablo Picasso, as well as all of literary Paris and the press. But as the procession reached the corner of Saint-Germain, the cortège was besieged by a noisy crowd celebrating the Armistice, a rival procession consisting of men and women waving their arms, singing, dancing and kissing.[46]

This was too much for Cendrars, who indignantly left the cortège with his lover, Raymone, and the artist Fernand Leger. 'It was fantastic', Cendrars said. 'Paris celebrating. Apollinaire lost. I was full of melancholy. It was absurd.'[47]

After a warm drink to protect themselves from the flu, they took a cab to Père Lachaise cemetery, only to find that they had missed the funeral. Trying to locate Apollinaire's grave in the vast cemetery they fell into two newly dug ones, much to the irritation of the gravediggers. But eventually the gravediggers took pity upon them and explained that they were unable to help: 'You understand, with the flu, with the war, they don't tell us the names of the dead we put in the ground. There are too many.'[48] Cendrars explained that they were looking for the grave of an important man, Lieutenant Guillaume Apollinaire, to fire a salvo over his tomb, but the gravediggers could do nothing. 'My dear sir,' said the head gravedigger, 'there were two salvoes. There were two lieutenants. We don't know which one you are looking for. Look for yourselves.'[49]

Then they spotted a grave nearby, with a lump of frozen earth that seemed to look like nothing so much as Apollinaire's head, with grass that resembled hair around the scar where he had been trepanned. Stunned by this optical illusion, Cendrars and his friends left the cemetery, which was rapidly becoming enveloped in a thick glacial mist.

'It was he,' insisted Cendrars. 'We saw him. Apollinaire isn't dead. Soon he will appear. Don't forget what I tell you.'[50]

For the rest of his life, Cendrars could never quite believe that

Apollinaire was dead. As far as he was concerned, 'Apollinaire inhabited not the kingdom of the dead but the kingdom of the shadows' and his strange funeral seemed like some sort of cosmic joke. That the incident took place near the tomb of Allan Kardec, founder of French spiritualism, added to Cendrars' impression of being sent a secret message from beyond the grave. Kardec's grave bears the motto, 'To be born, to die, to be born again and to progress without end. That is the law.'[51]

WHEN CAPTAIN J. Cook, RAMC, of the No. 18 Casualty Clearing Station at Arques, Pas-de-Calais, realized that he had an influenza epidemic on his hands, an extra clearing station was reopened at a former Christian Brothers' School near St Omer.[52] As 600 influenza patients a day poured in, additional beds were provided in marquees. Between thirty and forty nurses and forty medical staff were run ragged by the task of caring for their patients. At this point, Captain Cook noted sardonically, the English papers were publishing official statements to the effect that 'Up to the present the epidemic of influenza has not affected the British troops in France.'[53]

At No.4 General Hospital, Arques, VAD Kitty Kenyon told her diary that 'this new flu is knocking everyone everywhere over like ninepins'.[54] Kitty was particularly distressed by the death of an orderly, Franklin. 'He has been one of our orderlies for so long that it must have been hateful knowing all the last details and knowing that he would be carried out on a stretcher under a Union Jack, like so many men that he had accompanied himself. He was one of the nicest of our NCOs.'[55]

For probationer Margaret Ellis, stationed at No. 26 General Hospital at Camiers, nursing influenza patients was grim in the extreme. 'They were all incontinent so you were continually changing beds and washing. I remember doing one boy from head to foot, and ten minutes later I had to start doing it all over again.'[56]

Peggy Morton, a VAD at No. 55 General Hospital, Wimereux, recalled with horror the macabre symptoms of Spanish flu. 'I remember one man. I just happened to peep over the screen and an orderly was starting to wash him. The man's face was dark blue.' Peggy told the orderly to stop, and reported the case to Sister. The man died in the early evening, and by the following morning his body had already started to decompose. 'They called it influenza but it seemed to us to be some frightful plague.'[57]

This horror was shared by US Army Nurse Mary Dobson, who sailed out to Europe on a troopship. Mary and around twenty other nurses fell sick during the voyage, but there was nobody to look after them as hundreds of troops were sick as well. 'You had terrific pain all over your body, especially in your back and your head, and you just felt as if your head was going to fall off. The odor was terrible in that ship's infirmary – I never smelt anything like it before or since. It was awful, because there was poison in this virus.'[58] Eighty troops died on the voyage to Europe, but they were not buried at sea. Instead, they were to be taken to Brest and buried in military graves. Because the weather was so hot, all the food had to be removed from the ship's refrigerator and the bodies stored within.

The pervasive dread that Spanish flu was not influenza at all, but something more sinister, had begun to circulate in France. Credibility for this theory rested on the fact that 'the phenomena of asphyxia and cyanosis which followed the pulmonary complications of flu could give the dying a blackish facial color which recalled some manifestations of cholera'.[59] The French linguist Albert Dauzat provided one example from the Issoire region of the Auvergne, central France, when a local butcher, named only as 'B', received the news that his son had died of pneumonia on the Alsace front.

'The chaplain who announced the death to the parents, with the usual tactful phrases, specified that the young soldier had succumbed to pulmonary flu.' Despite the fact that there was little doubt about the matter, the rumour spread that B's son had died of cholera.

Several persons, who like me had seen the letters, reported: 'You don't die of flu. It must be cholera. The staff officers write what they want to sick soldiers and chaplains.' Further, the father himself was not convinced: 'I believe truly,' he confided in me, 'that this Spanish flu was nothing else but cholera. A nursing orderly from the front, who was here recently on leave, told me that the bodies that were taken away were covered with black spots. That's clear, isn't it?'[60]

According to Rasmussen, the 'cholera legend' was an example of 'mass thinking', a belief that, against all scientific fact, influenza was actually a form of cholera. Another example of the sheer horror of the spread of Spanish flu and its explosive nature, can be seen in the evidence of a doctor in the village of Cuttoli, Corsica.

A resident of Cuttoli, M. D., traveled to Ajaccio one Saturday with his daughter-in-law, for dental treatment. Three days after his return, on the Monday, a child died. M. D. died shortly afterwards. For family reasons, M. D.'s body was not buried as quickly as usual.

A close relative was awaited, he came, the coffin was opened, people rushed to the corpse for a final embrace, nine members of the family caught the infectious flu and succumbed. A particular detail, on the very day of M. D.'s funeral a confirmation service took place in the church where the dead man's body had rested for around an hour and a half. The faithful went in front of Mgr the Bishop and then returned together into the church to take part in two religious ceremonies. A few days later, 250 people were attacked by broncho-pneumonia and took to their beds, then 450 out of a population of 1,100 inhabitants, finally 600 cases were recorded with 54 deaths.[61]

In the field hospitals, death may have become commonplace, but it never lost its sting. Probationer Margaret Ellis, of No. 26 General Hospital, Camiers, came to hate the sight of a Union Jack, 'because they always used one to cover them as they carried them out on a stretcher'.[62]

One of the most tragic accounts came from Sister Mary McCall, of No. 4 General Hospital, who remembered: 'A very young bride, who'd been brought out to see her wounded husband. She had probably caught the infection before she left, because not long after she arrived in the ward she collapsed.' The young woman died a day or two later, 'and it was terribly tragic for the poor husband. Then later he caught it and died too.'[63]

Even the Armistice came as little comfort to many of the nurses of France. Margaret Ellis recalled bitterly that 'on the day the Armistice was declared, there wasn't one man in the ward who knew. They were all delirious, not conscious enough to know, too ill. There wasn't one man who understood. Not *one* man.'[64]

J. S. Wane, who had left Cambridge University to serve as a civilian clerk with the army, left a first-hand account of suffering from Spanish flu in France. Already noting the presence of 'internal trouble' on 4 November, Wane had recovered sufficiently to enjoy the Armistice celebrations on 11 November, but they were followed by 'a period of long illness'. 'I woke with a stiffness in the chest, and a bad head developed later. All afternoon I worked very mechanically . . . I crawled downstairs to pay the servants and went to bed.' Later, a passing RAMC orderly took his temperature, which was 102°, and

I was removed by stretcher and ambulances on a moonlit night to No. 19 C.C.S., as an influenza case, and crept into a sheeted bed in a marquee. Memory is not very clear about succeeding days. The influenza began to abate, on a light diet, and the old C.O. said to me after two days there 'my disease had nearly run its course'. Temperature on 13th, 101.2 and 102.6, on 14th, 100.2 and 100. Major Clark, who was then my M.O., a curly-haired man, seemed fairly casual.[65]

On 14 November, Wane's twenty-fifth birthday, he received some letters from home and his mother sent him a watch.

On the 15th (evening) I was 103.2 and remained henceforth over 103. On the 17th, Dr Gurling being now in charge of my case, they began to take my temperature every four hours. On the 18th, Dr G's notes first report pneumonia (left lung): that evening I touched 105.2, and the senior sister asked for Mother's address. My memory is vague. An orderly – a Durham miner – used to sponge me, and I remember him pitying my burning hands. Then there was a late afternoon when I asked for the Sister, and was told she could not come for over an hour. I forget what I needed, but I felt very ill, and then alone I can recall my reason straying, for I had some confused ideas about Chinese Labor Corps. 19–21st: temp. varying from 100 to 104, and occasional sleeping drafts. I could feel my lung was wrong, and tried to restrict my breathing. 22nd: right lung also affected, yet I did not seem worse. The sisters gave me aspirin, & Mist Amm & Carb, [ammonium carb, a traditional treatment for cardiac issues] *and deadly nightshade. About now, I was carried into another marquee. One officer, Smith, was there. He shouted two nights and I was drugged to sleep. The third night he died about 9 p.m. I never knew, till Sister Kewley (nights) told me, when I was back in the original marquee. On the 23rd, after eleven days of high fever, my temperature fell to 99.2 and did not rise again more than a point or two over normal. Sister Kewley was from 'near Manchester' and 'homely and very kind.' Gurling came and stethoscoped me daily:- one time he said to the sister – 'And here we have the most uncomplaining man on earth.'*[66]

Eventually, when he was well enough to travel, Wane was carried by stretcher to No. 10 Ambulance Train. There was food but no washing facilities. Wane was taken to Rouen, and thence ambulance and a 'long dark drive' to No. 8 General Hospital. He stayed there two nights and was then to be sent down to Trouville 'because evacuation to England was easy from there'. Wane noted with relief that he was to be treated by a 'pro-alcohol doctor'.[67] Next, he went to No. 74 General Hospital and was transferred to No. 1 Officers ward, 'a Nissan hut which was 12 days my home'.[68]

Private Richard Foot also managed to leave an account of his experiences.[69] Within days of the Armistice, Private Foot's 62nd Division was ordered to march into Germany with the Army of Occupation. This was a very considerable honour, extended to only two Territorial Army Divisions, the other being 51st Highland Division, with whom sixty-two had shared the successful battles at Havrincourt in 1917 and the Marne in 1918. But, in the weeks before the end of the war, this honour was to prove as costly in casualties as any battle.

> During a march from Maubeige to the Rhine bridgehead at Cologne, some 200 miles, reaching the Eifel west of Cologne on Christmas Eve, D/310 lost more men to flu and its consequences than had been killed in the previous 22 months of front line action. With the weather cold, often snowy, often wet it proved difficult to get a pneumonia case to hospital. There were temporary hospitals set up along the way with doctors 'working wonders' but they were walking away from their well organized hospitals and the Railways were not in a sufficient state of repair to allow hospital trains to get through to the forward marching army.[70]
>
> The lucky ones among us who survived the flu were those who were dropped out in a sympathetic warm French, Belgian, or German household, and sheltered till the fever had passed. I was one of the lucky ones.[71]

Private Foot was taken ill at the village of Thy-le-Château. He recalled walking and leading his horse all day and feeling very ill in the afternoon. To make matters worse, he 'had to stand to the salute for half an hour while brigade filed past to the sound of the National Anthem in waltz time,' swaying on his feet with sickness and exhaustion.[72] In his billet above the village bakery, Private Foot had a bottle of five grain tablets of quinine sulphate and a thermometer. Running a temperature of 105° he took thirty grains and passed out. Private Foot's battery went on ahead without him and he stayed there, warm in bed, taking his quinine, for three days until the fever had gone. Then he was lucky enough to get a ride forward in a motor truck and caught up with the Battery fifty miles further along the road.[73]

Sergeant Fitter Othen, from Botley, Hampshire, was among those who were not so lucky. Sergeant Othen was 'a gentle, competent man who had been with the Battery since its formation, and, as his technical capacity required, had been constantly with the guns in action'.[74] Private Foot saw Sergeant Othen into a horse ambulance when he got the flu, 'and he pressed my hand in gratitude as we parted. He died before they got him to a hospital.'[75]

Private Foot's testimony from this dark period of his life ended on a lighter note, with a comical account of a stolen pig, secretly butchered by the farrier, which the Battery officers roasted and served up to their men on Christmas Day. German prisoners of war witnessed the scene with incredulity, as they had never seen their officers treat their men with such informality.

FURTHER AFIELD, IN Salonica, Nurse Dorothy Sutton became a patient and battled against Spanish flu. In a letter home to her mother in High Wycombe, Buckinghamshire, Dorothy wrote:

I have been in bed for three days since I last wrote with 'Flue.'
It has played havoc among the troops out here this summer,
very few have escaped, & the death toll from Pneumonia alone
has been higher than it has ever been since this expedition was
started. I am quite alright again now thogh [sic] *& have been on*
duty again for three days. I was in bed when [the Armistice] *was*
signed, but I heard the salute fired . . . So I knew that once again
the fighting had ceased.[76]

The end of the war had come at last, to the relief of millions; but
the Spanish Lady had no intention of giving up the fight.

CHAPTER EIGHTEEN

Armistice Day

———•———

O N THE MORNING of 11 November 1918, Caroline Playne travelled to Chancery Lane in the City of London, from her home in Hampstead. At first, this journey seemed to be nothing out of the ordinary.

> *Starting from Hampstead to go by omnibus to Chancery Lane that morning, I noticed how everything appeared to be proceeding as 'for the duration' of the war, till we were near Mornington Tube Station. Suddenly maroons went off, a startling explosion just above us. An air-raid, another air-raid! A woman ran out of a house and gazed anxiously at the sky. But before one could recollect that it might mean the Armistice, people were pouring out of buildings, streaming into the streets. The war was ended. Tools must have been downed in no time. Crowds grew bigger every minute.*[1]

The majority of celebrations did not cause alarm, although a celebratory flare fired from the roof of the Air Ministry provoked a cry of 'Air raid! Take cover!' from one senior official.[2] Church bells rang out accompanied by bursts of patriotic singing, tug-boats hooted along the river and, just after eleven, a crowd swelled outside the Mansion House, 'until it filled the heart of

London'.[3] The *Daily Express* reported that 'heartful cheering was followed by a mighty burst of song, of sacred song, the swelling glorious chords of the Doxology – "Praise God from whom all blessing flow".'[4] The newspaper also reminded readers that 11 November was 'Martinmas, the feast-day of the great soldier-saint of France'.[5]

Parliamentary sketch writer Michael MacDonagh was startled by 'The booming of maroons, fired from police and fire-brigade stations, the loud reports of those near at hand being faintly re-echoed by others afar off . . . I rushed out and enquired what was the matter. "The Armistice!" they exclaimed. "The War is over!"'[6] But MacDonagh, while excited by 'the joyous nature of the event' also admitted to feeling ambivalent: 'I felt no joyous exultation. There was relief that the War was over, because it could not now end, as it might have done, in the crowning tragedy of the defeat of the Allies.'[7]

MacDonagh's sentiments were shared by many on Armistice Day. The Great War with Germany was over but the Spanish Lady had not relinquished her hold over London; over two thousand families had lost loved ones to influenza in the past fortnight. Others had been plunged into grief by telegrams from the Admiralty or the War Office telling them that a beloved husband, son or brother would never return home. As far as they were concerned, the Great War had been a tragedy, leaving them so distraught that they wished for nothing more than to spend Armistice Day alone. The Dean of Rochester stoically led a service of Armistice thanksgiving in his cathedral, within hours of learning that his son had died at sea.[8]

After four years of war, the Armistice left some individuals distinctly underwhelmed. Virginia Woolf, writing the closing chapters of her novel *Night and Day*, glanced out of the window to see a housepainter at work across the road. As the celebratory maroons went up, Woolf 'saw the housepainter give one look at the sky and go on with his job'.[9] Woolf, following suit, went back to her novel. The poet Robert Graves, having learned of the deaths of friends, including Wilfred Owen, went out walking near his camp in Wales, 'cursing and sobbing, and thinking of the dead'.[10]

While many continued to experience terrible suffering and loss, there was also a huge collective will to mark the end of the war with wild celebrations. Armistice Day proved to be just the excuse Londoners needed for a massive party. The festivities outdid the proceedings of 'Mafeking Night' (when Londoners had celebrated the relief of the siege of Mafeking during the Second Boer War on 1 January 1900) for magnificence. 'Today's orgy of rejoicing far transcended the other in complete surrender of self-control,' wrote MacDonagh. 'It was enacted in dozens of streets in the City and West End, and there was not a suburb that did not emulate in its little way the uproar of Central London.'[11] The overall effect was reminiscent of the England of long ago. 'It was quite old English. It was Bank Holiday on Hampstead Heath on a vastly stupendous scale.'[12] Even the reserved Caroline Playne allowed herself to become swept up in the excitement:

> There was great liveliness, calls, cries, whistles and hooters sounding... Chancery Lane was very lively... At the corner of Chancery Lane, a stout policeman on point duty was surrounded by girls all clamouring to dance with him. The London bobby rose to the occasion – without a word he took on one after another for a turn round on the narrow pavement as they stood, whilst

his countenance remained impassive. Custom and convention melted away as if a new world had indeed dawned. Officers and privates mixed in equal comradeship. Privates drilled officers, munitionettes commanded platoons made up of both. The spirit of militarism was turned into comedy.[13]

According to Michael MacDonagh, London 'lost all control of itself'.[14]

I hastened from Westminster, feeling assured that the Houses of Parliament and Buckingham Palace would this day, more than ever, be the centres of interesting happenings. The tramcar was packed, all the passengers obviously deeply moved, whether they were chattering and laughing or self-absorbed and silent. The children were let loose from all the schools. As we were passing an elementary school in Kennington Road near 'The Horns', the boys and girls came rushing out, yelling and jumping like mad. There were also many signs that business was being suspended. Shops were being closed and shuttered as on Sundays. Who, indeed, could settle down to work on such a day? Boy scouts on bicycles dashed past us sounding the 'All Clear', as they had so often done after an air-raid.[15]

MacDonagh even spotted an evening newspaper billboard at Westminster Bridge Underground Station, the first he had seen in years, due to the paper shortage. 'It was a heartening sign of London's return to normal life. And what news it proclaimed! "Fighting has ceased on all Fronts!" Hurrah!'[16]

At the Houses of Parliament in Westminster itself, the great bell Big Ben was preparing to strike after four years of silence.

I looked up at the clock. It was less than five minutes to the midday hour. Men from Dent & Co., of Cockspur Street, the custodians of the clock, had just completed the work of putting into action again the apparatus for striking the hours, though not the more complicated mechanism for the chiming of the quarters. Then when the hands of the dials pointed to XII, Big Ben struck the hour, booming it in his deep and solemn tones, so old and so familiar. It was a most dramatic moment. The crowd that had assembled in Parliament Square stood silent and still until the last stroke of the clock, when they burst into shouts of exultation.[17]

Although the day was grey and overcast, with the threat of rain, no one minded the weather. Parliament Street and Whitehall were packed with people, and the streets were hot with excitement. London was possessed by an impulse to 'let business go hang, to get into the streets and yell and sing and dance and weep – above all, to make oneself supremely ridiculous'.[18]

In the thick of the crowd outside the Houses of Parliament, numerous omnibuses, taxicabs and motor cars moved with difficulty, crawling up and down the thoroughfare, all packed with soldiers and civilians, not just inside but on the roofs and cabs as well, 'shouting, yelling, singing snatches of songs and gesticulating as wildly as the pedestrians on the footways – only the more so. Not only did everyone seem bent on bursting their throats in an effort to contribute to the din, but everything that could be banged, blown and rattled seemed to have been pressed into service for a like purpose.'[19]

Among the uproar, MacDonagh could hear

the hooting of motors, the ringing of handbells, the banging of tea-trays, the shrilling of police whistles, and the screaming of toy trumpets in the resulting infernal orchestra. Among the many ludicrous incidents to be observed were a colonel in uniform squatted on the top of a motor-car sounding a dinner-gong and a parson marching at the head of a group of parishioners singing lustily with a Union Jack stuck in the top of his silk hat.[20]

If anyone had any doubts about the war being over, 'the mad follies of the girl clerks of the Government offices in Whitehall must have removed it. They actually showered down upon our heads from the windows masses of official forms relating to the War. Think of it!'[21]

Vast crowds gathered outside Buckingham Palace, waving miniature flags and joining in with a collective staccato cry of 'We want King George!' and the Victoria Memorial was almost obliterated by the swarms of people climbing on it.[22] The King and the Queen appeared on the balcony of the Palace to a tumultuous greeting, as the crowd sang 'Land of Hope and Glory', and then 'Tipperary', which evoked sad memories. 'How many of the boys who sang it in the earlier years of the War will be coming home?' MacDonagh wondered.[23]

In Trafalgar Square, munitions girls who had left their factories in their caps and overalls at the sound of the maroons were romping with soldiers.[24] A rollicking band of young subalterns appeared, blowing police whistles and dancing around a big teddy-bear on wheels decorated with Union Jacks. A group of American soldiers, who had evidently made a raid on a Lyons' or A.B.C. teashop, held waitresses' trays, which they beat like tambourines while singing 'Yankee Doodle'. Taxi cabs crawled by, each with a colonial soldier and a girl sprawling on the roof.[25]

Members of the Stock Exchange, wearing silk hats and frock coats, marched up Northumberland Avenue from the Embankment heading up a 'band' composed of tin-kettles containing stones, the music produced being 'an infernal rattle'.[26]

Witnessing the scenes, MacDonagh felt as if London was engaged in nothing so much as an enormous family party, 'a stupendous house-warming'[27] celebrating the reopening and occupation of a new London and an era of peace and security, after years of care and worry. Everyone taking part was, as befitted such an unparalleled occasion, in extravagantly irresponsible high spirits, 'utterly forgetful of self-propriety, pretentiousness, absorbed in the desire to contribute something to the Pandean frolic'.[28]

The police and the army had agreed that existing bans on bonfires and fireworks would be lifted. This meant that, after dusk, the citizens of Hythe in Kent were able to burn the Kaiser in effigy, although in reality, 'the most hated man in England' was dining as guest of his Dutch host, Count Bentinck, at Amerongen that night.[29] As restraints had also been lifted on domestic lighting, the big cities were brightened for the first time since 'dim glimmer' was imposed with the onset of the Zeppelin raids. Later that night, the Government not only suspended DORA (the Defence of the Realm Act) but put on a brilliant searchlight display.[30]

A crowd of Londoners and servicemen on leave filled Trafalgar Square, often linking hands, singing and swaying. To the writer Osbert Sitwell, serving as a captain with the Grenadier Guards, 'they moved . . . as in a *kermesse* painted by Breughel the Elder'.[31] Captain Sitwell, accompanied by the ballet impresario Sergei

Diaghilev and the dancer-choreographer Leonide Massine, who had been in London performing with the *Ballets Russes*, joined a party at the Adelphi, between Trafalgar Square and the Thames.[32] Fellow guests included D. H. Lawrence and his German-born wife Frieda, cousin of the flying ace Baron von Richthofen, who had been killed seven months before. Close by, in the Union Club overlooking Trafalgar Square, T. E. 'Lawrence of Arabia' attended a quieter celebration, dining with two archaeologists, pre-war friends now in uniform.[33]

Lieutenant Duff Cooper of the Grenadier Guards was in no mood to celebrate but felt compelled to go out. He dined at the Ritz with his fiancée, Lady Diana Manners: 'There was an enormous crowd, the intervals between the courses were interminable and the food when it came was cold and nasty', Duff Cooper confided in his diary. 'I could not enjoy myself and as soon as possible Diana and I slipped away and came back to St James's Street. The streets were full of wild enthusiasm. Diana shared the melancholy with which these filled us – and once she broke down and sobbed.'[34]

The following morning, Duff woke up with a fever, and lay in bed reflecting on 'what a cruel irony it would be to survive the war only to die from flu in his own London flat'.[35] The following month, Duff's sister, Steffie, developed pneumonia after suffering from flu: 'In Dover Street I met Neil Arnott the doctor who told me that Steffie had died not many minutes ago. Her temperature had gone down last night and she had seemed better, but they now knew that her lungs were full of poison and the case was hopeless.'[36]

In Colorado, Katherine Anne Porter immortalized her own reaction to the Armistice in *Pale Horse, Pale Rider*. As Katherine's alter-ego, Miranda, lay in bed, she was awoken by pandemonium in the streets outside the hospital: 'Bells screamed all off key, wrangling together as they collided in mid air, horns and whistles mingled shrilly with cries of human distress; sulphur colored light exploded through the black window pane and flashed away in darkness.'[37]

When Miranda asked what was happening, her nurse, Miss Tanner, replied: 'Hear that? They're celebrating. It's the Armistice. The war is over, my dear.'[38]

But Miranda, who had lost her lover, Adam, to Spanish flu, was in no mood to celebrate. As a ragged chorus of old ladies sent up a ragged recital of 'Oh Say, Can You See?' their voices almost drowned by the bells, Miranda turned her face away. 'Please open the window, please,' she begged. 'I smell death in here.'[39]

The announcement of the Armistice left Miranda numb: 'No more war, no more plague, only the dazed silence that follows the ceasing of the heavy guns; noiseless houses with the shades drawn, empty streets, the dead cold light of tomorrow. Now there would be time for everything.'[40]

In New Haven, Connecticut, John Delano, who had lost many playmates in the epidemic, heard the sounds of the Armistice:

The firehouses blew their whistles and the factories blew their steam whistles and people ran into the streets banging pots and pans together. The boys were coming home! We had a big parade down Grand Street in New Haven and all the military men marched past in their uniforms, their tin hats, and their leggings. Everyone was waving flags, crying and hugging and kissing.[41]

Dan Tonkel, in Goldsboro, North Carolina, was awoken before dawn by his father's pool buddies, who wanted to borrow the large American flag draped across the outside of his store. A few hours later, the flag was on a pole, leading a victory parade as it marched through the town. To Dan, it was a 'joyous' time: 'People poured into the streets, forgetting their fears, hugging and kissing. It was a joyous, joyous time. Throngs paraded through Goldsboro.'[42]

After the parade, life in Goldsboro returned rapidly to normal. 'It was like you'd flipped a switch. Businesses and theaters opened up again. We went back to school. The farmers started coming back with their wagons of produce, and other vendors showed up within a week or two.'[43]

Columba Voltz, recovering from Spanish flu in Philadelphia, along with her parents, was no longer troubled by the funereal 'BONG, BONG, BONG' of the passing bells. Instead: 'The church bells began to ring again so gloriously. I think every church bell in Philadelphia rang that day. It was the most beautiful thing. Hearing the bells, everyone came out of their houses, congregating again, forgetting about the flu, so happy the war was ending. I felt all the joy come back into my life.'[44]

Street life also returned to normal in Anna Milani's lively Italian community: 'All the children were outside again playing. The fisherman came by with his wagon, selling fresh fish. The pushcart salesman was selling his vegetables. My mother came out – all the mothers came out – buying their fish and vegetables.'[45]

At the end of his feature on the Armistice Day celebrations, Michael MacDonagh concluded: 'For long have we been under the shadow of Death and Destruction. Our faces are now set forward – looking towards the Light of Life. At least such of us from whom the Light is not veiled by a mist of tears for those who will not return from the War.'[46]

Tragically, this 'Light of Life' would not shine upon everyone. As Dr Victor Vaughan observed, 'in November the Armistice was signed but there can be no armistice between medicine and disease'.[47]

The Spanish Lady did not disappear at the end of the war. In Manchester, she stalked through the crowds gathering in Albert Square to celebrate the Armistice, despite Chief Medical Officer of Health Dr. James Niven's warnings about the consequences of such mass gatherings. While the *Manchester Evening News* feared that 'by leaving their homes it is quite probable that many millions of microbes have been passed to one another',[48] Niven's advice went unheeded as thousands of people poured into the city to celebrate. By the last week of November 1918, Niven had recorded 383 influenza deaths in one week, twice the number who had perished in the last week of June. 'A real calamity had befallen the city.'[49]

In Canada, the Spanish Lady travelled home with returning soldiers, while in New Zealand, she triggered the fatal outbreak of 'Armistice Flu'.

CHAPTER NINETEEN

BLACK NOVEMBER

————◆·◆————

T HE NEWS THAT an Armistice was to be signed reached New Zealand at nine o'clock on Tuesday, 12 November 1918. As the news spread, the main streets of every city and town were jammed with people and scenes of wild celebration.[1] Trams stopped running, shops and businesses stood empty, court sessions were suspended and cinema managers 'abandoned any idea of entertaining the public'. Daily life ground to a halt, but it was joy that brought the streets to a standstill, and not the Spanish Lady. 'Everybody in the streets seemed to have a flag, and everybody in this case meant thousands.'[2]

In Christchurch, Stan Seymour, a carpenter's apprentice aged sixteen, recalled:

> *I remember being in Cathedral Square for the Armistice celebrations. It was the biggest crowd I'd ever seen. There were a lot of men in uniform, just returned from overseas, and the crowd was quite drunk with rejoicing. There were people hugging and kissing total strangers. The crowd was so tightly packed that people's elbows jabbed my ribs, and big boots trod on my toes . . .*[3]

According to Alex Dickie, a young lad from Gore, the following day was declared a general holiday and the celebrations took the form of a sports carnival at the Showgrounds.

We pupils of the Gore School marched there and the railway locomotives kept up their almost non-stop 'Hip, hip, hurrah' whistling. As we marched along, our master, 'Snowy' Nelson, flanked himself alongside each class in turn to tell us not to return to school next day and to wait for a notice when to return. That was the start of a long summer vacation.[4]

But this enticing prospect would prove to be anything but enjoyable. A sudden epidemic of influenza had closed the schools, and while some people were dancing in the streets to celebrate the Armistice, others were already in mourning. Laura Hardy, a housewife from Onehunga, then an outer suburb of Auckland, recalled that on Armistice Day, 'funerals were passing our house continually all day. Coffins were turned out by the hundred and were just made of rough boards . . . To this sad and sorrowing community came the news of the Armistice. There were few families which felt like rejoicing.'[5]

Kate Shaw's brother, Sergeant Angus Carnachan, was a young soldier in Featherston Military Camp when the news of the Armistice came through. Angus, who had not quite recovered from an attack of influenza, went into town to join in the celebrations, suffered a relapse and died. Kate recalled a 'nightmare journey' by train the following day as she travelled to collect her sister-in-law. 'All along the line we saw funeral after funeral, victims of the epidemic.'[6]

In Christchurch, young Stan Seymour was one of the first to help when Spanish flu hit his neighbourhood, a well-to-do area of town called Fendalton. Stan accompanied his mother on visits to the sick, carrying groceries and cleaning their houses. After a few days, even the most affluent homes began to stink of rotting food and overflowing chamber pots. 'I can remember my mother rolling up the long sleeves of her dress and grimly setting to work, to clean up sordid messes . . .' Stan recalled.[7]

One smell was worse than the rest combined. 'In houses where someone had died and the body was awaiting removal, there was quite a different smell, not the same as the rotting food and unemptied chamber pots, but quite distinctive.'[8]

New Zealand's doctors and nurses, their ranks already culled by the war, struggled to cope with the pandemic. One of the most outstanding was Dr Margaret Cruikshank, only the second woman to graduate in medicine from the Otago Medical School, in 1897, the first to register as a doctor and the first to enter general practice. She had also attended medical school in Edinburgh and Dublin.[9] When Dr Cruikshank's colleague, Dr Barclay, volunteered for the Medical Corps, Dr Cruikshank took sole charge of their practice, and took over Dr Barclay's car. Dr Cruikshank worked tirelessly during the outbreak, and when her driver came down with influenza, she used her bicycle for calls within the town, and a horse for those further afield.[10]

Dr David Lloyd Clay, of Wellington, had already survived one influenza epidemic and initially had no fears when the new outbreak hit Wellington in 1918. As a medical student at the Manchester Infirmary during the 1889–90 Russian flu epidemic, when 8,800 people died in England and Wales, Dr Clay believed he knew his enemy. 'They were mostly the very elderly and complications were rare,' he said of his British patients. But Dr Clay watched with mounting concern as he realized that this new strain of influenza presented disturbing features.

This 1918 flu seemed clinically quite different . . . Early in the case the patient showed signs of distress. Grave and alarming symptoms appeared in 24 to 36 hours. The headache was intense. The delirium was sometimes quiet, at other times violent, and at other times almost maniacal. The patient had excruciating pains in the chest. A common expression among patients was, 'Doctor, they have taken out the lining from my inside!' Men cried out in their pain, most especially in the severer cases. The temperature rose to about 104°, and as the cough became worse, bleeding started from the nose, the lungs and sometimes from the rectum.[11]

Dr Clay was desperately overworked during the epidemic. On the fourth day after Spanish flu appeared in Wellington, he worked for 22 hours without a break, visiting 152 houses and travelling 150 miles. He had his work cut out for him, with an average of two cases in every house.[12]

Young Arthur Cormack saw his home town transformed within days of the Armistice games in Gore:

The main street had the appearance of being a real ghost town. More than half the businesses were closed, and those that were open might as well be closed too, for there were no people about apart from Boy Scouts gathering for their late-afternoon tour of duty. The scouts did a marvellous job taking cooked food to stricken households. This food was prepared in the Cookery Technical block behind the Gore High School by Miss MacHutchison and Mrs Pigeon. They and their helpers rendered a service that just couldn't be rendered in words.[13]

The service was much needed. One lady recalled one case

That has stayed in my memory through all the years told of a little boy who, feeling the pinch of hunger, went to ask the butcher for some meat. He then asked the butcher how to cook it. The butcher asked why his mother wouldn't be cooking it. The little boy replied that his parents had been asleep in bed for two days. The butcher accompanied the lad home to find that they were asleep permanently.[14]

In Christchurch, Stan Seymour, who had been helping his mother care for the influenza patients, became a victim of Spanish flu himself:

I had a very high fever with tremendous sweating. My pajamas and bedclothes became completely sodden. Mother said she could wring the moisture out of my pajamas. I can recall her sponging me down to reduce the fever. Delirium was another distinctive symptom . . . I'd never had dreams like these before or since: they were terrifying, whirling, out-of-control dreams, with horrible fantasies.

I developed tremendous swellings under my armpits, so big that I couldn't lay my arms along my sides, and big purple-black blotches on my thighs. To any educated person, these were just like the symptoms of the medieval Black Death. Some people at the time said it was only flu, but it seemed more like a plague.

Stan had his own theories as to the origins of this mysterious and deadly disease, sentiments which echo those of victims from Europe, South Africa and the United States: 'I still reckon it had something to do with the First World War, all those bodies rotting in the open air in no man's land . . .'[15]

Syd Muirhead of Oamaru, South Island, recalled his father return home from work earlier than usual, flushed and running a high temperature:

Mother immediately packed him off to bed in the front room, which was reserved for visitors or special occasions, with extra towels, a basin and a container for formalin, a formaldehyde solution used as disinfectant. Dad indicated that he could not eat or drink – he had lost his voice – but Mother insisted that he have a plate of gruel. With pencil and paper and hand signals, Dad indicated that he had a bottle of whiskey planted in a cupboard for just such an emergency, and if she would add some to the gruel he would eat it. In all innocence, Mother tipped half a bottle of neat whiskey into the gruel. Dad drank it quickly and very soon broke out in a sweat. He perspired copiously and the bedclothes had to be changed several times. He seemed to be delirious, and his remarks on regaining his voice were quite incoherent for some time. But he made a quick recovery and always maintained that it was the quantity of whiskey and the shock and impact that brought about this miraculous recovery.[16]

Laura McQuilkin, a waitress at the Empire Hotel, 'got the flu very bad'.

It came on very sudden one night after giving myself a bath. I got into bed and left the window wide open. Different people in the hotel were yelling out, 'Laura, come here, you're

*wanted', but I stayed under the blankets, fresh air blowing
over me all night.*

*Next morning, Mr. Ken the chemist and a doctor came
through the hotel spraying everyone with formalin. I told them I
could see playing cards all over the ceiling. My tongue was very
big. Mr. Ken brought quinine medicine for me. They wanted to
move me over to the Winter Show building, but I told them to
leave me alone where I was.*

*They said afterwards I was turning black and they thought
I was a goner. There were several others who died; the boss's
wife, a housemaid, a barman and barmaid were all carried
out on stretchers. But I survived. I went home for a week to see
Mother, and it had been just as bad in the Wairarapa.*[17]

For overworked doctors and nurses the proceedings were
occasionally diverted by scenes tinged with black comedy.
At Christchurch Hospital, Nurse Winifred Muff treated a
honeymooning couple who had been admitted after collapsing at
Addington Races.

*The wife was taken back to her hotel, but nobody knew where
it was. The husband was admitted to my ward. He was very
delirious, singing hymns one minute, cursing the next. He got
out when no one was looking and, in his nightshirt, ran out of
the grounds to the Riccarton Hotel. The porters went to fetch
him with a wheelbarrow because there was no other transport
available. He died later that same day.*[18]

Another delirious patient, a wealthy farmer, told Nurse Muff:
'Don't stop me! I have to go twenty miles for a bedpan. My man
has a horse waiting for me.'[19]

These events may not have seemed amusing at the time, but once the nurses went for their break and exchanged stories, 'we saw the funny side of things', such as the doctor who came in with a sticky stethoscope. He had been examining an old lady and listening to her chest, but when he went to get up, the stethoscope stayed stuck fast. 'Treacle,' she said, 'it's very good for a cold!'[20]

Dorothy Hoben of Wellington, a volunteer nurse at a temporary hospital set up at the former Thorndon Normal School, recalled: 'One night the ambulance men brought in a fat old woman who must have weighed at least sixteen stone and was incredibly dirty. We thought she had black stockings on, until we discovered it was dirt! . . . She was so very, very ill. At least the poor old soul died clean.'[21]

In some cases, New Zealand's Spanish flu epidemic brought out the good in people, in unexpected ways. Peggy Clark, of Te Awamutu, remembered that:

During the worst of the crisis a man claiming to be a doctor appeared on the scene and worked ably and selflessly among the victims. Many years later Dad received a letter from the Palmerston North courthouse asking for information about this 'doctor', who had named Dad as a referee. It turned out that he was an escaper from Waikeria Prison in 1918 and had no medical qualifications whatsoever. Apparently he was in trouble again. Dad was pleased to write back his admiration of the man's work in the epidemic.[22]

In some cases, madness seemed the only sane response to the ongoing horror. Jean Forrester, *née* Quoi, of Auckland, was a member of the St John Ambulance Brigade and worked in an emergency hospital set up in Seddon Memorial Tech. One of Jean's patients, described as 'a Hindu man', 'was delirious and kept asking if it was four o'clock, as he was going to die then. Four o'clock came and went, but he did not die. He just couldn't accept that he hadn't died, and became so deranged in his ravings that he was removed to the mental hospital.'[23]

Maurice O'Callaghan, of the St John Ambulance Brigade, Auckland, made a horrific discovery when called to a house in Grey Lynn: 'We found a man who had been dead three days. His body was in the bed, and his wife was lying in the same bed, not dead but driven out of her mind with a dead husband and could not get up . . .'[24]

Volunteer nurse Ivy Landreth, of Owaka, South Otago, remembered one horrific night when a man cut his throat and died while she was on duty. 'My brother was one of those who had to deal with him. I remember my brother saying he had never experienced anything so bad all the time he was at the war, in spite of the fact that he had lost his left arm at Passchendaele.'[25]

In New Zealand, as in other parts of the world, the pandemic was responsible for many poignant scenes of family tragedy. At Kouipapa, Catlins District, Sister May Newman, a hospital nurse, was ordered by the police to work in an emergency hospital. This was in spite of the fact that the Newman family home had just burned to the ground and May was supposed to be caring for her motherless siblings. One afternoon their brother, Douglas Newman, was discovered collapsed by the side of the road with his horse standing by. Douglas was taken to hospital at Owaka, where it emerged that May, too, had become a patient. May had been on duty on the night when another patient had cut his own throat, and had held his head down while the doctor stitched his throat back together. Douglas survived, but when he recovered it was to be told that May had passed away. Douglas maintained that May had died as a result of the nursing duties she had been compelled to take on. 'This man was breathing directly onto my sister's face,' he said, 'and this I believe was the reason she caught the plague.'[26]

When Spanish flu hit the Hawkins family, dairy farmers in Limehills, near Winton, Southland, almost everyone fell sick. Edith Hawkins, a child at the time, remembered her mother refusing to go to bed but sitting up with her four-month-old son, Jim, who did not have influenza. Occasionally, she would sprinkle sulphur over the hot coals to fumigate the house and Edith enjoyed 'watching the pretty colors this made as it burned'.[27]

The family soon recovered with the exception of Edith's father, who died on 24 November, aged just thirty-three.

We were lucky to get a coffin right away, though it was a lady's coffin covered in pale blue velvet. Grandad Holland and Grandad Anderson harnessed up old Sandy the horse and yoked him into the spring cart that Dad used for carting the milk to the factory. Friends helped lift the casket into the cart. The two men sat one on each side of it at the front.[28]

As Edith sat on the doorstep, her mother stood in the doorway, 'holding a twin by each hand, and we watched them drive away down the road, round the corner and out of sight'.[29]

Just as they had done in North America and South Africa, the native population endured a considerably higher death rate than the white settlers. In the epidemic of 1918–19 a total of 8,573 New Zealanders died. This included 2,160 Maori out of an estimated

Maori population of 51,000.[30] According to Geoffrey W. Rice, author of *Black November: The 1918 Influenza Pandemic in New Zealand*, there was 'a huge difference between European and Maori death rates' in New Zealand, and the 'Maori were seven times more likely than Europeans to die from the flu'.[31] On 22 November 1918, the *Pukekohe and Waiuku Times* carried this desperate plea for help:

> *Te Awamutu is pitiable. There is no business being done and the deaths are appalling. The great trouble here is the scattered nature of the settlement. Families are stricken and lie about until almost past hope before they are discovered … It is simply horrible.*
>
> *The Maoris at Parawere are suffering badly and there is very little hope for them as there are very few people left even to attend to white people. They are talking of opening the town hall as a temporary hospital similar to Te Awamutu, but there is no help available.*
>
> *Do not let this plague get the upper hand in Pukekohe. Take drastic measures.*[32]

Julius Hogben, running an emergency hospital in Thames, was in charge of a ward to which most of the Maoris were sent. Many would only go to hospital as a last resort. 'They said that if you went there you would die, and, because of the advanced stage of the disease they were in on arrival, some of them did. Apart from influenza, some of them were suffering from malnutrition.'[33]

One fourteen-year-old boy was admitted described as 'skin and bone and sores', and died within a day. It later emerged that, during the previous winter, he had lived on little more than dried shark.[34] Florence Harsant, of Tanoa, Northland, recalled a certain air of fatalism among the Maoris: 'To show you how quickly it took its victims, a Maori neighbor of ours called Andrew passed the house on horseback one day when mother was on the veranda. "Goodbye, missus, goodbye," he called out. "I's sick, I won't be here tomorrow." And indeed next morning he was dead.'[35]

Nursing patients in the more remote areas of New Zealand presented a considerable logistical challenge. Ivy Driffell, of Rawene, Hokianga, was a young nurse in Hokianga Hospital in 1918:

> I was just a young nurse but, being a good rider, was sent to a very backblock Maori settlement, first having to cross the Hokianga River by launch from Opononi and then ride over sandhills and beach ... There were no doctors, chemists or antibiotics, just a bottle of brandy and lots of aspirins, and the use of our own judgement. Numbers of Maoris died before we arrived and many after.
>
> I rode forty-odd miles daily, there were so many side tracks. One home I went to, a father, mother and small boy were down, the boy obviously dying, so I gave him all I could and had to leave him. Next morning he had died and the parents had been carried on stretchers up a ladder into a large corn crib. Up I went and saw that the father was not so bad but the mother was failing. I gave her all I could, then talked to the old man and gave him a brandy and aspirin. He was furious and said, 'That's not fair, you gave her more than me!' She died that night.[36]

Florence Harsant, a 'Maori Organizer' for the Women's Christian Temperance Movement, had grown up fluent in the language as her father taught in a Maori school. She remembered a doctor telling her that the influenza epidemic 'was the nearest thing to the Black Plague he had ever seen'.[37]

One of Florence's duties was to cut the Maori women's hair, as the doctor insisted that 'the weight of the hair and the heat it generated would not help their high temperatures'.[38]

One girl, a bride of one month, had the most lovely head of long brown hair, her husband's pride and joy. No matter what we did, we could not get her temperature down. At last the doctor told me her hair must be cut off. I broke the news to her husband, and while tears rolled down his cheeks (and, I must admit, mine too) I cut those lovely tresses away. I gathered up her hair and gave it to him. Hair is very sacred to the Maoris. He wept as he took it away to bury it. After sponging her down, then attending to some other patients, I came back to find that her fever had dropped. She was one who lived.[39]

As usual, the outbreak took its toll on the medical profession, too. Dr Charles Little had served the district between Waikari and Waiau and was married to Hephzibah, a nurse at Christchurch Hospital. They had both worked tirelessly during the early stages of the epidemic, and both contracted influenza. Hephzibah died on 22 November, in the same hospital where she had trained, and Dr Little died of pneumonia four days later. A stunned community built a hospital in their memory, with a statue of Dr Little gazing out at the community for which he gave his life; tellingly, there is no statue to Hephzibah.[40] However, Dr Margaret Cruikshank, revered in the district as a dedicated general practitioner, was commemorated in a statue at Seddon Park, Waimate, in 1923.

Dr Cruikshank had died of pneumonia on 28 November, and her funeral was one of the largest ever seen in Waimate.[41]

Over in Australia, public health officials were confident that they had prevented the arrival of Spanish flu. Warned from afar as the epidemic advanced across Europe, Africa and North and South America, Australians had the opportunity to arm themselves and enact strict quarantine measures. Initially, this had proved successful. But in January 1919 the first cases of killer influenza were reported in the *Sydney Morning Herald*, and within weeks Australia's most populated city had fallen victim to the Spanish Lady. The *Herald*, realizing that the city was in terrible danger, issued this edict:

TO THE PEOPLE OF NEW SOUTH WALES

A danger greater than war faces the State of New South Wales and threatens the lives of all. Each day the progress of the battle is published in the Press. Watch out for it. Follow the advice given and the fight can be won.[42]

Stressing that 'the many shall not be placed in danger by the few', the paper urged readers to wear a mask. 'Those who are not doing so are not showing their independence – they are only showing their indifference for the lives of others – for the lives of the women and the helpless little children who cannot help themselves.'[43]

Strict quarantine regulations introduced into Sydney doubtless saved lives. As in the United States, all places of public entertainment were closed, along with bars and even public telephones; church services and race meetings were banned. The wearing of masks in public became compulsory.

But even Sydney could not outwit the Spanish Lady. The mortality rate climbed, and by the end of the year 3,500 Sydney residents had died, among the total 12,000 Australians who had lost their lives, illustrating that it was impossible to isolate a continent from Spanish flu, however strict the quarantine procedures.

CHAPTER TWENTY

Aftermath

※

THE ARMISTICE DID not bring about the demise of the Spanish Lady. Instead, after a vicious campaign against humanity in the closing months of 1918, she lingered on wretchedly like an unloved invalid for the best part of another year. At the first peacetime Christmas in four years, the London *Times* commented ruefully that 'Never since the Black Death has such a plague swept over the world; never, perhaps, has a plague been more stoically accepted.'[1]

Two weeks later, one of Britain's youngest war heroes became one of the Spanish Lady's last victims of the year. William Leefe Robinson VC, the first British pilot to shoot down a German aircraft over Britain, died of influenza on 31 December 1918, aged just twenty-three. Known as 'Billy', Leefe Robinson was born on his father's coffee estate in Coorg, India, on 14 July 1895.[2] Sent to public school in England, Billy proved to be sporty rather than academic, and attended Sandhurst military academy before being gazetted into the Worcestershire Regiment in December 1914. The following March, Billy joined the Royal Flying Corps in France, qualifying as a pilot in September 1915. Billy had an absolute passion for flying: 'You have no idea how beautiful it is above the clouds . . . I love flying more and more every day, and the work is even more interesting than it was,' he wrote in a letter home.[3]

Billy was posted to No. 39 Home Defence Squadron, a night-flying squadron near Hornchurch in Essex, and had his first chance to shoot down a Zeppelin in April 1916 but could not get his aircraft into position for an effective attack. However, on the night of 23 September, he was given another chance. Engaged on a routine 'search and find' operation flying at around 10,000 feet between the airfield and Joyce Green, Billy spotted a Zeppelin at 1.10 a.m., caught in two searchlight beams over Woolwich, south-east London. He set off in pursuit but lost the Zeppelin in thick cloud.[4] By this time, the searchlights over Finsbury Park, north London, had spotted another airship, one of sixteen on a mass raid, and anti-aircraft guns opened fire. Billy was low on fuel but he gave chase, joined by two comrades. As anti-aircraft fire lit up the sky, the airship unloaded its deadly cargo and soared higher. Billy emptied two drums of ammunition into the airship, but it flew on, apparently indestructible. He made another attack from astern and fired his last drum into the airship's twin rudders.

'When the colossal thing actually burst into flames of course it was a glorious sight,' Billy later wrote to his parents. 'Wonderful! It literally lit up all the sky around and me as well of course – I saw my machine as in the fire light – and sat still half dazed staring at the wonderful sight before me, not realizing to the least degree the wonderful thing that had happened!'[5]

'My feelings?' Billy continued. 'Can I describe my feelings? I hardly know how I felt as I watched the huge mass gradually turn on end, and – as it seemed to me – slowly sink, one glowing, blazing mass – I gradually realized what I had done and grew wild with excitement.'[6]

The airship burst into flames and plunged to earth, as thousands of Londoners looked on and cheered. It eventually crashed into a field in Cuffley, Hertfordshire. In fact, it had been a wooden-frame Schütte-Lanz machine, not strictly a Zeppelin, but this distinction was of little importance to the public and politicians. While Billy was back at Sutton's Farm writing his report and sleeping, the excitement of 'Zepp Sunday' broke out across London, and Billy woke up to find that he had become a hero. Within forty-eight hours, he had been awarded a Victoria Cross, the first man to receive one for action over the United Kingdom, and one of only nineteen awarded to airmen during the First World War. After receiving his VC from King George at Windsor Castle, Billy modestly told the press that, 'I only did my job.'[7]

He was recognized now wherever he went, whether in uniform or in mufti. People turned and stared, policemen saluted him, porters and waiters bowed and scraped, babies, flowers and even hats were named after him. As Billy himself commented, 'Oh, it's too thick!'[8] His fame also made him a magnet for young women, but he never seemed to complain about that. Soon after being awarded his VC, he was sent back to France as a flight commander and shot down by Manfred von Richthofen, the 'Red Baron', in 1917.[9]

Taken prisoner by the Germans, Billy attempted to escape four times in as many months, was court martialled and placed in solitary confinement. Sent on to Holzminden prison camp, in Lower Saxony, which was notorious for its brutality, Billy's health suffered. By the time he was released, on 14 December 1918, he had become desperately weak. As if this was not enough, he contracted influenza and, in his delirium, relived the horrors of his captivity. One of the greatest heroes of the First World War, Billy died on New Year's Eve, 1918.[10] Many other anonymous prisoners of war from both sides died of Spanish flu, among them 30,000 Austrian troops who perished between August 1918 and August 1919.[11]

Billy had become yet another victim of 'the appalling outbreak of "influenza"', as *The Illustrated London News* referred to it. 'From the high North to the Tropics its victims are to be counted by the thousand, and it is still at its deadly work.'[12]

Among the Spanish Lady's 1919 victims were the mother and sister of baby John Burgess Wilson, whose father arrived home in Manchester from the army to discover:

> *My mother and sister dead ... The Spanish Influenza pandemic had struck Harpurhey. There was no doubt of the existence of a God; only the Supreme Being could contrive so brilliant an afterpiece to four years of unprecedented suffering and devastation. I apparently was chuckling in my cot while my mother and sister lay dead on a bed in the same room.*[13]

The fact that baby John was 'chuckling' when his father arrived home instead of 'howling for food' was thanks to Dr James Niven; Manchester's Chief Medical Officer had mobilized mass provisions of food, particularly baby food, throughout the city as a response to the deadly second wave. A kindly neighbour had fed Baby Burgess Wilson a bottle of Glaxo baby food shortly before being struck down herself. The baby survived, and grew up to be novelist Anthony Burgess, author of *A Clockwork Orange*.[14]

In March 1919, Clementine Churchill's nanny Isabelle was struck down with Spanish flu. In her delirium, Isabelle took little Marigold Churchill, daughter of Clemmie and Winston, into bed with her. Clementine retrieved the child and spent the night running up and downstairs between the two. Marigold survived, but Isabelle perished.[15]

Spanish flu was implicated in an outbreak of murder suicides, apparently caused by the depression that was a common feature of disease. Newspapers on both sides of the Atlantic carried stories of men and women who attempted to slay their families. In the East End of London an infected docker, James Shaw, killed himself and one child with a knife; an older daughter ran away and escaped.[16]

Sir Mark Sykes' death at the Paris Peace Conference on 16 February 1919, and his posthumous contribution to influenza research, has already been discussed. But the warm weather and confluence of delegates from all over the world contributed to ideal conditions for the spread of influenza in a city that had already experienced an influenza epidemic. It was at this same conference that American President Woodrow Wilson fell sick, although the actual nature of his illness remains a matter of conjecture. Wilson was taken ill at the conference on 3 April 1919 with what appeared to be the symptoms of gastric flu.[17] After spending five days in bed, Wilson returned to the table on 8 April. But the President seemed utterly changed by the experience. Wilson's secret service man, Edmund Starling, noted that Wilson seemed to have lost his 'old quickness of grasp',[18] while Herbert Hoover observed that negotiating with Wilson was like pushing against 'an unwilling mind'.[19] Others commented on Wilson's drooping left eye and facial spasms. Nevertheless, Wilson's physician, Cary Grayson, informed Prime Minister David Lloyd George and other delegates that the President had suffered an attack of influenza.[20] It was a convincing scenario: even before he reached flu-ridden Paris,

Wilson had sailed to Europe aboard the *George Washington*, upon which eighty doughboys had perished from influenza in a single crossing a few weeks earlier. Among those who cheered as Wilson drove through the streets of Paris was Private Pressley, the same young soldier who had witnessed influenza in London and survived his own bout of Spanish flu in France.[21] But Woodrow Wilson's attack of 'influenza' may have been nothing more than a cover-up. Wilson, who was being treated for hypertension, had already suffered a number of strokes, but the public could not be allowed to know this: such a revelation would have shattered confidence in their leader, the man with the plan to end all wars. Dr Grayson was very conscious that his patient had undergone a serious episode, noting a curious scene during which Wilson rearranged the furniture in his Paris apartment, claiming that he didn't like the way the colours of the furniture appeared to fight against each other. 'The greens and the reds are all mixed up here and there is no harmony. Here is a big purple, high-backed covered chair, which is like the Purple Cow, strayed off to itself, and it is placed where the light shines on it too brightly.'[22] Wilson appeared to recover within a few days, but he was never quite the same again. The following September, Wilson suffered a catastrophic stroke and was forced to retire from public life.

Medical researchers had battled throughout 1918 to find a cure for a disease that they could scarcely identify, and in some cases the doctors themselves became victims. One such was Major H. Graeme Gibson, RAMC, who died in February 1919 at the No. 2 Stationary Hospital, Abbeville, along with two colleagues.

Major Gibson was commemorated in his obituaries as a 'martyr to science'. Working alongside Major Bowman of the

Canadian Army Medical Corps, and Captain Connor of the Australian Army Medical Corps, Major Gibson had:

> *Completed the discovery of what is very probably indeed the causative germ of this influenza epidemic. A preliminary note regarding this germ was published by these doctors on 14 December 1918, in the* British Medical Journal, *and thus Major Graeme Gibson's work takes precedence over later publications. At the time, however, the proof of the discovery was not complete. It has now been completed, as we understand; and Major Gibson's death furnishes a part of the evidence. His eagerness and enthusiasm led him to work so hard that he finally fell a victim to the very virulent strains of the germ with which he was experimenting. He himself caught the influenza, and pneumonia followed.*[23]

Sir Walter Morley Fletcher, the dynamic secretary of the Medical Research Council, was shocked by the deaths of Gibson and his colleagues, as they were 'all bowled over with this beastly thing'.[24] Gibson and his team were not the only victims; further correspondence to and from Fletcher indicates that many researchers were struck down with influenza, adding sick leave to the list of obstacles to developing a vaccine.[25]

Research into the causes of the Spanish Lady was not without its bizarre moments. On one occasion a monkey, destined to be used as a test subject, escaped from the laboratory. According to Fletcher:

> *Next day he was seen in New Scotland Yard, presumably about to report himself to the police. Chased by a policeman he crossed*

Whitehall, and was run over by a motor-bus. When they tried
to pick up the dead body, he came to life and ran up the façade
of the Home Office, to the great delight of a large crowd. He was
found dead at the top of the Home Office that evening, dead, but
not dishonoured.[26]

Walter Fletcher lived through the Spanish flu epidemic, but his
health had already been compromised by double pneumonia and
pleurisy in 1916. A typical example of a doctor making a terrible
patient, Fletcher undermined his health with his remorseless
work ethic and never fully recovered from the operation to drain
his lungs; an infection at the wound site eventually killed him at
the age of sixty-three.

Throughout the Spanish flu epidemic, Fletcher's dedication
to combating the disease had been absolute. 'That late summer
and autumn saw the appalling ravages of the black influenza
pandemic,'[26] wrote Fletcher's wife, Maisie. 'Walter himself
fortunately escaped, but he was terribly concerned about it, and
from then on he initiated a real attack on the disease.'[27] This
was to be Fletcher's life's work, an 'attack' on influenza 'which
was to include all the work done on dogs' distemper, and the
starting of the Field Laboratories up at Mill Hill where the vast
Laboratory of the Medical Research Council was to be built
thirty years later'.[28]

For some individuals, Spanish flu bequeathed such a legacy
of pain that they could not live with the consequences, even
when the pandemic had ceased. Dr James Niven, Manchester's
Chief Medical Officer of Health, had done much to contain
the first wave of influenza when it hit the city in June 1918.
His practical measures and recommendations to the city

authorities saved many lives. But Manchester's city fathers ignored Niven's advice to ban Armistice celebrations, with the result that the death rate soared following the mass gatherings of 11 November. In the years that followed, Niven became increasingly despondent, despite his outstanding professional reputation and achievements. On 28 September 1925, Niven travelled to the Isle of Man and checked into a hotel. Two days later, his body was discovered in Onchan Harbour. Niven had taken an overdose, and swum out to sea.

For others, though, it was a happier story. Vera Brittain, having served as a VAD in France and London, returned to her studies at the University of Oxford after the war and wrote about her experiences in *Testament of Youth*, one of the most graphic memoirs of the First World War. J. S. Wane, the army clerk who had chronicled his attack of Spanish flu in his diary while serving in France, also managed to complete his degree. Wane eventually returned home to England in the autumn of 1918, to be reunited with a young woman who, if not exactly his sweetheart, appeared to have been waiting for him. On Friday 31 January 1919, Wane recorded the experience of at last being able to graduate from Cambridge University: 'The degrees were given in the Senate House at 2: I wore uniform, and we three went up together to the throne, holding Joey's hand.' ('Joey' was Vice Chancellor Sir Arthur Everett Shipley, and the hand-holding refers to the ancient Cambridge tradition of holding the VC's hand as the degree is conferred.)[29]

What of the USS *Leviathan*, the stricken ship which had carried flu-ridden doughboys to France? Following the Armistice, the vessel was decommissioned. She had one other claim to fame when a future film star served on board as a coxswain between 27 November 1918 and February 1919. His name was Humphrey Bogart.[30] After a complete refit, the *Leviathan* returned to civilian life as an American passenger ship, her war service making her, if anything, more popular than in her glamorous pre-war days. She flourished during Prohibition, moored in waters outside US jurisdiction to serve 'medicinal alcohol' to all who sailed out to her. But in the end it was the Great Depression, and not the German U-boats, that brought about her downfall. High-maintenance and too expensive to operate, the USS *Leviathan* made her final voyage on 14 February 1938 to the breaker's yard at Rosyth, Scotland, where she was broken up for scrap. Nothing of the ship now remains, apart from the memories of those who served on her, and this celebratory address:

> We view the grandeur of thy bulk,
> And gaze with wonder and with awe,
> At thy great magnitude and might,
> Which surpass visions we foresaw.[31]

In Philadelphia, life swiftly returned to normal for Columba Voltz and her friend Katherine. Soon they were playing their old familiar games again, and roller skating through the park. 'Everything seemed so marvelous. I knew my uncles would be coming home from army camps; and they hadn't gotten sick. Everyone in our family had recovered from the flu and nobody else I knew was sick. We were all very, very happy. The war was over and the flu was practically gone. Peace and health had returned to the city.'[32]

But Anna Milani never forgot the loss of her little brother, Harry: 'I keep thinking about it. My brothers and sisters – there are eight of us living now – we talk about the flu, how we were all sick, what we went through. We talk about Harry.'[33]

For Mary McCarthy, the loss of her parents and her comfortable, middle-class family life proved more difficult to comprehend. Mary recalled visiting her parents' grave with her brothers as

> *a regular Sunday activity, which involved long streetcar trips or endless walking or waiting, and that had the peculiarly fatigued, dusty, proletarianised character of American municipal entertainment. The two mounds that were our parents associated themselves in our minds with Civil War cannon balls and monuments to the doughboy dead; we contemplated them stolidly, waiting for a sensation, but those twin grass beds, with their junior-executive headstones, elicited nothing whatever.*[34]

In retrospect, Mary credited Spanish flu for changing the course of her existence. If her parents had lived, Mary believed, her own life would have been far more conventional: marriage to an Irish lawyer, rounds of golf and membership of a Catholic book club.[35] As it was, the controversial author of *The Group* became an intellectual firebrand and mainstay of *The Partisan Review* and *The New York Review of Books*. Mary's pragmatism was a very different response from that of William Maxell, who became Mary's editor at the *New Yorker*. William recalled a poignant sense of loss when his own mother and new-born sibling died from the disease: 'From that time on there was a sadness which had not existed before, a deep down sadness that never went away. We aren't safe. Nobody's safe. Terrible things can happen to anyone at any time.'[36]

CHAPTER TWENTY-ONE

'VIRAL ARCHAEOLOGY'

⪼•⪻

PRIVATE HARRY UNDERDOWN, the English soldier who died at No. 24 Hospital in February 1917, now rests in peace beneath his plain white headstone in Étaples military cemetery, blissfully unaware of his status as the potential 'Patient Zero'.[1]

While the body of Harry lies undisturbed, the bodies of many other victims may hold the secret of the deadly virus, providing more information about the aetiology and causes of Spanish flu to avert the threat of future pandemics. This form of research has been conducted over the past seventy years, first by Swedish medical student Johan V. Hultin, later by Jeffery Taubenberger of the Armed Forces Institute of Pathology, Washington, DC and Professor John Oxford of the Royal London Hospital Medical School. While these men and their teams sought answers from the preserved bodies of influenza victims, it was not until the virus took a new and unexpected form, killing a three-year-old child in Hong Kong in 1997, that influenza research took on a new urgency.

In 1950, Johan V. Hultin (born 1925) had been attending medical school at the University of Uppsala 'as part of a special program in Swedish medical schools that allowed students to leave halfway through their studies to pursue other interests and to return with no loss in standing'.[2] Hultin had already decided to investigate the body's immune reaction to influenza. Immigrating to the United States, Hultin enrolled in the microbiology department of the University of Iowa. It was here that Hultin was introduced to Professor William Hale, an eminent virologist from Brookhaven National Laboratory, then at Camp Upton, Long Island. Over lunch, Professor Hale made an offhand remark about the 1918 influenza epidemic. It was a remark that was to change the course of Hultin's life forever.

'Everything has been done to elucidate the cause of that epidemic,' Hale said. 'But we just don't know what caused that flu. The only thing that remains is for someone to go to the northern part of the world and find bodies in the permafrost that are well preserved and that just might contain the influenza virus.'[3]

This statement was Hultin's light-bulb moment. Speculating that clues to the genetic code of Spanish flu might be found in the bodies of its victims, Hultin learned about the devastating outbreaks of Spanish influenza in Alaska in 1918, where its victims had been buried in the 'permafrost' – that is, ground, including rock or soil, at or below the freezing point of water: 0° C (32° F).

Having found the subject of his doctoral thesis, Hultin travelled to the northern coast of Alaska to exhume the bodies in a bid to isolate the virus. Using a combination of local records and weather charts to pinpoint the burial sites, Hultin also had to take into account the changeable nature of permafrost itself. This naturally occurring process brought with it its own problems. The sequence of freeze and thaw was likely to affect the condition of the human remains. Hultin was taking a tremendous risk: he had no guarantee his project would succeed, or that he would find any well-preserved bodies, let alone suitable tissue samples.

Hultin applied to the National Institute for Health for funding but never received a response. However, according to Hultin, the US government got wind of his plans and carried out a research expedition of its own.[4] In 1951, the US military planned a $300,000 mission code-named Project George, to exhume Spanish flu victims from the Alaskan permafrost.[5] If this strikes the reader as unlikely, it is worth bearing in mind that these events occurred in the context of the Cold War. In 1918, 450,000 Russians had been killed by Spanish flu. In the event of the Soviet Union developing its own strain of the virus and using it as a biological weapon against the United States, the consequences were unthinkable.

Ostensibly top-secret, Project George was discovered by officials at the University of Iowa and, within a day, Hultin found himself on his way to Nome, Alaska, with his associates Dr Albert McKee and Dr Jack Layton and $10,000 of funding.[6] The team landed in Nome but, when they started to excavate, they soon discovered that the permafrost had been fractured by a small creek, which had changed course. As a result, any bodies buried in the permafrost would have decayed and not be suitable for sampling.

As the virologist Jeffery Taubenberger later observed, the term 'permafrost' is a misnomer. Permafrost operates in a series of continual cycles, 'where the temperature kind of goes just above and just below freezing. With biological material, freezing and thawing is the very worst thing you can do, because ice crystals form and poke holes in membranes of cells, and it causes all sorts of damage. So, basically, nothing biological survives freezing and thawing.'[7]

Undeterred by their lack of success, Hultin and his team hired a pilot and flew to the Seward Peninsula in search of further burials, as the military personnel engaged in Project George arrived in Nome with a full complement of drilling and excavation equipment. While the army found nothing but bones, Hultin's team travelled to Brevig Mission, previously known as Teller Mission, where 85 per cent of Brevig Mission's inhabitants had died of Spanish flu in one week in November 1918.[8] Bodies were exhumed and tissue samples taken from lungs, kidneys, spleens and brains, packed and sent to Iowa. The results, however, were disappointing. Despite comprehensive analysis, no traces of the live virus were discovered.[9]

Nearly half a century later, Dr Jeffery Taubenberger, chief of the division of molecular biology at the Armed Forces Institute of Pathology, was casting around for a new research project. The AFIP, located on the campus of the Walter Reed Army Medical Center in Washington, had been established by a Civil War general in 1862 as an army pathology museum designed to combat 'diseases of the battlefield'. With its vast library of tissue samples and expertise at analysing tissues for the diagnosis of disease, the AFIP was a valuable resource for researchers and clinicians alike, regarded as 'a stalwart of the international biomedical community'.[10] Every year, the AFIP received at least 50,000 requests for second opinions on difficult cases from external pathologists, and its employees, including experts in many areas of human and animal pathology, 'made major or minor changes to roughly half of the cases they acted on'.[11]

Although the director still reported to the Surgeon General of the Army and not the commander at Walter Reed, the institute had expanded its research remit. In 1991, Tim O'Leary was appointed chair of the department of cellular pathology and set out to create a 'molecular diagnostic pathology component, with the idea that molecular biology tools would be useful as an adjunct in anatomical surgical pathology'.[12]

As a result, Jeffery Taubenberger and his team were engaged on research projects into the genetic structure of breast cancer and the recovery of the RNA virus from the decomposed flesh of dead dolphins, to determine whether the dolphins had died of a measles-type virus or a condition known as 'red tide', a harmful algal bloom toxic to sea life. Taubenberger's team, consisting of doctors Amy Krafft and Thomas Fanning and microbiologist Ann Reid, were given the challenge of resurrecting the virus from several decomposed tissue samples using a technique known as PCR or Polymerase Chain Reaction.

When the AFIP was threatened with funding cuts in 1995, Taubenberger and his colleagues responded by looking at how they could apply PCR to the immense warehouse of tissue samples at the institute.

'It was just kind of a hobby project idea,' Taubenberger admitted. 'I had a brainstorming session with Tim O'Leary, and the idea that we came up with was to go after the 1918 flu . . . the 1918 flu would be something that would be enormously useful, potentially of practical importance.'[13]

Taubenberger had learned briefly about the Spanish flu pandemic of 1918 in medical school, but knew little about it. After reading Alfred Crosby's *America's Forgotten Pandemic*, Taubenberger became intrigued by the sheer scale of the pandemic and the way it had faded so quickly from the 'cultural memory'.[14] Working for an army research laboratory, Taubenberger was particularly astonished by the toll taken on the US army.

The US entered World War I very late compared to the European combatant countries, so there were far fewer US military casualties – about 100,000 in total in World War I. But of those, over 40,000 died of influenza. So 40% of people who were young, healthy, well-fed, 18 to 25-year-old strapping American GIs dropped dead of flu in 1918. Which is an absolutely unbelievable number, when you think about that![15]

Resolving to find the remains of the Spanish flu virus, Taubenberger ordered up tissue samples from seventy-seven soldiers who had died in the pandemic. Taubenberger's team searched for samples of victims who had succumbed to the initial viral infection and not the subsequent bacterial pneumonia. Seven samples seemed promising.

It was an exciting moment when the cases showed up on his desk. 'There they were!' he said. 'Having not been touched in 80 years!'[16]

These samples consisted of tiny scraps of lung tissue, preserved in formaldehyde embedded in pieces of paraffin wax. Taubenberger and his team then attempted to 'develop techniques to tease out fragments of the virus's genome from these tissues'.[17]

After seventy negative results, the researchers almost abandoned the project, but it proved so fascinating that they were reluctant to stop. 'And the more we read about this virus and the outbreak and the devastating impact it had, the more committed we became to get the project to work.'[18]

By this stage, research into the causes of Spanish flu had become something of an obsession for Taubenberger. 'It just got impossibly too much,' he admitted. 'Breast cancer was the first to go, then dolphin viruses and T-cell development. And flu just kind of took over my life!'[19]

Research into the origins of the Spanish Lady was also lengthy and time consuming. 'This kind of "viral archaeology" is extraordinarily painful! And very slow,' Taubenberger commented. 'It's not like you can just go to the freezer and pull out the virus. We have to find autopsy cases.'[20]

The breakthrough came a year later, in July 1996. Dr Amy Krafft began examining a sample of preserved lung tissue from the body of Private Roscoe Vaughn. Private Vaughn had been just twenty-one years old when he fell sick on 19 September 1918, at Fort Jackson, South Carolina. A week later, at 6.30 a.m. on 26 September, Private Jackson died of pneumonia. At 2 p.m. that same day an autopsy was performed on Private Vaughn's body and a pathological specimen removed from his lung.[21] Now, eighty years after his death, Private Vaughn was to play his part in helping to solve the mystery of the Spanish Lady.

Vaughn's contribution to medical science lay in the unusual manner in which his body had responded to Spanish flu. Taubenberger was struck by the way his case looked under the microscope.

What was recognized clinically is that he had developed a pneumonia of his left lung [and the right lung was seemingly normal]. *Now it's quite common to have pneumonia of just one lung, not necessarily both. And at the time of autopsy that was confirmed – he had massive bacterial pneumonia of his left lung that was fatal, and his right lung was almost completely normal.*[22]

This went unnoticed at the time of the autopsy, 'but what was there if you looked at the sections quite carefully were little tiny areas of very acute inflammation around the terminal bronchioles in that lung that were characteristic of very early phases of the influenza viral replication'.[23]

Private Vaughn was also unusual because he demonstrated an 'asynchrony' in the way that the disease developed,

> *in that he got influenza infection, and then had a bacterial pneumonia in his left lung which overtook the viral infection and killed him, but the influenza virus infection of his right lung was somehow delayed by several days. So when he died it left a snapshot of the very earliest stages of the virus infecting the lung. It was a very subtle change, and it took me a while to look at enough autopsies to get a sense of that. Influenza does not have characteristic changes that allow you to be confident, to just look under the microscope and say, 'This is definitely influenza.' You can sort of suspect it, but you can't be certain. But there was something about that case that just struck me as an excellent example, and so once I'd identified it, we extracted RNA, did our test and, boom! We found influenza virus RNA!*[24]

Given that the quality of genetic material recovered was, in Taubenberger's words, 'horrible!' the team had the daunting task of attempting to carry out 'large-scale sequencing of the virus to try to work out what it was'.[25]

Concerned that there was not enough material for testing, Taubenberger put aside the material from Private Vaughn and looked for other cases. Another specimen was located, which had come from another person who had died on the same day, but in a different camp. This too was positive, so the team now had two cases.[26]

Taubenberger and his colleagues published their initial findings, 'just little tiny fragments of sequence of the virus from our pathology material from the AFIP',[27] in *Science* magazine in 1997. It was at this point that Johan Hultin, now aged seventy-three, read the article and wrote to Taubenberger, explaining his own research. When Taubenberger requested the opportunity to look at Hultin's old material from Alaska he discovered, to his horror, that it had been destroyed, just a few years earlier.

Hultin proposed that they return to Alaska to exhume more bodies and obtain further frozen material, upon which they could perform molecular analysis at Taubenberger's AFIP laboratory, an activity that would not have been possible in 1951. The structure of DNA had not even been determined until 1953. There was no stopping Hultin. Despite being seventy-three years of age, he set off for Brevig Mission, equipped with little more than a camera, a sleeping bag and two bags of tools. Hultin funded the entire expedition himself, but it was a decidedly low-tech affair and Hultin slept at night on the floor of the local school. Taubenberger did not accompany him, and perhaps this was advantageous, as, given the sensitive nature of the work, many people in the community remembered Hultin and were content to allow him to excavate. 'They had been children and they were now the elders in this community,' said Taubenberger, 'remembering him 45 years later. He got permission to do an exhumation and he sent us material.'[28]

Brevig Mission's seventy-two influenza victims had been buried in a mass grave in 1918, marked with two large wooden crosses. With the help of four young men, Hultin began to dig until they had excavated a trench twenty-seven feet long, six feet wide and seven feet deep. At first it seemed as if, once again,

Hultin was to be disappointed. He discovered skeletons, but no remains containing soft tissue. But then they uncovered the body of an obese woman, whose fat had preserved her organs from the depredations of permafrost.

'I sat on a pail and looked at this woman. She was in a state of good preservation. Her lungs were good. I knew that this is where the virus would be.'[29]

Hultin named the woman 'Lucy', after the famous prehistoric skeleton recovered in Ethiopia in 1974. Taking samples of Lucy's organs, Hultin packed them in preservative. To prevent the samples from being lost, Hultin sent four identical sets over four days, courtesy of UPS, Fed Ex and the US Postal Service. He closed the grave and planted two new crosses there, which he had made himself in the woodwork department of the local school.

Hultin had made a significant discovery. Although three tissue samples proved negative, Ann Reid identified traces of the influenza virus in 'Lucy's' samples. They proved identical to the RNA from Private Roscoe Vaughn. Soon afterwards, a third match was made from a sample from Private James Downs, who had died of influenza at Camp Upton, New York, on 26 September 1918, aged thirty. It was 'Lucy', however, who provided the missing link.[30]

'Using the frozen material it became possible to sequence the entire genome of the virus,' said Taubenberger.

We ended up sequencing the hemagglutinin gene, the sort of main gene of the virus, from all three of the cases. And what we found, amazingly, was that they were basically identical, one to the other – that out of 1700 bases in this gene, these three cases differed from each other by only one nucleotide. So we knew

that this was really the pandemic virus; there was no question
that this was the virus. And using the frozen material it became
possible to sequence the entire genome of the virus.[31]

Hultin's earlier research was vindicated: he and Taubenberger's team had found the Spanish flu virus.

'It took an enormous amount of effort on our part, from 1997 through early 2005, to fully sequence the genome of the virus,' said Taubenberger. 'One of the things we concluded from this study was that this was a sort of bird flu virus that adapted somehow to humans.'[32]

How that pandemic virus was transferred from animals to people is another question which is still hotly debated. Taubenberger, in common with other virologists, is at the forefront of trying to find the answer to this dark riddle, equipped with a technique that enables scientists to create influenza viruses from cloned genes. A number of scientists arrived at this technique, known as 'reverse genetics', simultaneously. 'Drs. George Brownlee at Oxford, Peter Palese at Mount Sinai, and Yoshi Kawaoka in Wisconsin kind of all independently worked on this,'[33] Taubenberger explained.

Having sequenced the virus, 'through the wizardry of modern molecular biology',[34] scientists then tested it on animals in 'high containment' laboratories at the Center for Disease Control in Atlanta and at a laboratory in Winnipeg, Canada, where the 1918 virus has been put into macaques.

As to what made the Spanish flu pandemic so deadly, and why the virus killed so many healthy young people, Taubenberger subscribed to the theory that the virus provoked an auto-immune response known as a cytokine storm. Ironically, the healthier the patient, the more likely they were to die. The 1918 H5N1 produced a marked inflammatory response, causing secondary damage to the patients' lungs. 'It's not the virus that kills you but your own body's immune response,' explained Taubenberger.[35]

Mercifully, the twentieth century has not seen another pandemic on the scale of 1918's Spanish flu. In 1957, there was an outbreak of Asian flu (H2N2) and in 1968 of Hong Kong flu (H3N2). There was a 'pseudopandemic' in 1947 with low death rates, an epidemic in 1977 that was a pandemic in children, and an epidemic of swine influenza in 1976 which was feared to have pandemic potential.[36] But the 1918 pandemic appeared to have been a unique event, a combination of circumstances which, it was hoped, would never occur again. As a result, by 1997 research into the origins of Spanish flu might have been regarded as a somewhat *recherché* project, an academic quest with little relevance to contemporary life. Research funding was in jeopardy, with the finance director's blue pencil hovering over the APIT budget. But then, just as Taubenberger and his team were publishing their first research findings in March 1997, a three-year-old child in Hong Kong got infected with an H5N1 bird flu virus and died.

CHAPTER TWENTY-TWO

THE HONG KONG CONNECTION

———•◆•———

ON 9 MAY 1997, a little boy fell sick in Hong Kong. Normally lively and robust, three-year-old Lam Hoi-ka was struck down suddenly with a fever and sore throat. Lam's anxious parents called their doctor only to be told that Lam was experiencing a routine childhood malady and would recover within a day or two. Lam's symptoms suggested an upper respiratory infection, common among children the world over and the kind of illness a busy doctor sees dozens of times a day.

But, five days later, Lam had not recovered and so his parents took him to the local community hospital.[1] Staff there could not identify the cause of his symptoms but they were sufficiently concerned to admit Lam to the Queen Elizabeth Hospital in Kowloon, where the doctors were once again unable to make a diagnosis. But something clearly was wrong: Lam was going downhill rapidly. The little boy could not breathe without a ventilator, and the best guess was that he was suffering from viral pneumonia. As if this was not bad enough, Lam had also developed Reye's syndrome, a rare disease which generally afflicts children and teenagers and can be fatal. Reye's, which often succeeds viral infections such as influenza or chicken pox, causes fluid on the brain, which puts pressure on the nerves that control breathing and heart rate. Once this happens, the patient dies.[2] Lam was dosed with antibiotics to treat his pneumonia, but then developed 'disseminated intravascular coagulopathy', in which the blood clots like curdled milk. Normal clotting is disrupted, leading to severe bleeding from several sites.[3] Lam suffered massive organ failure and died a week after he had been admitted. Lam's devastated parents and shocked medical staff were left wondering how on earth, in the final decade of the twentieth century, a healthy little boy could fall sick and die so quickly.

On 20 May 1997, the day before Lam Hoi-ka died, doctors took a specimen of throat wash from his windpipe for analysis. This specimen went to Hong Kong's Department of Health for testing, as a matter of routine. Laboratory staff investigated the specimen and concluded three days later that Lam had died of influenza. However, despite extensive testing, chief virologist Dr Wilina Lim could not determine the type of influenza that had killed the little boy. Tests had eliminated H3N2, the descendant of Hong Kong's 1968 epidemic. Nor was the H1N1 virus of an outbreak in 1977 to blame.[4] Unperturbed, Lim sent the specimen to the World Health Organization's Collaborating Centres devoted to research into deadly diseases, based in London, Tokyo, Melbourne and at the Center for Disease Control in Atlanta, Georgia. Like international terrorism, pandemic disease is a constant high-level threat, and these centres are the early warning stations for pandemics, keeping a lookout for newly evolving strains of deadly viruses, including influenza, SARS and Ebola. Thousands of samples are sent every year for testing. Lim also sent a sample to eminent virologist Jan de Jong at the Dutch National Institute of Public Health near Utrecht.

On Friday 8 August, de Jong rang Lim telling her that he was flying straight to Hong Kong, but not saying why. When Lim picked him up from the airport, de Jong explained the reason for his sudden visit.

'Do you have any idea what virus you sent me?' he asked her.

Lim replied that she thought it was an H3, but one that had evolved so much that she could not identify it through laboratory tests.

'No,' de Jong said. 'It was an H5.'[5]

As expert virologists, they both knew what this meant. H5 was bird flu, but bird flu that had just killed another human being. Was Hong Kong on the verge of a pandemic?

Meanwhile, at the Center for Disease Control in Atlanta, Nancy Cox, chief of the influenza division, had just returned from vacation and resumed analysis of the thousands of specimens sent in from all over the world. As far as Cox was concerned, the Hong Kong sample was just another specimen, waiting its turn. A month passed before Cox's team examined it. When Cox saw the test results, she was horrified. Just like de Jong, Cox confirmed that Lam Hoi-ka had died of bird flu, in Asia, long considered to be the epicentre of influenza by scientists.

Cox's first duty was to protect her staff. The research operation was moved to a biosafety level three-plus containment facility and their existing protective equipment was increased so that they worked in heavy layers of hoods and masks, like the modern equivalent of Jacobean plague doctors.[6] The similarities did not end there, with Cox fearing that the world was poised on the verge of a deadly plague.

To confirm that Lam Hoi-ka had died of bird flu, and that the sample had not become contaminated, all the tests were run again. The laboratory in Hong Kong still had samples of Lam Hoi-ka's throat wash, and these were tested. The result was the same: bird flu.

Now that two different teams, de Jong's in Utrecht and Cox's in Atlanta, had confirmed that Lam Hoi-ka died of bird flu, it was vital to find out how he had become infected. Dr Keiji Fukuda, a colleague of Cox's, maintained that according to his research, a human being had never been infected with bird flu before.[7] This was regardless of the research being conducted by Taubenberger in the United States. If this *was* bird flu, he asked, was it unique, 'or was there a new epidemic brewing?'[8] It was impossible to think of an influenza pandemic without invoking the spectre of Spanish flu.

In order to determine how Lam Hoi-ka had become infected, or whether his specimens had become contaminated in Hong Kong, a team of scientists from the World Health Organization arrived in Hong Kong, including Fukuda and pre-eminent bird flu expert Robert Webster.

Fukuda and his colleagues carried out a meticulous examination of conditions at the Queen Elizabeth Hospital in Kowloon, inspecting the health of the staff who had cared for Lam Hoi-ka, the equipment used to treat him and the health status of any fellow patients. Next, Wilina Lim's government laboratories were investigated, but once again, Fukuda and his colleagues found nothing amiss, concluding that 'the government labs were very clean, very well organized'.[9] Lim and her team had clearly done everything to minimize contamination. Fukuda spoke to Lam Hoi-ka's doctor, who confirmed that Lam had been a normal healthy little boy with nothing in his medical history to suggest such a tragedy. The next step was to discover how and when Lam had been exposed to the H5 virus. Had he visited a farm, or mixed with a schoolmate whose family were poultry workers? Again, the investigation drew a blank until it was discovered that his school had played host to a clutch of baby chickens a few days before Lam's death. The chicks had been placed in a pen under a lamp in a corner of the classroom, and the children were encouraged to hold them and even give them names. But the chicks had died within hours. Could these chicks have been the cause of Lam's death from H5?[10] Extensive tests failed to confirm the presence of H5N1, and yet those doomed chicks seemed to suggest the source of Lam's fatal infection.[11]

Lam Hoi-ka's death from the H5 virus was a medical mystery. But there appeared to be one grain of comfort in all this. Despite fears of a pandemic, the infection had not spread, and no other deaths from bird flu were reported. By September, Nancy Cox at the Center for Disease Control in Atlanta, Georgia, had concluded that Lam Hoi-ka's death was an isolated incident. However, just before Thanksgiving, Cox received a phone call from Hong Kong telling her that additional cases of bird flu had been confirmed.[12] The first of these was a two-year-old boy from Kennedy Town, in the north-west of Hong Kong Island, on 8 November. The boy was admitted to the Queen Mary hospital on 7 November, as he had a weak heart, but he recovered within two days and was discharged. A specimen from the boy's nose and throat tested positive for H5.[13] On 24 November, a thirty-seven-year-old man from Kowloon was admitted to Queen Elizabeth hospital with the new strain of influenza, and on 26 November a thirteen-year-old girl from Ma On Shan in the New Territories was admitted to the Prince of Wales Hospital with headaches, a cough and a fever.[14] On 21 December, she died there. In Kowloon, a fifty-four-year-old man fell ill on 21 November and died of pneumonia at the Queen Elizabeth Hospital on 6 December.[15]

The sixth case was a twenty-four-year-old woman from Tsuen Wan, in the New Territories. She was admitted to hospital on 4 December after falling ill with dizziness and fever, and became so sick that she spent months on a respirator before being discharged the following April.[16] Two other victims fell ill on 4 December, a five-year-old girl from Ap Lei Chau, just off the south side of Hong Kong Island, and a six-year-old girl from Kowloon.[17] Both girls spent December in hospital, along with a ten-year-old boy from Tsuen Wan who came down with the symptoms on 10 December and a two-year-old boy from Ap Lei Chau.[18] On 15 December, a nineteen-year-old girl from Tsuen Wan fell ill and started coughing up sputum; she was to spend almost six months in hospital.[19]

On 16 December, three people developed influenza: a baby boy from Kowloon and a baby girl from the New Territories both became unwell but survived; a woman of sixty did not, dying two days before Christmas.[20] On 17 December, a twenty-five-year-old girl from Yuen Long fell ill, and died in January with acute respiratory distress and pneumonia; on the same day in Kowloon, a thirty-four-year-old woman suffered kidney failure and her lungs filled with fluid; she too died in January.[21]

The seventeenth victim was a girl of fourteen, who fell sick in Kowloon with influenza symptoms as well as histiocytosis, a disease of the bone marrow cells, on 23 December.[22] Five days later a three-year-old boy presented with the same symptoms.[23] By 28 December, eighteen people, including the first victim,

Lam Hoi-Ka, had fallen victim to the mysterious new strain of influenza and six were dead or dying. A mortality rate of one in three was a terrifying prospect.[24] An outbreak of bird flu was apparently under way, much to the horror of Dr Wilina Lim and her colleagues. 'That month was terrible,' she said. 'It wasn't clear where these viruses were coming from, but these people were getting sick, there were new cases day by day and we were really under a lot of stress.'[25] In a state of panic, even those with the mildest symptoms laid siege to their doctors; Dr Lim's laboratory was inundated with samples. And then the unthinkable happened. Dr Lim's sixteen-year-old daughter fell ill with a sore throat. At first, Dr Lim suggested that her daughter was merely 'swinging the lead' in order to avoid her piano lesson. In normal circumstances, the doctor would have encouraged her daughter to get up and attend the lesson anyway. Instead, she told her daughter to stay in bed. 'Because there was that worry. I was frightened. A lot of people were.'[26] Mercifully, Dr Lim's teenage daughter survived her attack of suspected bird flu.

Dr John LaMontagne, Mexican-born deputy director of the National Institute of Allergy and Infectious Diseases, learned about the outbreak during an official visit to India. 'I had remembered that there was a case in May, but this was a six-month interval. The fact that it had come back after six months was very worrisome to me.'[27] Was the outbreak about to replicate the chilling first and second waves of the 1918 Spanish flu pandemic? If so, medical scientists had no time to lose in coming up with a vaccine.

LaMontagne's immediate response was to try to develop a vaccine in sufficient quantities to protect the entire world, if necessary – a massive logistical operation. Meanwhile, in Hong Kong, the number of cases increased. Eighteen people were hospitalized between November and the end of December. Eight patients had to be placed on respirators, and six died.[28] Just as in 1918, it was mainly young adults who perished, a pattern chillingly reminiscent of Spanish flu. As LaMontagne negotiated with the drug companies to prepare a vaccine, and found them reluctant to do so in case their laboratories became infected with H5N1, the Australian virologist Kennedy Shortridge took a walk through the 'wet markets' of Hong Kong.

Every day, crates of live chickens arrived in Hong Kong from the Chinese countryside. They were sold in 'wet markets' in the centre of the city, and slaughtered in front of their buyers; the Hong Kong Chinese liked their birds fresh. Hygiene consisted of a brief wash down with cold water, and given that the virus grows in the chicken's intestines, this was sufficient to cause an infection.[29] While raw chicken is a notorious source of food poisoning such as salmonella, campylobacter and *E. coli*, the concept that humans could die of chicken influenza was another matter entirely.

On a walk through a wet market one morning, Shortridge, who had isolated the H5N1 virus in Asia, witnessed something that made his blood run cold. 'We saw a bird standing up there, pecking away at its food, and then very gently lean over, slowly fall over, to lie on its side, looking dead. Blood was trickling from the cloaca. It was a very unreal, bizarre situation. I had never seen anything like it.'[30] After seeing the same thing happen to another chicken, and another, Shortridge concluded: 'We were looking at chicken Ebola . . . When I saw those birds dying like that, it really hit home what might have happened in the 1918 pandemic. My God. What if this virus were to get out of this market and spread elsewhere?'[31]

It emerged that Hong King's bird population had been blighted by bird flu for months. The first chickens died on a farm near the rural town of Yuen Long. The infection quickly spread to a second and then a third farm, each time with grisly results. One farmer recalled seeing his birds beginning to shake as thick saliva dripped from their mouths. The wattles on other birds turned green or black, giving the chickens the appearance of feathered zombies. Some hens started laying eggs that had no shells. Others fell dead on the spot, asphyxiated from blood clots lodged in their windpipes. By the time of Lam Hoi-ka's death, nearly 7,000 birds had succumbed.[32] It had, as Fukuda put it, happened not in the lab, but out in the wild.[33]

If the nightmare prospect of a bird flu epidemic was to be avoided, there could be only one solution. After learning that, despite previous measures, chickens at a farm in Yuen Long in the New Territories had tested positive for the virus and that a large number of chickens had died at the Cheung Sha Wan poultry wholesale market in Kowloon, possibly from the virus, Margaret Chan, Hong Kong's then director of public health, closed the territory's wet markets and initiated a mass poultry cull.[34]

Hong Kong's Agriculture Department suspended the city's daily import of 75,000 live chickens from mainland China and on 29 December 1997, Steven Ip, Secretary for Economic Services, announced that 'we will start destroying all the chickens in Hong Kong Island, Kowloon Island, and the New Territories'.[35]

According to Elisabeth Rosenthal of the *New York Times*, this was a grisly operation, extreme, but necessary. An army of government clerks was mobilized across the territory to collect all the birds from 160 chicken farms as well as from more than 1,000 chicken wholesalers and retail chicken stalls. The birds were killed by market owners, or carted away by local authorities and euthanized with poison gas. Their corpses were disinfected, wrapped in plastic and taken to landfill sites. Geese and ducks that had been in close contact with the chickens were also killed.[36]

The slaughter of the innocents presented a biblical sight:

At 8 a.m. today, after receiving brief instructions from a blue-uniformed poultry inspector, the four workers at the outdoor store called Fai Chai Lam Cheung Kai set out to complete the morning's grim task. Working with skilled bare hands, the workers lifted dozens of chickens, ducks, pigeons and quail out of stacked metal cages, arched back each bird's neck, and deftly pulled a sharp knife over the veins and arteries. As blood oozed forth, they tossed the birds – a few with wings still flapping – into several large plastic garbage bins. The inspector said he would return later with disinfectant and plastic bags.

The store's owner, Mr. Tam, who refused to give reporters his full name, remained surprisingly upbeat despite this horrific event.

'We knew this would happen sooner or later and there's good and bad to it,' said Mr. Tam, as he slit a bird's neck. 'Hopefully it will calm people's fears so business will pick up. But it will take three months to replace all my chickens, and how will I pay rent until then?'

Mr. Tam said his business had fallen by 90 percent in the last month and the government had promised him $3.87 for each chicken, but he normally sold them for twice as much.[37]

Hong Kong's draconian response to the threat of bird flu appeared to have been successful, at least at the time. Subsequently, the World Health Organization has recorded 598 cases since 2003, with 352 deaths. Most deaths from bird flu are in Egypt, Indonesia, Vietnam and China. So far, the virus has not adapted to spread easily between humans.[38] However, the resurgence of human infections in Thailand and Vietnam in 2003, followed by outbreaks on chicken farms across Asia, the Middle East and Eastern Europe in 2005, made H5N1 a household name and even inspired a blockbuster movie, Steven Soderbergh's 'bio-thriller', *Contagion*.[39]

Tragic as it was, the Hong Kong bird flu outbreak of 1997 constituted a wake-up call for epidemiologists and public health authorities, allowing pandemic civil contingency plans to be put in place. In Great Britain, for instance, anyone who arrived at Heathrow Airport from Hong Kong with a respiratory infection during the 1997 outbreak was immediately quarantined. The Hong Kong outbreak also focused attention on the terrifying prospect of another pandemic on the scale of 1918.

'This was the first time that there was evidence that a bird virus could actually infect a human and cause disease,' commented Jeffery Taubenberger. 'The two stories – the 1918 and the H5N1 bird flu story – have kind of intertwined with each other and so there was this enormous upsurge of interest in influenza. People were worried that what the H5N1 virus was doing was paralleling what 1918 did – causing high mortality in young people.'[40]

Meanwhile, virologist Professor John Oxford, a world expert on Spanish flu, saw the Hong Kong outbreak as 'a dress rehearsal for the real thing'.[41] While the Hong Kong H5N1 virus had been hitting the headlines worldwide, and Taubenberger's team were attempting to sequence the genome behind the 1918 flu pandemic, Professor Oxford had been involved in another investigation. His task was to seek out the origins of the Spanish Lady in Spitzbergen, Norway.

CHAPTER TWENTY-THREE

SECRETS OF THE GRAVE

I N AUGUST 1998, while Hong Kong came to terms with the aftermath of the bird flu outbreak, and Jeffery Taubenberger's team deciphered the origins of the 1918 pandemic from its victims, another group of 'viral archaeologists' set off for Spitsbergen Island in Norway's Svalbard archipelago. Their mission was to recover tissue samples from the preserved bodies of miners buried in the permafrost of the Norwegian Arctic. Professor John Oxford, virologist at the Royal London Hospital Medical School, aimed to solve the riddle of the original Spanish flu epidemic in order to avoid such outbreaks in the future. In other words, how did the avian strain of flu leap the species barrier to mutate into the virus of 1918? The Hong Kong H5N1 outbreak of 1997 had lent the issue a new urgency.

Professor Oxford had become involved with the project after being approached by Dr Kirsty Duncan, a Canadian geologist who developed a fascination with the Spanish flu pandemic after reading Alfred Crosby's book on the subject at the age of twenty-six in 1993. 'I said to my family, "I'm going to find out what caused this."'[1] Following five years of painstaking research, Duncan had pinpointed a graveyard in Longyearbyen, a small coal-mining town on Spitsbergen Island. It was here, in 1918, that the bodies of seven miners had been buried in the Arctic permafrost, and Duncan believed their remains might provide clues to the origins of the Spanish Lady. Having been introduced to Jeffery Taubenberger, Duncan hoped he would lend his expertise to the Spitsbergen expedition. However, just as the Spitsbergen expedition was about to leave, the breakthrough in Taubenberger and Hultin's research occurred, and he decided to withdraw from the project, much to Duncan's dismay.[2]

The Spitsbergen expedition included Professor Oxford, bird flu expert Dr Robert Webster, and Dr Rod Daniels of the National Institute for Medical Research at Mill Hill, an influenza expert with experience of working with highly contagious viruses in Category Four laboratories.[3] Professor Oxford's wife Gillian and their daughter Esther also joined the team, and Esther Oxford provided a vivid account of subsequent events for the *Independent* newspaper.

Daniels and Oxford had been working together to analyse lung tissue samples from victims of the 1918 influenza epidemic stored at the Royal London Hospital. Unfortunately, according to Esther Oxford, 'the samples were preserved in formalin which made it impossible to extract an accurate "footprint" of the genetic structure of the 1918 virus. The point of the Svalbard project was to find fresh tissue samples which had not been affected by chemical treatment.'[4]

'If we identify the "deadly motif", we will be able to target that gene in the development of new anti-viral drugs,' said Professor Oxford.[5] This meant that any future outbreak of a similarly lethal virus could be effectively controlled:

Once we know which part of the virus causes morbidity, then when a new influenza virus arises unexpectedly, like the one

*in Hong Kong, the first thing you do is look at the genes in that
new virus and say to yourself, 'How do those genes compare to
the 1918 genes?' If you see they are exactly the same, you are
in trouble. That would be the moment to pour resources into
preventing a pandemic. If on the other hand, you find that the
genetic structure is not related, you can relax a little bit.*[6]

Excavating the miners' bodies would be the task of the London
Necropolis Company, a professional exhumation team originally
founded in 1852,[7] and now empowered to exhume and rebury
human remains at sites where new roads, housing or commercial
developments were planned.[8]

When Dr Kirsty Duncan had set out to find remains of
Spanish flu victims in the Norwegian permafrost, she had
not undertaken an easy task. There were no medical records
dating back to 1918, the hospital having been destroyed.
Neither were there parish records, as the first pastor did not
arrive until 1920, and there were no government records, as
Svalbard only became part of Norway in 1925. But, through
research, Duncan discovered that there were diaries, written
by the chief engineer of a coal-mining company. These diaries
were in the custody of a local schoolteacher, and he agreed to
translate them. From the diaries, the graves of seven miners
were identified with ground-penetrating radar. Their remains
were buried at the foot of the mountains in the 'freezing, windy
valley of Longyearbyen'.[9]

The expedition and subsequent excavation was far from
straightforward. There were anxieties among the scientists that
the specimens might have been ruined when the permafrost
melted. In addition, an international media circus had

descended on the quiet town of Longyearbyen, eager for the latest discoveries. As if these factors were not enough, there were tensions among the members of the expedition. Various sources, including Esther Oxford and Duncan herself, have testified to the clash of personalities that marred the project. The eminent scientists, it seemed, were sceptical of Duncan's amateur status, glamorous appearance and 'emotional' graveside press conferences, in which, while blinking back tears, she begged for dignity to be accorded to the miners' bodies. This was never in doubt, with the excavation conducted in an atmosphere of respect for the influenza victims. Duncan, for her part, came to feel increasingly patronized and marginalized by a scientific establishment that refused to give her credit for the time and effort she had devoted to the project. Duncan later referred to the expedition as 'the most unpleasant experience of my life'.[10]

On the eighth day of excavating the pit where the miners were buried, Dr Daniels' spade hit the lid of a box. This seemed too early; the mass grave was only half a metre deep, and still in the sloppy active layer of permafrost. But, much to Professor Oxford's dismay, the box turned out to be a coffin. 'When I first saw that coffin, I didn't think it was one of our coffins,' he said. 'I didn't want to think it was the first coffin. I could see the project vanishing down the tube.'[11]

After some discussion, the team decided that the coffin did not belong to one of the miners, and that it would be safe to continue digging. But the following day a second coffin was found at the same level, then a third, then a fourth. The team continued to dig until they had uncovered seven coffins, hoping against hope that these were not the coffins of the miners. 'Even when we had the seven there was no clear indication that they were our seven,' said Rob Daniels. 'It was only when we found some newspaper in the coffins, dated 1917, that we realized these were probably our men. Up until that point there was always the hope that there would be another seven bodies further down.'[12]

To make matters worse, one of the coffins had burst, and turned out to be full of grit and sand, raising queries about the suitability of the tissue samples. When the coffins were opened, they revealed six skeletons, one family having refused permission to examine the remains.

The sight was, in the words of Esther Oxford, a 'pitiful' one.[13] The seven coal-miners, all young men, had been buried naked, wrapped in nothing but newspaper. There were no personal items, no pieces of clothing; little care had been taken in arranging the bodies. Only one had his hands crossed over his crotch. The rest lay with their hands by their sides. All were submerged in water and coated with a fine, clay-like substance. The coffins were packed tightly into the grave.[14] 'I thought they would be more separate,' said Professor Oxford. 'But there wasn't an inch between each coffin.'[15]

Autopsies were conducted in a respectful atmosphere by Barry Blenkinsop, an assistant pathologist from the Chief Coroner's office in Ontario, Canada, and his colleague, Charles Smith.

With the tenderness of a father, Blenkinsop lay beside each of the six bodies on a platform of wood planks, and using three tools – a scalpel, a knife and a pair of forceps – he gently lifted out lumps of organs, carefully removed the layer of silt, then placed them reverently in the sample jars. He also took samples of bone marrow, hair ('blond' through loss of pigment), and small artefacts such as bits of newspaper or rope.[16]

Despite the silt in the coffins and the condition of the bodies, the team remained in good spirits. It was decided that the excavation would continue, as radar indicated ground disturbance two metres deep, leading to speculation that other bodies were buried further down.

But the mood didn't last. That night, an event took place that might have been foreseen, given the unstable nature of permafrost. The pit walls filled with water and the pit collapsed overnight. The following day, the site was abandoned, and Esther Oxford watched as the gravediggers from Necropolis filled in the hole. 'It was the collapse of a dream for my dad,'[17] wrote Esther.

Professor Oxford's own response was more pragmatic. While accepting that the Spitsbergen project was now untenable, he turned his attention to other less expensive and time-consuming forms of 'viral archaeology' back in England, such as analysis of two bodies found buried in lead near St Bartholomew's Hospital 200 years earlier, including a boy who died of smallpox. In an interview conducted in 2016, Professor Oxford told me that, for his purposes, the best clinical data came from 'path labs, human tissue harvested from PMs at Bart's and the Royal London'.[18] This was also an efficient method of bypassing ethical issues and issues such as obtaining permission from families for exhumations. While agreeing that Jeffery Taubenberger has had 'good results with "lung blocks," a piece of tissue the size of a sugar cube taken from larger lung samples, the problem with this is you only get a small perception of the pathology of the lung. It's better to have the entire lung or even the body to examine the pathology of the infection.'[19] To this end, Professor Oxford and his colleagues embarked on further projects such as the investigation into the remains of Sir Mark Sykes, the diplomat who died at the Paris Peace Conference in 1919, an exhumation with which this book began. Leading up to this, Professor Oxford and his colleagues had embarked on another project, taking specimens from the bodies of nine victims of the 1918 pandemic buried in lead-lined coffins in south London and Oxford. Professor Oxford had located the grave sites by asking a funeral company to review its records of young people who died in the autumn of 1918 and by checking the death certificates of ten likely to be best preserved because they had been buried in lead. One Spanish flu victim in particular, Phyllis Burn, buried in Twickenham Cemetery in 1918, seemed likely to offer valuable specimens. 'Her family were very well off,' Professor Oxford told me, 'they owned a motor car, very unusual in those days. So they buried her in a lead-lined coffin placed in a brick vault, as befitting her status.'[20] As a result, it was hoped that Phyllis Burn's remains might be sufficiently preserved to provide internal tissue samples 'which could give vital information about the influenza virus – with the potential to save millions of lives'.[21]

The brief life of Phyllis 'Hillie' Burn provides a poignant coda to this book. In many respects, Hillie was a typical victim of Spanish flu, young, healthy, and, as a VAD, sacrificing her life for the war effort. This would have come naturally to a young woman who was the daughter of an army officer, Major James Montague Burn, and raised in the tradition of duty and service.

Phyllis Burn was born in 1898 and grew up with her two sisters, Nellie and Jessie, in a large house in Strawberry Hill, Twickenham, south-west London. Theirs was a happy, carefree childhood, until tragedy struck when their father died of cancer on 17 March 1912, aged just forty-five.[22]

When war broke out two years later, Phyllis and her sister Nellie signed up to the Volunteer Aid Detachment and together they nursed injured British soldiers returning from France for medical treatment. Phyllis was young and healthy, but on 28 October she fell sick with a headache and chills, classic symptoms of Spanish flu. Realizing that she was ill, Phyllis immediately moved out of the family home to save her mother and sisters from becoming infected. Phyllis went to stay with a neighbour, Janet Newton, in Southfield Gardens, Twickenham. Two days later, at Janet Newton's house, Phyllis died. She was just twenty years old.[23]

Phyllis was buried in Twickenham Cemetery, with a carved gravestone reading 'In Sweet and Loving Remembrance of Phyllis "Hillie", eldest daughter of Fanny Isabella Burn'.[24]

In 2004, Mrs Hilary Burn-Callander, widow of Phyllis's nephew, Roderick, still remembered what a tragedy Phyllis's death was for her family. 'It was a terrible tragedy for the family to lose a daughter after losing the father,'[25] she said. 'Phyllis was really loved by her sisters. After Phyllis's death, they lived very quietly. They never got over her death.'[26]

When Mrs Burn-Callander was first contacted by Professor Oxford, for permission to exhume Phyllis's body, she admitted she felt 'baffled'.[27] But Professor Oxford 'explained that there was a good chance that her chest cavity has been preserved and that the virus could still be there and that it was important to help prevent another pandemic. If that's what scientists need to stop any future lethal outbreak, then it has to be done. I hope that after all these years, Phyllis can stop this happening again.'[28]

Sadly, Phyllis proved unable to make a posthumous contribution after all. After her body had been exhumed, it emerged that Phyllis's coffin was not, in fact, made of lead. As she had been buried in wood, no usable samples could be retrieved. Despite this disappointing development, Professor Oxford and his team have continued with their research undaunted, in the knowledge that finding a solution to the riddle of pandemic influenza is increasingly vital.

Spanish flu killed upwards of 100 million souls during 1918–19. As Professor Oxford told me, we will never know the true figures for certain as so many deaths went unrecorded. But knowing our enemy, finding out who the Spanish Lady and her descendants really were, is vital in order to prevent another devastating type of pandemic.

The threat of another influenza pandemic remains a very real one. 'We are like vulcanologists,'[29] Professor Oxford told an interviewer back in 2000. 'We are sitting on our volcano, and we don't know when it is going to erupt.'[30]

The threat of pandemic flu is as severe as that of a terrorist attack. According to Professor Oxford, the impact of a flu pandemic in Great Britain would be the equivalent of blowing up a nuclear power station.[31] The police, hospital staff and military and local authorities therefore conduct regular contingency exercises in preparation for such an event.

Quarantine plans are tested, antibiotics, analgesics and anti-viral inoculations are stockpiled, and, chillingly, leisure centres and stadiums are designated as emergency morgues. Planning is the key to survival. And even this may not be enough: the influenza virus, 'that clever little virus!' as Taubenberger called it, mutates constantly, meaning that a new version of the shape-shifting Spanish Lady could one day return. Back in 2013, the AIR Worldwide Research and Modeling Group 'characterized the historic 1918 pandemic and estimated the effects of a similar pandemic occurring today using the AIR Pandemic Flu Model'.[32] In the model, it was found that a modern-day Spanish flu event would result in 188,000–337,000 deaths in the United States alone.[33]

Although Spanish flu was once the forgotten tragedy, so traumatic that it was apparently wiped from the collective memory, the pandemic now fascinates a generation of medical researchers, writers and historians. And the Spanish Lady's victims are beginning to get the memorials that they deserve. One cold November afternoon, I visited the chapel of the Royal London Hospital in Whitechapel to view the Johannes Schreiter memorial windows, one of which is dedicated to the victims of Spanish flu. The chapel is now the medical school library and a new generation of students sat industriously at their books and laptops. Professor Oxford had described the stained-glass window to me during our interview, an abstract stained-glass triptych designed by Caroline Swash to honour the staff and patients who lost their lives in 1918. The design is based on the 'W' diagram of the waves of Spanish flu, and as I walked past, the colours flickered and changed with the light. For Professor Oxford, this window is a memorial to the courage and resilience of those who fought against killer influenza.

'Who are we?' he had asked me. 'We don't know until we are up against it.'[34]

The fight against flu, says Professor Oxford, had been characterized by 'tiny daily acts of heroism by men and women. In 1918 there were more acts of heroism on the Home Front than on the Western Front.'[35]

NOTES AND REFERENCES

Introduction: An Ill Wind

1. http://news.bbc.co.uk/1/hi/england/humber/7617968.stm.
2. http://www.independent.co.uk/life-style/health-and-families/health-news/a-cure-for-flu-from-beyond-the-grave-933046.html.
3. Ibid.
4. Ibid.
5. Ibid.
6. Michael B. A. M. Oldstone, *Viruses, Plagues, and History: Past, Present and Future*, revised edition, Oxford: Oxford University Press, 2009, pp. 177–8.
7. Ibid.
8. Joan Eileen Knight, 'The Social Impact of the Influenza Pandemic of 1918–19: With Special Reference to the East Midlands', PhD thesis, University of Nottingham, (2015), p. 1.
9. Ibid., p. 2.
10. Ibid., p. 4.
11. Ibid., p. 4.
12. Ibid., p. 4.
13. Ibid., p. 5.
14. Ibid., p. 6.
15. Ibid.
16. Interview, Jeffery Taubenberger, Senior Investigator in the Laboratory of Infectious Diseases at the National Institute for Allergy and Infectious Diseases; Interview location: The National Institutes of Health campus in Bethesda, Maryland, United States, 27 November 2007; https://www.pathsoc.org/conversations/index.php?view=article&catid=65%3Ajeffery-taubenberger&id=92%3Ajeffery-taubenberger-full-transcript&option=com_content.

17. Ibid.
18. Ibid.
19. Ibid.
20. Ibid.
21. Ibid.
22. Ibid.
23. Lynette Iezzoni, *Influenza 1918: The Worst Epidemic in American History*, New York: TV Books, 1999 (1619 Broadway New York NY 10019).
24. Mark Honigsbaum, *Living With Enza: The Forgotten Story of Britain and the Great Flu Pandemic of 1918*, London: Macmillan, 2009, pp. 122–3.
25. *Manchester Evening News*, 13 November 1918.
26. Oldstone, *op. cit.* p. 178.
27. Dr Basil Hood, 'Notes on Marylebone Infirmary (later St. Charles Hospital) 1910–1941', Contemporary Medical Archives Centre, Wellcome Library GC/21, p. 91.
28. https://www.history.navy.mil/research/library/online-reading-room/title-list-alphabetically/i/influenza/a-winding-sheet-and-a-wooden-box.html.
29. Alfred W. Crosby, *America's Forgotten Pandemic: The Influenza of 1918*, Cambridge: Cambridge University Press, 2003, p. 133.
30. Howard Phillips, 'Black October: The Impact of the Spanish Influenza Epidemic of 1918 on South Africa', PhD dissertation, University of Cape Town, 1984.
31. Crosby, *op. cit.*, p. 83.
32. http://ec2-184-73-198-63.compute-1.amazonaws.com/wgbh/americanexperience/features/biography/influenza-victor-vaughan/?flavour=full.
33. Iezzoni, *op. cit.*, p. 51.
34. Roosevelt, Eleanor, *The Autobiography of Eleanor Roosevelt*, London: Hutchinson, 1962, p. 86.
35. John Grigg, *Lloyd George: War Leader, 1916–1918*, London: Penguin Books, 2003, p. 593.
36. Jay Parini, *John Steinbeck: A Biography*, London: Heinemann, 1994, p. 33.
37. Katherine Anne Porter, *Pale Horse, Pale Rider: Three Short Novels*, New York: The Modern Library, Random House, 1936.

38. Thomas Wolfe, *Look Homeward, Angel*, http://gutenberg.net.au/ebooks03/0300721.txt.

39. Mohammad Hossein Azizi MD, Ghanbar Ali Raees Jalali MD and Farzaneh Azizi, 'A History of the 1918 Spanish Influenza Pandemic and its Impact on Iran', *History of Contemporary Medicine in Iran*, http://www.ams.ac.ir/AIM/010133/0018.pdf.

40. Iezzoni, *op. cit.*, p. 128.

41. J. S. Oxford, R. Lambkin, A. Sefton, R. Daniels, A. Elliot, R. Brown and D. Gill, 'A Hypothesis: The Conjunction of Soldiers, Gas, Pigs, Ducks, Geese and Horses in Northern France during the Great War Provided the Conditions for the Emergence of the "Spanish" Influenza Pandemic of 1918–1919', *Vaccine* 23 (2005), 940–5, online version, Elsevier, 11 September 2004.

42. Crosby, *op. cit.*, p. 9.

43. Iezzoni, *op. cit.*, p. 156.

44. Phillips, *op. cit.*, p. 263.

45. Geoffrey W. Rice, *Black November: The 1918 Influenza Pandemic in New Zealand*, Christchurch: Canterbury University Press, 1988, p. 118.

46. Lucinda Gosling, *Great War Britain: The First World War at Home*, London: The History Press, 2014, p. 91.

47. Isobel Charman, *The Great War: The People's Story*, London: Random House, 2014, p. 417.

48. Vera Brittain, *Testament of Youth*, London: Virago Press Limited, 1978, p. 402.

Chapter One: A Victim and a Survivor

1. See J. A. B. Hammond, William Rolland and T. H. G. Shore, 'Purulent Bronchitis: A Study of Cases Occurring Amongst the British Troops at a Base in France', *The Lancet* 190 (14 July 1917), pp. 41–6.

2. http://ww1centenary.oucs.ox.ac.uk/body-and-mind/the-influenza-pandemic-of-1918/.

3. Ibid.

4. Ibid.

5. Ibid.

6. Ibid.

7. Ibid.

8. See Hammond, Rolland and Shore, *op. cit.*

9. Ibid.

10. Ibid.

11. See A. Abrahams, N. Hollows and H. French, 'Purulent Bronchitis: Its Influenza and Pneumococcal Bacteriology', *The Lancet* ii (1917), pp. 377–80.

12. See Hammond, Rolland and Shore, *op. cit.*

13. See Mark Honigsbaum, *Living with Enza: The Forgotten Story of Britain and the Great Flu Pandemic of 1918*, London: Macmillan, 2009, p. 26.

14. Ibid.

15. Ibid.

16. See Hammond, Rolland and Shore, *op. cit.*

17. See Abrahams, Hollows and French, *op. cit.*

18. See Douglas Gill and Gloden Dallas, 'Mutiny at Étaples Base in 1917', *Past & Present* 69 (November 1975), pp. 88–112, published by Oxford University Press on behalf of The Past and Present Society Stable; http://www.jstor.org/stable/650297. Accessed: 22 August 2016 12:04 UTC.

19. See Honigsbaum, *op. cit.*, p. 21.

20. Michael Woods, 'How to Brew Flu: Put Ducks, People and Pigs Together', PG Notes, 29 April 2001, http://old.post-gazette.com/healthscience/20010429chinafluhealth3.asp.

21. See Oxford, Lambkin, Sefton, Daniels, Elliot, Brown and Gill, *op. cit.*

22. See Woods, *op. cit.*

23. Ibid.

24. See Gill and Dallas, *op. cit.*

25. Ibid.

26. Lady Baden-Powell, *Window on My Heart*, London: Hodder & Stoughton, 1987.

27. See Gill and Dallas, *op. cit.*

28. Ibid.

29. Ibid.

30. Ibid.

31. Ibid.

32. Ibid.

33. See Vera Brittain, *Testament of Youth*, London: Virago Press Limited, 1984, p. 386.
34. Wilfred Owen, *Collected Letters*, ed. H. Owen and J. Bell, London: Oxford University Press, 1967, p. 521.
35. See Brittain, *op. cit.*, p. 362.
36. Ibid., p. 381.
37. See Honigsbaum, *op. cit.*, p. 18.
38. See Brittain, *op. cit.*, p. 372.
39. Ibid., p. 380.
40. See Honigsbaum, *op. cit.*, p. 19.
41. See Brittain, *op. cit.*, p. 402.
42. Ibid.

Chapter Two: 'Knock Me Down' Fever

1. John M. Barry, *The Great Influenza: The Epic Story of the Deadliest Plague in History*, London: Penguin Books Ltd, 2005, p. 93.
2. Ibid.
3. https://acanadiannaturalist.net/2012/12/06/influenza-part-ii-a-rural-doctor-and-the-roots-of-the-spanish-flu/.
4. *Santa Fe Monitor*, 14 February 1918.
5. Ibid.
6. Ibid.
7. Ibid.
8. *Public Health Reports* 33, Part 1, 5 April 1918, p. 502.
9. *Santa Fe Monitor*, 21 February 1918.
10. Ibid.
11. See Victor C. Vaughan, *A Doctor's Memories*, Indianapolis: The Bobbs-Merrill Company Publishers, 1926, p. 424.
12. Ibid., p. 428.
13. Ibid., p. 423.
14. https://www.kshs.org/kansapedia/camp-funston/.
15. Ibid.
16. James H. Dickson, 356th Infantry Regiment, 89th Division, letter home.
17. First Lieutenant Elizabeth Harding, http://www.kancoll.org/khq/1958/58_1_omer.htm.

18. George E. Omer, Jr, 'An Army Hospital: From Horses to Helicopters', http://www.kancoll.org/khq/1958/58_1_omer.htmEquus magazine.

19. James E. Higgins, *Keystone of an Epidemic*, https://www.readings.com.au/products/15569909/keystone-of-an-epidemic-pennsylvanias-urban-experience-during-the-1918-1920-influenza-epidemic, p. 32.

20. George E. Omer, Jr, 'An Army Hospital: From Horses to Helicopters', http://www.kancoll.org/khq/1958/58_1_omer.htm.

21. First Lieutenant Harding, *op. cit.*

22. Mark Honigsbaum, *Living with Enza: The Forgotten Story of Britain and the Great Flu Pandemic of 1918*, Basingstoke, Hampshire: Macmillan, 2009, p. 41.

23. Ibid.

24. See Carol R. Byerly, *Fever of War: The Influenza Epidemic in the U.S. Army during World War I*, New York and London: New York University Press, 2005, p. 60.

25. First Lieutenant Harding, *op. cit.*

26. See Honigsbaum, *op. cit.*

27. George E. Omer, Jr, 'An Army Hospital: From Horses to Helicopters', See *Equus* magazine, *op. cit.*

Chapter Three: The Killer Without a Name

1. Carol R. Byerly, *Fever of War: The Influenza Epidemic in the U.S. Army during World War I*, New York University Press, 2005, p. 14.

2. Ibid.

3. Ibid.

4. Ibid., pp. 14–15.

5. See Alfred W. Crosby, *America's Forgotten Pandemic: The Influenza of 1918*, new edition, Cambridge: Cambridge University Press, 2003, p. 25.

6. See Lynette Iezzoni, *Influenza 1918: The Worst Epidemic in American History*, New York: TV Books, 1999, p. 25.

7. Ibid.

8. Ibid., p. 26.

9. http://history.amedd.army.mil/booksdocs/wwi/1918flu/ARSG1919/ARSG1919Extractsflu.htm#G. Camp Sherman Division Surgeon Report.

10. See *Public Health Reports* 33, 5 April 1918.

11. See Jay Parini, *John Steinbeck: A Biography*, London: Heinemann, 1994, p. 33.

12. Ibid.

13. Ibid., pp. 33–4.

14. Ibid., p. 34.

15. See Ethan Blue, 'The Strange Career of Leo Stanley: Remaking Manhood and Medicine at San Quentin State Penitentiary, 1913–1951', *Pacific Historical Review* 78 (2) (May 2009), pp. 210–41. Published by University of California Press Stable; http://www.jstor.org/stable/10.1525/phr.2009.78.2.210. Accessed 20 June 2017.

16. Ibid.

17. Ibid.

18. Ibid.

19. L. L. M. D. Stanley (Resident Physician), 'Influenza at San Quentin Prison, California', *Public Health Reports (1896–1970)* 34 (19) (9 May 1919), pp. 996–1008, Sage Publications Inc.

20. Ibid.

21. Ibid.

22. Ibid.

23. Ibid.

24. Blue, *op. cit.*

25. Ibid.

26. Ibid.

27. Stanley, *op. cit.*

28. Ibid.

29. Ibid.

30. Ibid.

31. Ibid.

32. Ibid.

33. Ibid.

34. Ibid.

35. Blue, *op. cit.*

36. Ibid.

37. Iezzoni, *op. cit.*, p. 35.

Chapter Four: The Invisible Enemy

1. Michael B. A. M. Oldstone, *Viruses, Plagues, and History: Past, Present and Future*, revised edition, Oxford: Oxford University Press, 2009, p. 172.
2. Ibid.
3. Ibid.
4. Michael Bresalier, 'Fighting Flu: Military Pathology, Vaccines, and the Conflicted Identity of the 1918–19 Pandemic in Britain', *Journal of the History of Medicine and Allied Sciences* 68 (1) (January 2013), pp. 87–128.
5. Alfred W. Crosby, *America's Forgotten Pandemic: The Influenza of 1918*, new edition, Cambridge: Cambridge University Press, 2003, p. 25.
6. Niall Johnson, *Britain and the 1918–19 Influenza Pandemic: A Dark Epilogue*, Routledge Studies in the Social History of Medicine, Abingdon, Oxon: Routledge, 2006, p. 67.
7. See Vera Brittain, *Testament of Youth*, London: Virago Press Limited, 1984, p. 420.
8. Ibid.
9. Crosby, *op. cit.*, p. 25.
10. Victor C. Vaughan, *A Doctor's Memories*, Indianapolis: The Bobbs-Merrill Company, 1926, p. 430.
11. Colonel A. B. Soltau, 'Discussion on Influenza', *The Royal Society of Medicine*, http://journals.sagepub.com/doi/pdf/10.1177/003591571901200515.
12. Ibid.
13. Ibid.
14. Ibid.
15. Ibid.
16. Ibid.
17. Ibid.
18. See Crosby, *op. cit.*, p. 25.
19. Ibid.
20. Ibid.
21. Ibid., p. 26.
22. Malcolm Brown, *The Imperial War Museum Book of 1918: Year of Victory*, London: Sidgwick & Jackson, 1998, p. 171.

23. *The Times*, 29 June 1918, p. 6.

24. N. P. A. S. Johnson, 'The Overshadowed Killer Influenza in Britain in 1918–19', in *The Spanish Influenza Pandemic of 1918–19: New Perspectives*, ed. Howard Phillips and David Killingray, Routledge Studies in the Social History of Medicine, Abingdon, Oxon: Routledge, 2003, p. 146.

25. S. F. Dudley, 'The Influenza Pandemic as Seen at Scapa Flow', *Journal of the Royal Naval Medical Service* V (4) (October 1919).

26. Ibid.

27. Brown, *op. cit.*, p. 171.

28. Carol R. Byerly, *Fever of War: The Influenza Epidemic in the U.S. Army during World War I*, New York University Press, 2005, p. 72.

29. Mark Honigsbaum, *Living with Enza: The Forgotten Story of Britain and the Great Flu Pandemic of 1918*, Basingstoke, Hampshire: Macmillan, 2009, p. 46.

30. Ryan Davis, *The Spanish Flu: Narrative and Cultural Identity in Spain, 1918*, New York: Palgrave Macmillan, 2013, p. 35 (St Martin's Press LLC, 175 Fifth Avenue, New York, NY 10010).

31. Ibid., p. 35.

32. *British Medical Journal*, 8 June 1918, p. 653.

33. See Davis, *op. cit.*, p. 37.

34. Ibid., pp. 35–6.

35. Ibid., p. 75.

Chapter Five: One Deadly Summer

1. Mark Honigsbaum, *Living with Enza: The Forgotten Story of Britain and the Great Flu Pandemic of 1918*, Basingstoke, Hampshire: Macmillan, 2009, p. 61.

2. *The Times*, 23 July 1918, p. 8.

3. Lindy Woodhead, *Shopping, Seduction and Mr. Selfridge*, London: Profile Books, 2012, p. 146.

4. *Detroit Free Press*, 2 June 1918, p. C1.

5. Sam Webb, 'The forgotten grave of Mr Selfridge: Tombstone to mark burial place of famous shop owner left in a dilapidated and sorry state', *Daily Mail*, 4 June 2013.

6. Niall Johnson, *Britain and the 1918–19 Influenza Pandemic:*

A Dark Epilogue, Routledge Studies in the Social History of Medicine, Abingdon, Oxon: Routledge, 2006, p. 156.

7. *Nottingham Journal and Express*, 2 July 1918, p. 3.
8. Ibid.
9. *The Times*, 22 June 1918, p. 6.
10. *The Times*, 5 July 1918, p. 3.
11. Honigsbaum, *op. cit.*, p. 50.
12. *Yorkshire Telegraph*, 3–5 July 1918.
13. *Leicester Mercury*, 1 July 1918, p. 2.
14. Ibid., 2 July 1918, p. 2.
15. *Loughborough Herald and North Leicestershire Gazette*, 4 July 1918, p. 5.
16. Ibid., 11 July 1918, p. 5.
17. *Nottingham Journal and Express*, 4 July 1918, p. 3.
18. *Nottingham Journal and Express*, 10 July 1918, p. 1.
19. *Leicester Evening Mail*, 10 July 1918, p. 1.
20. *Salford Reporter*, 29 June 1918.
21. Ibid.
22. Honigsbaum, *op. cit.*, p. 51.
23. Ibid.
24. Ibid.
25. *Manchester Guardian*, 20 July 1918.
26. https://www.illustratedfirstworldwar.com/learning/timeline/1918-2/spanish-flu-peaks/.
27. *The Times*, 25 June 1918.
28. Ibid.
29. *Manchester Guardian*, 20 July 1918.
30. *Evening Standard*, 25 May 1918.
31. Ibid.
32. Ibid.
33. Ibid.
34. *Manchester Guardian*, 7 June 1917.
35. Ibid.
36. Ibid.
37. Ibid.
38. Ibid.
39. *Manchester Guardian*, 7 June 1918.
40. Ibid.

41. Ibid.
42. Caroline Playne, *Britain Holds On*, London: George Allen & Unwin, 1933, p. 333.
43. Ibid.
44. Ibid.
45. Ibid.
46. *Manchester Guardian*, 7 June 1917.
47. Ibid.
48. Ibid.
49. Caroline Playne, *op. cit.*
50. Robert Graves, *Goodbye to All That*, London: Penguin Books, 1960, p. 227.
51. Ibid., p. 228.
52. Malcolm Brown, *Imperial War Museum Book of 1918*, London: Sidgwick & Jackson, in association with the Imperial War Museum in association with Macmillan Publishers Ltd, 1998, p. 246.
53. Virginia Woolf, *Diary*, Vol. 1, 1915–19, 2 July 1918.
54. Lady Cynthia Asquith, *Diaries 1915–1918*, London: Hutchinson, 1968.
55. Alfred W. Crosby, *America's Forgotten Pandemic: The Influenza of 1918*, new edition, Cambridge: Cambridge University Press, 2003, p. 28.
56. Brown, *Imperial War Museum Book of 1918*, pp. 171–2.
57. Richard van Emden and Steve Humphries, *All Quiet on the Home Front: An Oral History of Life in Britain during the First World War*, London: Hodder Headline, 2004, p. 284.
58. Honigsbaum, *op. cit.*, p. 64.
59. Andrea Tanner, 'The Spanish Lady Comes to London: The Influenza Pandemic 1918–1919', *London Journal* 27 (2), 2002, p. 54; http://www.tandfonline.com.libezproxy.open.ac.uk/doi/abs/10.1179/ldn.2002.27.2.51.
60. Johnson, *op. cit.*, p. 46.

Chapter Six: Know Thy Enemy

1. Sandra M. Tomkins, 'The Failure of Expertise: Public Health Policy in Britain during the 1918–19 Influenza Epidemic', *Social*

History of Medicine 5 (3) (1992), pp. 435–54. DOI: https://doi-org.libezproxy.open.ac.uk/10.1093/shm/5.3.435.

2. Ibid.
3. Mark Honigsbaum, *Living with Enza: The Forgotten Story of Britain and the Great Flu Pandemic of 1918*, Basingstoke, Hampshire: Macmillan, 2009, p. 57.
4. Obituary Notice, Walter Morley Fletcher (1873–1933), *The Biochemical Journal* 27 (5) (1933), pp. 1333–6.
5. Ibid.
6. Ibid.
7. Ibid.
8. Maisie Fletcher, *The Bright Countenance: A Personal Biography of Walter Morley Fletcher*, London: Hodder & Stoughton, 1957, p. 129.
9. Ibid.
10. Ibid., p. 130.
11. Ibid.
12. Ibid.
13. Michael Bresalier, 'Fighting Flu: Military Pathology, Vaccines, and the Conflicted Identity of the 1918–19 Pandemic in Britain', *Journal of the History of Medicines and Allied Sciences* 68 (1) (2013), pp. 87–128. DOI: https://doi.org/10.1093/jhmas/jrr041.
14. Ibid.
15. Ibid.
16. Ibid.
17. Ibid.
18. Ibid.
19. Ibid.
20. Ibid.
21. Ibid.
22. Ibid.
23. Ibid.
24. Ibid.
25. Ibid.
26. Ibid.
27. Ibid.
28. Ibid.

29. Ibid.
30. Ibid.
31. Honigsbaum, *op. cit.*, p. 54.
32. Ibid., p. 55.
33. Ibid.

Chapter Seven: The Fangs of Death

1. *New York Times*, 11 July 1918.
2. John Tolland, *No Man's Land: The Story of 1918*, London: Book Club Associates, 1980, by arrangement with Eyre Methuen Limited 1980, p. 526.
3. Ibid., pp. 526–7.
4. Ibid., p. 527.
5. J. S. Wane, diary, Richard Collier Collection.
6. A. J. Jamieson, memoirs, p. 5, Richard Collier Collection.
7. Mridula Ramanna, 'Coping with the Influenza Pandemic: The Bombay Experience', in *The Spanish Influenza Pandemic of 1918–19*, ed. Howard Phillips and David Killingray, Routledge Studies in the Social History of Medicine, Abingdon, Oxon: Routledge, 2003, p. 87.
8. Ibid.
9. Ibid.
10. Ibid., p. 88.
11. Ibid.
12. Ibid.
13. Frederick Brittain, memoir, pp. 46–7, Richard Collier Collection.
14. Ibid.
15. Mohammad Hossein Azizi MD, Ghanbar Ali Raees Jalali MD and Farzaneh Azizi, 'A History of the 1918 Spanish Influenza Pandemic and its Impact on Iran', *History of Contemporary Medicine in Iran*, http://www.ams.ac.ir/AIM/010133/0018.pdf.
16. Ibid.
17. Ibid.
18. Sidney Peirce, *WW1 Recollections*, Richard Collier Collection, Imperial War Museum.
19. Ibid.
20. Ibid.

21. Lynette Iezzoni, *Influenza 1918: The Worst Epidemic in American History*, New York: TV Books, 1999, p. 39.
22. Ibid.
23. Alfred W. Crosby, *America's Forgotten Pandemic: The Influenza of 1918*, new edition, Cambridge: Cambridge University Press, 2003, p. 29.
24. Ibid.
25. Ibid.
26. Ibid.
27. Iezzoni, *op. cit.*, p. 47.
28. Crosby, *op. cit.*, p. 39.
29. Maria Porras Gallo and Ryan Davis, *The Spanish Influenza Pandemic of 1918–1919: Perspectives from the Iberian Peninsula and the Americas*, Rochester: Boydell & Brewer, 2014, p. 252.
30. Ibid.
31. Crosby, *op. cit.*, p. 39.
32. Ibid., pp. 39–40.
33. Ibid., p. 40.
34. Ibid.
35. Ibid., p. 46.
36. Ibid.
37. Iezzoni, *op. cit.*, p. 47.
38. Richard Collier, *The Plague of the Spanish Lady: The Influenza Pandemic of 1918–19*, London: Macmillan, 1974, p. 34.
39. Victor C. Vaughan, *A Doctor's Memories*, Indianapolis: The Bobbs-Merrill Company, 1926, p. 431.
40. Ibid., pp. 431–2.
41. Ibid., pp. 383–4.
42. http://amextbg2.wgbhdigital.org/wgbh/americanexperience/features/biography/influenza-victor-vaughan/?flavour=mobile.
43. Ibid.
44. R. N. Grist, 'Pandemic Influenza 1918', *British Medical Journal* (22–9 December 1979), pp. 1632–3.
45. Ibid.
46. Crosby, *op. cit.*, p. 9.
47. Ibid., p. 11.
48. Ibid., p. 9.
49. Iezzoni, *op. cit.*, pp. 66–7.

50. Ibid.
51. Ibid., p. 156.
52. Ibid.
53. Crosby, *op. cit.*, p. 11.
54. Ibid. *cit.*, p. 9.
55. Iezzoni, *op. cit.*, p. 174.

Chapter Eight: Like Fighting With a Ghost

1. Thomas Gray, *Ode on a Distant Prospect of Eton College*, https://www.poetryfoundation.org/poems/44301/ode-on-a-distant-prospect-of-eton-college.
2. Alfred W. Crosby, *America's Forgotten Pandemic: The Influenza of 1918*, new edition, Cambridge: Cambridge University Press, 2003, p. 46.
3. Ibid., pp. 46–7.
4. Lynette Iezzoni, *Influenza 1918: The Worst Epidemic in American History*, New York: TV Books, 1999, p. 56.
5. Crosby, *op. cit.*, p. 48.
6. Ibid.
7. Iezzoni, *op. cit.*, p. 47.
8. Ibid.
9. Ibid., p. 57.
10. Ibid., pp. 57–8.
11. Ibid., p. 78.
12. Crosby, *op. cit.*, p. 76.
13. Iezzoni, *op. cit.*, p. 50.
14. Ibid., p. 70.
15. Ibid.
16. Ibid., p. 51.
17. Ibid.
18. Ibid., pp. 51–2.
19. Ibid., p. 79.
20. Ibid., pp. 79–80.
21. Ibid., p. 80.
22. Ibid., p. 81.
23. Ibid., p. 88.
24. Ibid., p. 120.

25. Ibid., p. 136.
26. Crosby, *op. cit.*, p. 46.
27. Ibid., p. 159.
28. Eleanor Roosevelt, *The Autobiography of Eleanor Roosevelt*, London: Hutchinson & Co., 1962, p. 85.
29. Ibid.
30. Ted Morgan, *FDR: A Biography*, London: Grafton Books, 1986, p. 200.
31. Crosby, *op. cit.*, p. 68.
32. Ibid., p. 73.
33. Iezonni, *op. cit.*, p. 90.
34. Ibid., p. 90.
35. Ibid.
36. Ibid.
37. Ibid., p. 89.
38. Ibid., p. 91.
39. Ibid.
40. Ibid.
41. Ibid., p. 159.
42. Ibid., pp. 216–17.
43. Ibid., p. 159.

Chapter Nine: Eye of the Storm

1. Alfred W. Crosby, *America's Forgotten Pandemic: The Influenza of 1918*, new edition, Cambridge: Cambridge University Press, 2003, p. 70.
2. Lynette Iezzoni, *Influenza 1918: The Worst Epidemic in American History*, New York: TV Books, 1999, p. 46.
3. Crosby, *op. cit.*, p. 71.
4. Ibid.
5. Ibid., pp. 71–2.
6. Iezzoni, *op. cit.*, p. 63.
7. Crosby, *op. cit.*, p. 72.
8. Iezzoni, *op. cit.*, p. 63.
9. Ibid.
10. Ibid.
11. Ibid., pp. 63–4.

12. Crosby, *op. cit.*, p. 73.
13. Ibid., p. 74.
14. Iezzoni, *op. cit.*, p. 52.
15. Ibid., p. 146.
16. Ibid., p. 147.
17. Crosby, *op. cit.*, p. 75.
18. Ibid., p. 76.
19. Ibid., p. 78.
20. Ibid., p. 79.
21. Ibid.
22. Ibid., p. 81.
23. Ibid.
24. Ibid.
25. Iezzoni, *op. cit.*, p. 131.
26. Ibid., p. 132.
27. Crosby, *op. cit.*, p. 76.
28. Ibid., p. 77.
29. Iezzoni, *op. cit.*, p. 157.
30. Crosby, *op. cit.*, p. 77.
31. Ibid., p. 82.
32. Ibid.
33. Ibid.
34. Iezzoni, *op. cit.*, p. 134.
35. Ibid., p. 135.
36. Ibid.
37. Crosby, *op. cit.*, pp. 82–3.
38. Ibid.
39. Iezzoni, *op. cit.*, p. 149.
40. Ibid., p. 149.
41. Ibid., p. 150.
42. Ibid., pp. 149–50.
43. Ibid., p. 150.
44. Ibid., p. 152.
45. Ibid., p. 152.
46. Ibid., p. 163.
47. Ibid.
48. Ibid., p. 154.
49. Ibid., p. 163.

50. Ibid., p. 173.
51. Ibid., p. 170.
52. Ibid., p. 165.

Chapter Ten: A Winding Sheet and a Wooden Box

1. Alfred W. Crosby, *America's Forgotten Pandemic: The Influenza of 1918*, new edition, Cambridge: Cambridge University Press, 2003, p. 51.
2. https://www.history.navy.mil/research/library/online-reading-room/title-list-alphabetically/i/influenza/a-winding-sheet-and-a-wooden-box.html.
3. Ibid.
4. Ibid.
5. Ibid.
6. Ibid.
7. Ibid.
8. Ibid.
9. Ibid.
10. Lynette Iezzoni, *Influenza 1918: The Worst Epidemic in American History*, New York: TV Books, 1999, p. 120.
11. https://www.history.navy.mil/research/library/online-reading-room/title-list-alphabetically/i/influenza/a-winding-sheet-and-a-wooden-box.html.
12. http://waltdisney.org/blog/over-there-walt-disneys-world-war-i-adventure.
13. Stefan Kanfer, *Groucho: The Life and Times of Julius Henry Marx*, London: Penguin, 2000, pp. 55–6.
14. Ibid.
15. Ibid.
16. Iezzoni, *op. cit.*, p. 158.
17. Ibid., pp. 161–2.
18. Ibid., p. 165.
19. Ibid.
20. Ibid.
21. Ibid.
22. Ibid., pp. 165–6.
23. Ibid., p. 166.

24. Ann Herring and Lisa Sattenspiel, 'Death in Winter: Spanish Flu in the Canadian Subarctic', in *The Spanish Influenza Pandemic of 1918–19: New Perspectives*, ed. Howard Phillips and David Killingray, Routledge Studies in the Social History of Medicine, Abingdon, Oxon: Routledge, 2003, p. 156.

25. Ibid.

26. Ibid., p. 157.

27. Ibid., p. 158.

28. Ibid.

29. Ibid., pp. 158–9.

30. Ibid., p. 159.

31. Ibid.

32. Ibid., p. 161.

33. Ibid.

34. Joseph S. Lombardo and David L. *Buckeridge*, *Disease Surveillance*, eu.Wiley.com, p. 9.

35. FirstLieutenantHarding,http://www.kancoll.org/khq/1958/58_1_omer.htm.

36. Ibid.

37. http://cosmictimes.gsfc.nasa.gov/teachers/downloads/lessons/1919/letter_from_camp_funston.pdf.

38. Ibid.

39. Iezzoni, *op. cit.*, p. 66.

40. Ibid., p. 99.

41. Ibid., p. 100.

42. Ibid. p. 106.

43. Ibid.

Chapter Eleven: The Spanish Lady Goes to Washington

1. See Lynette Iezzoni, *Influenza 1918: The Worst Epidemic in American History*, New York: TV Books, 1999, p. 83.

2. Ibid.

3. Ibid., p. 84.

4. Ibid.

5. Ibid.

6. Niall Johnson, *Britain and the 1918–19 Influenza Pandemic:*

A Dark Epilogue, Routledge Studies in the Social History of Medicine, Abingdon, Oxford: Routledge, 2006, pp. 175–6.

7. Ibid.

8. Eleanor Roosevelt, *The Autobiography of Eleanor Roosevelt*, London: Hutchinson & Co., 1962, p. 86.

9. Ibid.

10. See Iezzoni, *op. cit.*, p. 85.

11. Ibid., p. 86.

12. Ibid.

13. Ibid., p. 87.

14. Ibid.

15. Ibid., p. 105.

16. Ibid.

17. Ibid., p. 154.

18. Ibid., p. 53.

19. Ibid., p. 118.

20. Thomas Wolfe, *Look Homeward, Angel*, 1929, eBook, http://gutenberg.net.au/ebooks03/0300721.txt.

21. Ibid.

22. Ibid.

23. Ibid.

Chapter Twelve: 'You Can't Do Anything for Flu'

1. *Nottingham Journal*, 9 December 1918.

2. Ibid.

3. Ibid.

4. 'Eat More Onions' campaign, http://influenza1918.weebly.com/flu-facts.html.

5. Lynette Iezzoni, *Influenza 1918: The Worst Epidemic in American History*, New York: TV Books, 1999, p. 119.

6. *Nottingham Evening Post*, 'Bygones' Supplement, 24 January 2009.

7. Niall Johnson, *Britain and the 1918–19 Influenza Pandemic: A Dark Epilogue*, Routledge Studies in the Social History of Medicine, Abingdon, Oxford: Routledge, 2006, p. 165.

8. Howard Phillips, 'Black October: The Impact of the Spanish

Influenza Epidemic of 1918 on South Africa', PhD dissertation, University of Cape Town, 1984, p. 276.

9. Ibid., p. 252.

10. Iezzoni, *op. cit.*, p. 119.

11. Ibid.

12. Ibid., p. 120.

13. Robert Graves, *Goodbye to All That*, London: Penguin Books, 1960, p. 233.

14. Johnson, *op. cit.*, p. 166.

15. Iezzoni, *op. cit.*, pp. 143–4.

16. Ibid., p. 144.

17. Ibid.

18. Ibid., p. 145.

19. Ibid., p. 195.

20. Nancy K. Bristow, 'You Can't Do Anything for Influenza: Doctors, Nurses and the Power of Gender during the Influenza Pandemic in the United States', in *The Spanish Influenza Pandemic of 1918–19: New Perspectives*, ed. Howard Phillips and David Killingray, Routledge Studies in the Social History of Medicine, Abingdon, Oxon: Routledge, 2003, p. 67.

21. Ibid.

22. Ibid.

23. Ibid., p. 119.

24. Ibid., p. 117.

25. Juliet Nicolson, 'The war was over – but Spanish Flu would kill millions more', *Daily Telegraph*, 11 November 2009.

26. F. W. P. Frewer, Letter, 11 May 1973, Richard Collier Collection.

27. Iezzoni, *op. cit.*, p. 141.

28. Ibid., p. 142.

29. Ibid.

30. Ibid.

31. Ibid.

32. Ibid., p. 143.

33. Ibid.

34. William Byam, *The Road to Harley Street: An Autobiography*, London: Geoffrey Bles, 1963, p. 223.

35. Ibid., p. 224.

36. Ibid.

Chapter Thirteen: 'Native Daughter Dies'

1. Lynette Iezzoni, *Influenza 1918: The Worst Epidemic in American History*, New York: TV Books, 1999, p. 89.
2. Ibid.
3. Ibid.
4. Ibid., p. 160.
5. Ibid., p. 129.
6. Ibid.
7. Ibid.
8. Ibid.
9. Alfred W. Crosby, *America's Forgotten Pandemic: The Influenza of 1918*, new edition, Cambridge: Cambridge University Press, 2003, p. 102.
10. Iezzoni, *op. cit.*, p. 130.
11. http://www.pressreader.com/usa/san-francisco-chronicle-late-edit ion/20150912/282016146108973.
12. Iezzoni, *op. cit.*, p. 129.
13. Ibid., p. 130.
14. http://www.pressreader.com/usa/san-francisco-chronicle-late-edit ion/20150912/282016146108973.
15. Ibid.
16. *San Francisco Chronicle*, 28 October 1918.
17. Iezzoni, *op. cit.*, p. 161.
18. Billy H. Doyle, *The Ultimate Directory of Silent Screen Performers*, pp. 30–1, Metuchen, New Jersey: Scarecrow Press, 1995.
19. Charles Affron, *Lillian Gish: Her Legend, Her Life*, University of California Press, 2002, p. 127.
20. *Seattle Post-Intelligencer*, 10 November 1918.
21. Ibid.
22. Mary McCarthy, *Memories of a Catholic Girlhood*, London: Heinemann, 1957, pp xxiii–iv.
23. Ibid., p. 7.
24. Ibid., p. 18.
25. Ibid.
26. Joan Givner, *Katherine Anne Porter: A Life*, revised edition, Athens, GA: University of Georgia Press, 1991, p. 124.
27. Ibid.

28. Ibid., p. 125.

29. Ibid.

30. Ibid., pp. 125–6.

31. Katherine Anne Porter, *Pale Horse, Pale Rider: Three Short Novels*, New York: The Modern Library, Random House, 1936, p. 255.

32. Givner, *op. cit.*, p. 126.

Chapter Fourteen: The Fatal Voyage

1. *Auckland Star*, 15 December 1917.

2. Ibid.

3. Ibid.

4. USS *Leviathan* ship's log.

5. *Auckland Star*, 15 December 1917.

6. Ibid.

7. USS *Leviathan* ship's log.

8. *Auckland Star*, 15 December 1917.

9. Benedict Crowell and Robert Wilson, *How America Went to War: The Road to France*, New Haven: Yale University Press, 1921, p. 441.

10. USS *Leviathan* ship's log.

11. Alfred W. Crosby, *America's Forgotten Pandemic: The Influenza of 1918*, new edition, Cambridge: Cambridge University Press, 2003, pp. 126–7.

12. Ibid., p. 127.

13. Ibid.

14. Ibid.

15. USS *Leviathan* ship's log.

16. Ibid.

17. Ibid.

18. Crosby, *op. cit.*, p. 124.

19. Office of the Surgeon General, *Medical Department US Army*, Vol. 6, p. 1106; Vol. 15, part II, pp. 1026–7.

20. John M. Barry, *The Great Influenza*, New York: Penguin, 2005, pp. 304–5.

21. *Auckland Star*, 15 December 1917.

22. *History of USS Leviathan, Cruiser and Transport Forces United States Atlantic Fleet, Compiled from the Ship's Log and Data*

Gathered by the History Committee on Board the Ship, Brooklyn, N. Y. Brooklyn Eagle Press 1919, pp. 157–8.

23. Barry, *op. cit.*, p. 305.
24. Ibid.
25. Ibid.
26. Crosby, *op. cit.*, p. 128.
27. *History of USS Leviathan*, p. 93.
28. Crosby, *op. cit.*, p. 129.
29. Ibid., pp. 129–30.
30. Ibid., p. 130.
31. Ibid.
32. Ibid., pp. 130–1.
33. Ibid., p. 131.
34. Ibid., p. 132.

Chapter Fifteen: Ship of Death

1. Alfred W. Crosby, *America's Forgotten Pandemic: The Influenza of 1918*, new edition, Cambridge: Cambridge University Press, 2003, pp. 132–3.
2. *History of the USS Leviathan*, p. 92.
3. Crosby, *op. cit.*, p. 132.
4. Ibid.
5. USS *Leviathan* ship's log.
6. Ibid.
7. Ibid.
8. Ibid.
9. John M. Barry, *The Great Influenza: The Epic Story of the Deadliest Plague in History*, London: Penguin, 2005, p. 306.
10. USS *Leviathan* ship's log.
11. *History of the USS Leviathan*, p. 93.
12. Ibid.
13. Ibid.
14. Ibid.
15. Ibid.
16. Crosby, *op. cit.*, p. 133.
17. Ibid., p. 134.
18. Ibid.

19. Ibid.
20. Ibid.
21. Ibid., p. 135.
22. Ibid.
23. Ibid., pp. 135–6.
24. Ibid.
25. Ibid.
26. Ibid., p. 137.
27. Ibid.
28. Ibid., p. 138.
29. Ibid.
30. Ibid., p. 125.

Chapter Sixteen: 'Like a Thief in the Night'

1. Richard Collier, *The Plague of the Spanish Lady: The Influenza Pandemic of 1918–1919*, London and Basingstoke: Macmillan Limited, 1974, p. 59.
2. *Rand Daily Mail*, 17 October 1918.
3. Howard Phillips, 'Black October: The Impact of the Spanish Influenza Epidemic of 1918 on South Africa', PhD dissertation, University of Cape Town, 1984, p. 11.
4. *Daily Dispatch*, 28 September 1918.
5. Phillips, *op. cit.* Testimony of Dr E. Oliver Ashe, p. 238.
6. *Daily Dispatch*, 28 September 1918.
7. Phillips, *op. cit.*, p. 24.
8. Ibid., p. 26.
9. Ibid.
10. Ibid., p. 27.
11. *Cape Times*, 7 October 1918.
12. *De Burger*, 14 October 1918.
13. *Cape Argus*, 10 October 1918.
14. Phillips, *op. cit.*, p. 33.
15. Ibid.
16. Ibid.
17. Ibid., pp. 34–5.
18. Ibid., p. 35.
19. *Cape Times*, 7 October 1918.

20. Phillips, *op. cit.*, p. 36.
21. *Tembuland News*, 8 November 1918.
22. *Cape Times*, 10 October 1918, Editorial.
23. The *Star*, 11 October 1918.
24. *Cape Argus*, 19 October 1918.
25. Phillips, *op. cit.*, pp. 45–6.
26. Ibid.
27. Ibid.
28. *Cape Argus*, 14 October 1918, Editorial.
29. Ibid.
30. Richard Collier Collection: Letter from Mrs M. B. Holmes, *née* Forman, 25 June 1972.
31. See Phillips, *op. cit.*, p. 47.
32. Ibid.
33. *Tembuland News*, 8 November 1918.
34. Phillips, *op. cit.*, p. 49.
35. Ibid.
36. Ibid., p. 51.
37. Ibid., p. 52.
38. The *Star*, 11 November 1918 (letter from D. H. Poole).
39. Ibid.
40. Ibid.
41. Phillips, *op. cit.*, p. 20.
42. *De Burger*, 25 October 1918, p. 2.
43. M. Fraser and A. J. Jeeves (eds), *All That Glittered: Selected Correspondence of Lionel Phillips*, Cape Town: Oxford University Press, 1977, p. 318.
44. Ibid.
45. Phillips, *op. cit.*, p. 84.
46. Ibid., p. 85.
47. Ibid., p. 242.
48. Ibid.
49. Ibid.
50. Ibid., p. 243.
51. Ibid., p. 263.
52. Ibid., p. 275.
53. Ibid., p. 281.
54. Ibid., p. 244.

55. *Diamond Fields Advertiser*, 26 October 1918, p. 7.
56. Phillips, *op. cit.*, p. 246.
57. Ibid.
58. Ibid., p. 247.
59. Ibid., p. 86.
60. Ibid., p. 100.
61. Ibid., p. 101.
62. Ibid.
63. Ibid., p. 101–2.
64. Ibid.
65. Ibid., p. 107.

Chapter Seventeen: The Dying Fall

1. *Manchester Guardian*, 12 and 14 September 1918.
2. John Grigg, *Lloyd George: War Leader, 1916–1918*, London, Penguin Books, 2003.
3. Ibid., p. 593.
4. Ibid.
5. Ibid.
6. Ibid., p. 595.
7. Ibid.
8. Ibid.
9. Ibid.
10. Ibid.
11. Mridula Ramanna, 'Coping with the Influenza Pandemic: The Bombay Experience', in *The Spanish Influenza Pandemic of 1918–19*, ed. Howard Phillips and David Killingray, Routledge Studies in the Social History of Medicine, Abingdon, Oxon: Routledge, 2003, p. 88.
12. Ibid., p. 89.
13. Ibid.
14. Ibid.
15. Ibid.
16. Ibid., p. 90.
17. Ibid.
18. Ibid.
19. Ibid.

20. Ibid.
21. *Nottingham Evening Post*, 'Bygones' Supplement, 'Spanish Flu Pandemic', 24 January 2009, p. 7.
22. Ibid., p. 8.
23. See Niall Johnson, *Britain and the 1918–19 Influenza Pandemic: A Dark Epilogue*, Routledge Studies in the Social History of Medicine, Abingdon, Oxon: Routledge, 2006, p. 56.
24. Caroline Playne, *Britain Holds On*, London: George Allen & Unwin, 1933, p. 380.
25. Ibid.
26. Lyn MacDonald, *The Roses of No Man's Land*, London: Penguin Books, 1980, pp. 324–5.
27. Edward Bujak, *Reckless Fellows: The Gentlemen of the Royal Flying Corps*, I. B. Tauris, 2015, p. 45.
28. Lucinda Gosling, *Great War Britain: The First World War at Home*, Stroud, Gloucestershire: The History Press, 2014, p. 91.
29. Ibid., p. 17.
30. Dr Basil Hood, *Notes on St. Marylebone Infirmary (later St. Charles Hospital) 1910–1941*, GC/21, Contemporary Medical Archives Centre, Wellcome Library, p. 130.
31. Ibid.
32. Ibid.
33. Ibid.
34. Ibid.
35. Ibid.
36. Frank Whitford, *Egon Schiele*, London: Thames & Hudson, 1981, p. 195.
37. Ibid.
38. Simon Wilson, *Egon Schiele*, Oxford: Phaidon Press Limited, 1980, p. 52.
39. Whitford, *op. cit.*, pp. 193–4.
40. Wilson, *op. cit.*, p. 7.
41. Whitford *op. cit.*, p. 195.
42. Jay Winter, *Sites of Memory, Sites of Mourning*, Cambridge: Cambridge University Press, 1995, pp. 18–20.
43. Ibid., p. 20.
44. Ibid.
45. Ibid.

46. Ibid., p. 21.
47. Ibid.
48. Ibid.
49. Ibid.
50. Ibid.
51. Ibid.
52. Lyn Macdonald, *The Roses of No Man's Land*, London: Penguin Books, 1993, p. 318.
53. Ibid., *op. cit.*, p. 318.
54. Ibid.
55. Ibid., p. 319.
56. Ibid.
57. Ibid.
58. Ibid., pp. 319–20.
59. Ibid., p. 322.
60. Anna Rasmussen, 'The Spanish Flu', in *The Cambridge History of the First World War*, Vol. III, *Civil Society*, ed. Jay Winter, Cambridge: Cambridge University Press, 2014, p. 343.
61. Ibid.
62. Ibid., p. 347.
63. Macdonald, *op. cit.*, p. 325.
64. Ibid., pp. 325–6.
65. Ibid., p. 328.
66. J. S. Wane, *Diaries*, Richard Collier Collection, box 44.
67. Ibid.
68. Ibid.
69. Richard Foot, *Once a Gunner*, Reminiscences of World War 1, Richard Collier Collection, Imperial War Museum.
70. Ibid., p. 108.
71. Ibid., pp. 108–9.
72. Ibid.
73. Ibid., p. 109.
74. Ibid., p. 110.
75. Ibid.
76. Miss Dorothy Sutton, letter, Richard Collier Collection, 17 November 1918.

Chapter Eighteen: Armistice Day

1. Caroline Playne, *Britain Holds On*, London: George Allen & Unwin, 1933, p. 393.
2. *The Times*, 12 November 1918.
3. *Daily Express*, 12 November 1918.
4. Ibid.
5. Ibid.
6. Michael MacDonagh, *In London During the Great War*, London: Eyre & Spottiswoode, 1935, pp. 327–8.
7. Ibid.
8. Alan Palmer, *Victory 1918*, London: Weidenfeld & Nicolson, 1998, p. 286.
9. Karen L. Levenback, *Virginia Woolf and the Great War*, Syracuse: Syracuse University Press, 1998, p. 146.
10. Robert Graves, *Goodbye to All That*, London: Penguin Books, 1960, p. 228.
11. MacDonagh, *op. cit.*, p. 330.
12. Ibid., p. 332.
13. Playne, *op. cit.*, p. 393.
14. MacDonagh, *op. cit.*, p. 328.
15. Ibid.
16. Ibid.
17. Ibid., pp. 328–9.
18. Ibid., p. 329.
19. Ibid.
20. Ibid.
21. Ibid., p. 331.
22. Ibid., p. 330.
23. Ibid., p. 331.
24. Ibid., p. 332.
25. Ibid.
26. Ibid., p. 333.
27. Ibid.
28. Ibid.
29. Alan Warwick Palmer, *Victory 1918*, London: Weidenfeld & Nicolson, The Orion Publishing Group Ltd, 1998, p. 286.
30. Ibid.

31. Ibid.
32. Ibid.
33. Ibid., p. 287.
34. Isobel Charman, *The Great War: The People's Story*, London: Random House, 2014, p. 417.
35. Ibid.
36. Ibid., p. 425.
37. Katherine Anne Porter, *Pale Horse, Pale Rider: Three Short Novels*, New York: The Modern Library, Random House, 1936, p. 255.
38. Ibid., p. 256.
39. Ibid.
40. Ibid.
41. Lynette Iezzoni, *Influenza 1918: The Worst Epidemic in American History*, New York: TV Books, 1999, pp. 175–6.
42. Ibid., p. 176.
43. Ibid., p. 182.
44. Ibid., p. 176.
45. Ibid., p. 183.
46. MacDonagh, *op. cit.*, p. 336.
47. Victor C. Vaughan, *A Doctor's Memories*, Indianapolis: The Bobbs-Merrill Company, 1926, p. 432.
48. *Manchester Evening News*, 12 November 1918.
49. Mark Honigsbaum, *Living with Enza: The Forgotten Story of Britain and the Great Flu Pandemic of 1918*, Basingstoke: Macmillan, 2009, pp. 101–2.

Chapter Nineteen: Black November

1. Hugh Cecil and Peter H. Liddle (eds), *At the Eleventh Hour: Reflections, Hopes and Anxieties at the Closing of the Great War, 1918*, Barnsley: Leo Cooper, 1998, p. 206.
2. Ibid.
3. Geoffrey W. Rice, *Black November: The 1918 Influenza Pandemic in New Zealand*, Christchurch, NZ: Canterbury University Press, 2005, p. 118.
4. Ibid., p. 247.
5. Cecil and Liddle (eds), *op. cit.*, p. 206.
6. Rice, *op. cit.*, p. 251.

7. Ibid., p. 118.
8. Ibid.
9. Ibid., p. 157.
10. Ibid.
11. Ibid., p. 241.
12. Ibid.
13. Ibid., p. 247.
14. Ibid.
15. Ibid., p. 118.
16. Ibid., p. 252.
17. Ibid., p. 248.
18. Ibid., p. 153.
19. Ibid.
20. Ibid.
21. Ibid., p. 105.
22. Ibid., p. 195.
23. Ibid., p. 83.
24. Ibid., p. 73.
25. Ibid., p. 187.
26. Ibid., p. 194.
27. Ibid., p. 198.
28. Ibid.
29. Ibid.
30. Cecil and Liddle (eds), *op. cit.*, p. 206.
31. Rice, *op. cit.*, p. 159.
32. Ibid., page 197.
33. Ibid., p. 208.
34. Ibid.
35. Ibid., p. 173.
36. Ibid., p. 163.
37. Ibid., p. 173.
38. Ibid.
39. Ibid.
40. Ibid., p. 158.
41. Ibid., p. 157–8.
42. See Kevin McCracken and Peter Curson, 'Flu Downunder: A Demographic and Geographic Analysis of the 1919 Epidemic in Sydney, Australia', in *The Spanish Influenza Pandemic of 1918–*

19: New Perspectives, ed. Howard Phillips and David Killingray, Routledge Studies in the Social History of Medicine, Abingdon, Oxon: Routledge, 2003 p. 112.

43. Ibid., p. 117.

Chapter Twenty: Aftermath

1. The *Times* 18 December 1918.
2. Michael Ashcroft, 'The Victoria Cross recipient who "only did his job"', *Daily Telegraph*, 1 November 2013.
3. Ibid.
4. Ibid.
5. Ibid.
6. Ibid.
7. Ibid.
8. Ibid.
9. Ibid.
10. Ibid.
11. Ibid.
12. https://www.illustratedfirstworldwar.com/learning/timeline/1918-2/spanish-flu-peaks/.
13. Niall Johnson, *Britain and the 1918–19 Influenza Pandemic: A Dark Epilogue*, Routledge Studies in the Social History of Medicine, Abingdon, Oxon: Routledge, 2006, p. 141.
14. Ibid.
15. Mary Soames, *Clementine Churchill*, 2nd revised edition, New York: Doubleday, 2002, p. 219.
16. Juliet Nicolson, http://www.telegraph.co.uk/news/health/6542203/The-war-was-over-but-Spanish-Flu-would-kill-millions-more.html, 11 November 2009.
17. Mark, Honigsbaum, *Living with Enza: The Forgotten Story of Britain and the Great Flu Pandemic of 1918*, Basingstoke: Macmillan, 2009, p. 138.
18. Ibid.
19. Ibid.
20. H. W. Brands, *Woodrow Wilson*, Time Books, New York: Henry Holt and Company, 2003, p. 123.

21. Alfred W. Crosby, *America's Forgotten Pandemic: The Influenza of 1918*, new edition, Cambridge: Cambridge University Press, 2003, p. 172.

22. Brands, *op. cit.*, pp. 123–4.

23. https://paperspast.natlib.govt.nz/newspapers/TC19190502.2.5.

24. Johnson, *op. cit.*, p. 144.

25. Ibid.

26. Ibid., p. 145.

27. Maisie Fletcher, *The Bright Countenance: A Personal Biography of Walter Morley Fletcher*, London: Hodder & Stoughton, 1957, p. 143.

28. Ibid.

29. J. S. Wane, Diary, Richard Collier Collection, Imperial War Museum.

30. See http://www.navsource.org/archives/12/171326.htm.

31. https://forgottenbooks.com/es/books/HistoryoftheUSSLeviathan_10213422.

32. Lynette Iezzoni, *Influenza 1918: The Worst Epidemic in American History*, New York: TV Books, 1999, p. 183.

33. Ibid., p. 184.

34. Mary McCarthy, *Memories of a Catholic Girlhood*, London: Heinemann, 1957, pp 12–13.

35. Ibid., p. xxiv.

36. Iezzoni, *op. cit.*, p. 185.

Chapter Twenty-One: 'Viral Archaeology'

1. Private Harry Underdawn is buried at Étaples Military Cemetery Nord-Pas-de-Calais.

2. Gina Kolata, *Flu: The Story of the Great Influenza Pandemic of 1918 and the Search for the Virus that Caused It*, New York: Touchstone, Rockefeller Center, 1999, pp. 85–6.

3. Ibid., p. 89.

4. Lynette Iezzoni, *Influenza 1918: The Worst Epidemic in American History*, New York: TV Books, 1999, p. 221.

5. Ibid.

6. Ibid.

7. Jeffery Taubenberger, Senior Investigator in the Laboratory of Infectious Diseases at the National Institute for Allergy and

Infectious Diseases. Interview location: The National Institutes of Health campus in Bethesda, Maryland, United States, Interview date: 27 November 2007.

8. Iezzoni, *op. cit.*, p. 222.

9. Ibid., pp. 221–2.

10. Alison McCook, 'Death of a Pathology Centre', *Nature* 476 (2011), pp. 270–2. DOI:10.1038/476270a http://www.nature.com/news/2011/110817/full/476270a.html.

11. Ibid.

12. Taubenberger, *op. cit.*

13. Ibid.

14. Ibid.

15. Ibid.

16. Ibid.

17. Ibid.

18. Ibid.

19. Ibid.

20. Ibid.

21. Iezzoni, *op. cit.*, p. 219.

22. Taubenberger, *op. cit.*

23. Ibid.

24. Ibid.

25. Ibid.

26. Ibid.

27. Ibid.

28. Iezzoni, *op. cit.*, p. 224.

29. Ibid., p. 225.

30. Taubenberger, *op. cit.*

31. Ibid.

32. Ibid.

33. Ibid.

34. Ibid.

35. Ibid.

36. Edwin D. Kilbourne, *Influenza Pandemics of the 20th Century*, https://www.ncbi.nlm.nih.gov/pmc/articles/PMC3291411/.

Chapter Twenty-Two: The Hong Kong Connection

1. Pete Davies, *Catching Cold: 1918's Forgotten Tragedy and the Scientific Hunt for the Virus that Caused It*, London: Penguin Books, 1999, p. 7.

2. Gina Kolata, *Flu: The Story of the Great Influenza Pandemic of 1918 and the Search for the Virus that Caused It*, New York: Touchstone, Rockefeller Center, 1999, p. 200.

3. M. Levi (2007). 'Disseminated Intravascular Coagulation', *Critical Care Medicine* 35 (9), pp. 2191–5.

4. Davies, *op. cit.*, p. 8.

5. Ibid.

6. Kolata, *op. cit.*, p. 225.

7. Ibid., p. 226.

8. Ibid.

9. Ibid., p. 228.

10. Simon Parkin, *Inception: The Avian Flu Outbreak in Hong Kong, 1997*, https://howwegettonext.com/inception-the-avian-flu-outbreak-in-hong-kong-1997-5c0de48f6781.

11. Davies, *op. cit.*, p. 18.

12. Kolata, *op. cit.*, p. 232.

13. Davies, *op. cit.*, p. 20.

14. Ibid., p. 21.

15. Ibid.

16. Ibid.

17. Ibid., p. 25.

18. Ibid.

19. Ibid.

20. Ibid.

21. Ibid.

22. Ibid.

23. Ibid.

24. Ibid., p. 27.

25. Ibid., p. 21.

26. Ibid.

27. Parkin, *op. cit.*

28. Kolata, *op. cit.*, p. 233.

29. Ibid.

30. Ibid., p. 236.

31. Ibid., p. 239.

32. Ibid.

33. Ibid., p. 26.

34. Parkin, *op. cit.*

35. Ibid.

36. Mark Honigsbaum, 'Robert Webster: We ignore bird flu at our peril', *Guardian*, 17 September 2011, https://www.theguardian.com/world/2011/sep/17/bird-flu-swine-flu-warning.

37. Kolata, *op. cit.*, p. 238.

38. Ian Sample, 'A history of major flu pandemics', *Guardian*, 28 March 2012, https://www.theguardian.com/world/2012/mar/28/history-major-flu-pandemics.

39. Mark Honigsbaum, 'Robert Webster: We ignore bird flu at our peril', *Guardian*, 17 September 2011, https://www.theguardian.com/world/2011/sep/17/bird-flu-swine-flu-warning.

40. Jeffery Taubenberger, Senior Investigator in the Laboratory of Infectious Diseases at the National Institute for Allergy and Infectious Diseases. Interview location: The National Institutes of Health campus in Bethesda, Maryland, United States, Interview date: 27 November 2007.

41. Professor John Oxford, interview with author, September 2016.

Chapter Twenty-Three: Secrets of the Grave

1. Pete Davies, *Catching Cold: 1918's Forgotten Tragedy and the Scientific Hunt for the Virus that Caused It*, London: Penguin Books, 1999, p. 120.

2. Gina Kolata, *Flu: The Story of the Great Influenza Pandemic of 1918 and the Search for the Virus that Caused It*, New York: Touchstone, Rockefeller Center, 1999 p. 273.

3. Esther Oxford, 'Secrets of the grave', *Independent*, 26 September 1998.

4. Ibid.

5. Ibid.

6. Ibid.

7. Candida Crewe, 'The London Necropolis', *The Spectator*, 23 March 1991, p. 26.

8. Davies, *op. cit.*, p. 147.
9. Oxford, *op. cit.*
10. Kolata, *op. cit.*, p. 280.
11. Oxford, *op. cit.*
12. Ibid.
13. Ibid.
14. Ibid.
15. Ibid.
16. Ibid.
17. Ibid.
18. Author interview with Professor Oxford, September 2016.
19. Ibid.
20. Ibid.
21. Barbara Davies, 'Revealed: face of the woman who could save us from bird flu; courage of tragic 1918 epidemic victim', *Daily Mirror*, 5 February 2004, https://www.thefreelibrary.com/Revealed%3A+face+of+the+woman+who+could+save+us+from+bird+flu%3B+COURAGE...-a0112921273.
22. Ibid.
23. Ibid.
24. Ibid.
25. Ibid.
26. Ibid.
27. Ibid.
28. Ibid.
29. Wendy Moore, 'Fever Pitch', *The Observer*, 26 November 2000.
30. Ibid.
31. Author interview with Professor Oxford, September 2016.
32. Nita Madhav and Molly J. Markey (eds), 'Modeling a Modern-Day Spanish Flu Pandemic', AIR's Research and Modeling Group, 21 February 2013.
33. Ibid.
34. Author interview with Professor Oxford.
35. Ibid.

BIBLIOGRAPHY

Books

Acton, Carol, *Grief in Wartime: Private Pain, Public Discourse*, Basingstoke: Palgrave Macmillan, 2007.

Baden-Powell, Lady, *Window on My Heart*, London: Hodder & Stoughton, 1987.

Barry, John M., *The Great Influenza: The Epic Story of the Deadliest Plague in History*, London: Penguin, 2005.

Brands, H. W., *Woodrow Wilson*, Times Books, New York: Henry Holt and Company, 2003.

Bristow, Nancy K., *American Pandemic: The Lost Worlds of the 1918 Influenza Epidemic*, New York: Oxford University Press, 2012.

Brown, Malcolm, *The Imperial War Museum Book of 1918 Year of Victory*, London: Sidgwick & Jackson, in association with the Imperial War Museum in association with Macmillan Publishers Ltd, 1998.

Brown, Malcolm, *The Imperial War Museum Book of the First World War: A Great Conflict Recalled in Previously Unpublished Letters, Diaries, Documents and Memoirs*, London: Sidgwick & Jackson, in association with the Imperial War Museum, 1991.

Brittain, Vera, *Testament of Youth*, London: Virago Press Limited, 1984.

Byerly, Carol R., *Fever of War: The Influenza Epidemic in the U.S. Army during World War I*, New York University Press, 2005.

Cannan, May, Bevil [*sic*] Quiller-Couch and Charlotte Fyfe (eds), *The Tears of War: The Love Story of a Young Poet and a War Hero*, Upavon, Wilts: Cavalier Books, 2002.

Cather, Willa, *One of Ours* (Introduction by Hermione Lee), London: Virago Press Limited, 1987.

Cecil, Hugh and Peter H. Liddle (eds), *At the Eleventh Hour Reflections: Hopes and Anxieties at the Closing of the Great War 1918*, Barnsley, Leo Cooper, an imprint of Pen & Sword Books Ltd, 1998.

Charles River Editors, *The 1918 Spanish Flu Epidemic: The History and Legacy of the World's Deadliest Influenza Epidemic*. Charles River Editors (October 8, 2014) Amazon Digital Services LLC.

Charman, Isobel, *The Great War: The People's Story*, London: Random House, 2014.

Clayton, Anthony, *Paths of Glory: The French Army 1914–18*, A Cassell Military Paperback, London: Orion Books Ltd, 2005.

Collier, Richard, *The Plague of the Spanish Lady: The Influenza Pandemic of 1918–1919*, London and Basingstoke: Macmillan Limited, 1974.

Crosby, Alfred W., *America's Forgotten Pandemic: The Influenza of 1918*, new edition, Cambridge: Cambridge University Press, 2003.

Cunningham, Andrew and Perry Williams (eds), *The Laboratory Revolution in Medicine*, Cambridge: Cambridge University Press, 1992.

Davis, Ryan A., *The Spanish Flu: Narrative and Cultural Identity in Spain, 1918*, New York: Palgrave Macmillan and St Martin's Press, 2013.

Fisher, Jane Elizabeth, *Envisioning Disease, Gender, and War: Women's Narratives of the 1918 Influenza Pandemic*, New York: Palgrave Macmillan, 2012.

Fletcher, Maisie, *The Bright Countenance: A Personal Biography of Walter Morley Fletcher*, London: Hodder & Stoughton, 1957.

Fraser, M. and A. J. Jeeves (eds), *All That Glittered: Selected Correspondence of Lionel Phillips*, Cape Town: Oxford University Press, 1977.

Grigg, John, *Lloyd George: War Leader, 1916–1918*, London: Penguin Books, 2003.

Gorham, Deborah, *Vera Brittain: A Feminist Life*, Oxford: Blackwell Publishers Ltd, 1996.

Graves, Robert, *Goodbye to All That*, London: Penguin Books, 1960.

Givner, Joan, *Katherine Anne Porter: A Life*, revised edition, Brown Thrasher Books, Athens, GA: The University of Georgia Press, 1991.

Honigsbaum, Mark, *A History of the Great Influenza Pandemics: Death, Panic and Hysteria, 1830–1920*, London: I.B. Tauris & Co. Ltd, 2014.

Honigsbaum, Mark, *Living with Enza: The Forgotten Story of Britain and the Great Flu Pandemic of 1918*, Basingstoke, Hampshire: Macmillan, 2009.

Humphries, Mark Osborne, *The Last Plague Spanish Influenza and the Politics of Public Health in Canada*, Toronto: University of Toronto Press, 2013.

Iezzoni, Lynette, *Influenza 1918: The Worst Epidemic in American History*, New York: TV Books, 1999.

Johnson, Niall, *Britain and the 1918–19 Influenza Pandemic: A Dark Epilogue*, Routledge Studies in the Social History of Medicine, Abingdon, Oxon: Routledge, 2006.

Kanfer, Stefan, *Groucho: The Life and Times of Julius Henry Marx*, London: Penguin Books Ltd, 2000.

Kolata, Gina, *Flu: The Story of the Great Influenza Pandemic of 1918 and the Search for the Virus that Caused It*, New York: Touchstone, Rockefeller Center, 1999.

Leake, R. E., *Letters of a V.A.D.*, London: Andrew Melrose Ltd, 1919.

Lee, Janet, *War Girls: The First Aid Nursing Yeomanry in the First World War*, Manchester: Manchester University Press, 2005.

Levenback, Karen L., *Virginia Woolf and the Great War*, Syracuse University Press, 1998.

Lombardo, Joseph S. and David L. Buckeridge, *Disease Surveillance: A Public Health Informatics Approach*, first online edition, eu.Wiley.com Wiley, 2006.

McCarthy, Mary, *Memories of a Catholic Girlhood*, London: Heinemann, 1957.

MacDonagh, Michael, *In London During the Great War: The Diary of a Journalist*, London: Eyre & Spottiswoode, 1935.

Macdonald, Lyn, *The Roses of No Man's Land*, London: Penguin Books, 1993.

Macdonald, Lyn, *To the Last Man: Spring 1918*, London: Viking Penguin Books Ltd, 1998.

Macnaughtan, S., *My War Experiences in Two Continents*, ed. Mrs Lionel Salmon, London: John Murray, 1919.

Macpherson, W. G., Herringham, W. P., Elliott, T. R. and Balfour, A. (eds), *Medical Services: Diseases of the War*, Vol. 1, London: His Majesty's Stationery Office, 1922.

Morgan, Ted, *FDR: A Biography*, London: Grafton Books, Collins Publishing Group, 1986.

Muir, Ward, *Observations of an Orderly: Some Glimpses of Life and Work in an English War Hospital*, London: Simpkin, Marshall, Hamilton, Kent & Co Ltd, 1917.

Oldstone, Michael B. A. M. *Viruses, Plagues, and History: Past, Present and Future*, revised edition, Oxford: Oxford University Press, 2009.

Palmer, Alan Warwick, *Victory 1918*, London: Weidenfeld & Nicolson The Orion Publishing Group Ltd, 1998.

Parini, Jay, *John Steinbeck: A Biography*, London: Heinemann, 1994.

Phillips, Howard and Killingray, David K. (eds), *The Spanish Influenza Pandemic of 1918–19: New Perspectives*, Routledge Studies in the Social History of Medicine, Abingdon, Oxon: Routledge, 2003.

Playne, Caroline, *Britain Holds On*, London: George Allen & Unwin, 1933.

Porter, Katherine Anne, *Pale Horse, Pale Rider: Three Short Novels*, New York: The Modern Library, Random House, 1936.

Rice, Geoffrey W. *Black November: The 1918 Influenza Pandemic in New Zealand*, Christchurch NZ: University of Canterbury Press, 2005.

Roosevelt, Eleanor, *The Autobiography of Eleanor Roosevelt*, London: Hutchinson & Co. (Publishers) Ltd, 1962.

Stevenson, D., *With our Backs to the Wall: Victory and Defeat in 1918*, London: Penguin Books, 2011.

Toland, John, *No Man's Land: The Story of 1918*, London: Book Club Associates by arrangement with Eyre Methuen Ltd, 1980.

Van Emden, Richard and Humphries, Steve, *All Quiet on the Home Front: An Oral History of Life in Britain during the First World War*, London: Headline Book Publishing, Hodder Headline, 2004.

Vaughan, Victor C., *A Doctor's Memories*, Indianapolis: The Bobbs-Merrill Company, 1926.

Waddington, Mary King (Madame Waddington), *My War Diary*, London: John Murray, 1918.

White, Jerry, *Zeppelin Nights: London in the First World War*, London: Vintage Books, 2015.

Whitford, Frank, *Egon Schiele*, London: Thames & Hudson, 1981.

Wilson, Simon, *Egon Schiele*, Oxford: Phaidon Press Limited, 1980.

Wolfe, Thomas, *Look Homeward, Angel*, 1929, http://gutenberg.net. au/ebooks03/0300721.txt.

Winter, Jay (ed.), *The Cambridge History of the First World War*, Cambridge: Cambridge University Press, 2014.

Winter, J. M., *Sites of Memory, Sites of Mourning: The Great War in European Cultural History*, Cambridge: Cambridge University Press, 1995.

Woodhead, Lindy, *Shopping, Seduction and Mr. Selfridge*, London: Profile Books, 2012.

PhD Theses

Knight, Joan Eileen, 'The Social Impact of the Influenza Pandemic of 1918–19: With Special Reference to the East Midlands', PhD thesis, University of Nottingham (2015); access from the University of Nottingham repository: http://eprints.nottingham.ac.uk/28545/1/ JOAN%20KNIGHT%20-%20THESIS.pdf.

Phillips, Howard, 'Black October: The Impact of the Spanish Influenza Epidemic of 1918 on South Africa', PhD dissertation, University of Cape Town, 1984.

Special Collections

Caroline Playne Collection, Senate House Library, University of London.

Richard Collier Collection, Imperial War Museum.

Contemporary Medical Archives Centre, Wellcome Library, 'Notes on Marylebone Infirmary (later St. Charles Hospital) 1910–1941', compiled by Dr Basil Hood – GC/21.

Journal Articles

Blue, Ethan, 'The Strange Career of Leo Stanley: Remaking Manhood and Medicine at San Quentin State Penitentiary, 1913–1951', *Pacific*

Historical Review 78 (2) (May 2009), pp. 210–41; published by University of California Press. Stable URL: http://www.jstor.org/stable/10.1525/phr.2009.78.2.210. Accessed 20 June 2017.

Bresalier, Michael, 'Fighting Flu: Military Pathology, Vaccines, and the Conflicted Identity of the 1918–19 Pandemic in Britain', *Journal of the History of Medicine and Allied Sciences* 68 (1) (January 2013), pp. 87–128; https://oup.silverchair-cdn.com/oup/backfile/Content_public/Journal/jhmas/68/1/10.1093/jhmas/jrr041/2/jrr041.pdf.

Dudley, S. F., 'The Influenza Pandemic as Seen at Scapa Flow', *Journal of the Royal Naval Medical Service*, V (4) (October 1919).

Gill, Douglas and Dallas, Gloden, 'Mutiny at Etaples Base in 1917', *Past & Present*, 69 (November 1975), pp. 88–112; published by Oxford University Press on behalf of The Past and Present Society; Stable URL: http://www.jstor.org/stable/650297. Accessed 22 August 2016.

Graeme Gibson, H., Bowman, F. B. and Connor, J. I., 'The Etiology of Influenza: A Filterable Virus as the Cause, With Some Notes on the Culture of the Virus By Noguchi's Method', *The British Medical Journal* 1 (3038) (22 March 1919), pp. 331–5. Stable URL: http://www.jstor.org/stable/20337178. Accessed 19 June 2017.

Hammond, J. A. B., Rolland, William and Shore, T. H. G., 'Purulent Bronchitis: A Study of Cases Occurring Amongst the British Troops at a Base in France', *The Lancet* 190 (14 July 1917), pp. 41–6.

Honigsbaum, Mark, 'Robert Webster: We ignore bird flu at our peril', *Guardian*, 17 September 2011, https://www.theguardian.com/world/2011/sep/17/bird-flu-swine-flu-warning.

Oxford, J. S., Lambkin, R,, Sefton, A., Daniels, R., Elliot, A., Brown, R. and Gill, D., 'A Hypothesis: The Conjunction of Soldiers, Gas, Pigs, Ducks, Geese and Horses in Northern France during the Great War Provided the Conditions for the Emergence of the "Spanish" Influenza Pandemic of 1918–1919', *Vaccine* 23 (2005), pp. 940–5, online version, Elsevier, 11 September 2004.

Raymond, J. K., 'Influenza on Board a Battleship', *Journal of the Royal Naval Medical Service* 5 (4) (October 1918).

Tanner, Andrea, 'The Spanish Lady Comes to London: The Influenza Pandemic 1918–1919', *London Journal* 27 (2) (2002).

Tomkins, Sandra M., 'The Failure of Expertise: Public Health Policy in Britain during the 1918–19 Influenza Epidemic', *Social History of Medicine* 5 (3) (1992), pp. 435–54. DOI: https://doi-org. libezproxy.open.ac.uk/10.1093/shm/5.3.435.

ACKNOWLEDGEMENTS

With thanks to the following individuals and institutions for their assistance in researching and writing *Pandemic 1918: The Story of the Deadliest Influenza in History*: Dr Michael Bresalier, Dr Mark Honigsbaum of the Wellcome Trust, Professor Geoffrey Rice of the University of Canterbury, New Zealand, Professor Howard Phillips, Dr Joan Knight of Loughborough University, Dr Richard Johnson, Charles Harrowell at Special Collections, Senate House Library, University of London, and the staff of Cambridge University Library, the Hallward Library and the Greenfield Medical Library, University of Nottingham, the Imperial War Museum and the Wellcome Library. Many thanks also to Fiona Slater and Louise Dixon at Michael O'Mara Books and Charles Spicer and April Osborn at St Martin's Press. Thanks are also due to my family and friends and to my agent Andrew Lownie for all their encouragement and support.

PICTURE CREDITS

First Section

Page 1 (top): Image courtesy of the National Museum of Health and Medicine, Armed Forces Institute of Pathology, Washington, D.C. / source Nicholls H (2006) *Pandemic Influenza: The Inside Story* (CC by 4.0)

Page 1 (bottom): Photo courtesy of Otis Historical Archives, National Museum of Health and Medicine, AFIP, Washington, D.C. (CC by 2.0)

Page 2 (top): Ministry of Health, Great Britain, *No. 4 Report on the Pandemic of Influenza 1918-19*, His Majesty's Stationery Office, London (1920)

Page 2 (bottom): From the *Los Angeles Evening Herald*, 22 October, 1918. *Chronicling America: Historic American Newspapers*, Library of Congress/ lccn / sn84025969

Page 3 (top): Photo courtesy of U.S. Naval History and Heritage Command, Washington, D.C. /NH 71 USS Leviathan (ID 1326)

Page 3 (bottom): © Corbis / Corbis via Getty Images

Page 4 (top): Photo from *My Chicago* by Anna Morgan, 1918

Page 4 (bottom): Mary Evans / Everett Collection

Page 5 (top): Hulton Archive / Getty Images

Page 5 (bottom): Art Collection 2 / Alamy

Page 6 (top): Photo courtesy of U.S. Naval History and Heritage Command, Washington, D.C. / NH 41731-A

Page 6 (bottom): © Illustrated London News / Mary Evans

Page 7 (top): Universal History Archive / UIG via Getty Images

Page 7 (bottom): © Illustrated London News / Mary Evans

Page 8 (top): Everett Historical / Shutterstock.com

Page 8 (bottom): © Illustrated London News / Mary Evans

Second Section

Page 9 (top): Old newspaper advertisement

Page 9 (bottom): Photo courtesy of State Library of Queensland, Brisbane

Page 10 (top): Photo courtesy of the Dublin Heritage Museum, California

Page 10 (bottom): U.S. National Archives / 165-WW-269B-25

Page 11 (top): U.S. National Archives / 165-WW-269B-16

Page 11 (bottom): Mary Evans Picture Library

Page 12 (top): Atomic / Alamy

Page 12 (bottom): Mary Evans Picture Library

Page 13 (top): Wellcome Collection (CC by 4.0)

Page 13 (bottom): From a 1942 advertisement for Dixie Cups, referring back to 1918

Page 14 (top): British Library, London, UK / © British Library Board. All Rights Reserved / Bridgeman Images

Page 14 (bottom): From *The Ogden Standard*, 29 January, 1916. *Chronicling America: Historic American Newspapers*, Library of Congress / lccn / sn85058396

Page 15 (top): Mary Evans Picture Library

Page 15 (bottom): Photo courtesy of Kansas State Historical Society

Page 16: The Influenza Pandemic Window from the Johannes Schreiter windows at the Medical Library, The Royal London Hospital, Whitechapel, designed by Caroline Swash, published for the hospital by Malvern Arts Press Ltd PO Box 3 Malvern WR14 1WW, photograph by Philip Vile

INDEX